MS Access 2000 Expert User

Self-Paced Training for MOUS

www.learnitbooks.com

Published by
GTSLearning International Limited

© GTSLearning International Limited 2001
ISBN 1 84005 246 5

First edition published 2000
Publication Number L106eng (101)

All rights reserved. No part of this book may be copied, photocopied or reproduced in any form or by any means without permission in writing from GTSLearning International Limited.

Author	**Kate Jennings**
Editor	James Pengelly

Copyright	This book is copyrighted © *GTSLearning International Limited 2001*. No part of this book may be copied, photocopied or reproduced in any form or by any means without the permission in writing from GTSLearning International Limited. Violation of copyright will lead to prosecution. All trademarks, service marks, products or services are trademarks or registered trademarks of their respective holders and are acknowledged by the authors.
Limitation of liability	Every effort has been made to ensure complete and accurate information concerning the material presented in this book. However, GTSLearning International Limited cannot be held legally responsible for any mistakes in printing or faulty instructions contained within this book. The authors appreciate receiving notice of any errors or misprints.
	Information in this book is subject to change without notice. Companies, names and data used in examples herein are fictitious unless otherwise noted.
	This book is designed to familiarise the user with the operation of software programs. We urge the user to review the manuals provided by the software publisher regarding specific questions as to the operation of the programs.
Publisher and Distributor	This courseware is owned and distributed internationally by **gtlearning**, the market-leading Education Services Provider, supplying a portfolio of courseware for IT skills and certifications to more than 500 **gtspartner** sites in more than 50 countries.

www.gtslearning.com   www.learnitbooks.com   www.ecdlcourseware.eu.com

Table of Contents

Introduction How This Book Works 1
    Learning Outcomes 2
    Assumed Knowledge 3
    The Data Disk 4
    Working Through the Lessons 5
    Review and Going Further 6
    Notes, Tips and Warnings 7
    Index and Glossary 7
    Mouse Conventions 8
    Keyboard Conventions 9

Lesson 1 Database Development 11
    Designing a Relational Database 12
    Normalisation of Data 13
    De-normalisation 16
    Queries, Forms and Reports 16
    Documenting the Database 17
    Database Terms 19

        Review 21

Lesson 2 Defining Relationships 25
    What are Table Relationships? 26
    Creating Relationships 27
    Referential Integrity 32
    Find Unmatched Query Wizard 34
    Cascade Update and Delete 38
    Join Types 40
    Subdatasheets 44

        Review 47

Lesson 3 Working with Field Properties 51
    Creating a Robust Database 52
    Setting Field Properties 52
    Data Type and Field Size 53
    Validation Rules 54
    Validation Text 55
    Table Level Validation 57
    Input Masks 58
    Format Property 60
    Lookup Fields 61
    Creating a Lookup List 61
    Indexes 68
    Other Useful Fields 70

Review and Going Further 71
    Using the Input Mask Wizard 75
    Creating a Lookup List from a Fixed Set of Values 76
    Modifying Tables and Fields 78

Lesson 4 Working with External Data 83
    Using External Data in Access 84
    Importing Data 84
    Linking Data 89
    The Linked Table Manager 91
    Exporting Database Records 92

Review 95

Lesson 5 Manipulating Data with Queries 99
    The Different Types of Queries 100
    Action Queries 101
    Planning an Action Query 101
    Make-Table Queries 102
    Append Queries 105
    Delete Queries 106
    Update Queries 108
    Creating Summary Queries 110
    Grouping in Queries 111
    Using Calculated Fields in a Query 113
    Calculations 113
    Combining Queries 116
    Filtering Query Results 119
    Parameter Queries 122
    Concatenation 125
    Crosstab Queries 126

Review and Going Further 133
    Between...And 137
    Display Only the Top Values 138

Lesson 6 Building and Modifying Forms 139
    Using Advanced Form Features 140
    Form Design Worksurface 141
    Form Sections 142
    Resizing Form Sections 144
    Form Controls 145
    Selecting Controls 147
    Form Properties 151
    Form Header 152
    The Formatting Toolbar 152
    Deleting Controls 154
    Undo 154
    Adding a Graphic to a Form 155
    Creating a Calculated Control 157
    Multi-Table Forms 160
    Working with Main and Subform Forms 163
    Using the SubForm Control 165

Review and Going Further 169

    Switchboard Forms.. 173

Lesson 7 Reports and Charts 177

    Customising Reports... 178
    Report Sections 178
    Applying Sorting and Grouping to Reports 179
    Modifying Field and Section Properties... 185
    Creating a Multi-Column Report.. 186
    Adding Calculations to a Report... 189
    Creating Charts 192
    Modifying the Chart.. 197
    Using the SubReport Control.. 202

    Review 205

Lesson 8 Publishing Data on the Internet....................................... 209

    Putting a Database on the Web.. 210
    Using Hyperlinks in Forms 211
    Exporting Datasheet Views to HTML 214
    HTML Templates 216
    Data Access Pages 219
    Creating a Grouped Data Access Page.. 225
    Modifying the Design of a Data Access Page... 227

    Review... 233

Lesson 9 Macros... 237

    What is a Macro? 238
    Access Applications 239
    Creating a Macro... 239
    Running a Macro 242
    Macro Examples 243
    Design Solving Macros.. 249
    Adding a Macro to a Command Button 252
    Using the Expression Builder to Build a Macro 254

    Review and Going Further 261

    Designing Menus Bars and Toolbars... 264
    Customising Menus and Toolbars 267
    Customising Startup 273

Lesson 10 Database Management 275

    Database Administration.. 276
    Setting a Database Password 277
    Backing Up a Database 281
    Restoring a Database from Backup 283
    Compacting and Repairing a Database.. 284
    Running Compact and Repair Automatically 285
    Encrypting and Decrypting a Database 286
    Splitting a Database... 288

Review and Going Further 291

Managing Shared Databases 295
Setting Default Locking Properties 298
Creating Groups and Users 299
Setting User Permissions 306
Assigning Ownership 307

Lesson 11 Database Utilities 309

The Table Analyzer 310
Replicating a Database 314
Synchronising Replicas 317
Converting Databases 322

Review and Going Further 325

Documenting the Database Structure 329
The Performance Analyzer 331

Appendices Glossary 333

Appendices Index 337

Appendices Going Further 341

Opportunities for Further Study 341
Further Titles in the LearnIT Series 342

Introduction: How This Book Works

This book is intended for existing users of Microsoft™ Access 2000 who want to learn more advanced features of the application. It aims to show you how to build more complex databases using Access' sophisticated tools by providing simple instructions and step-by-step examples that you can work through as often as required and at your own pace.

To complete this course successfully, you should already be confident in using the basic features of Access.

Read this chapter first to understand the learning objectives for the course and how it is organised.

This chapter covers the following topics:

- **Learning outcomes** and **certification** and features you must **already be able** to use

- Using the **data disk**

- How to **work through** the lessons, **review** sessions and **going further**

- About **notes** and **tips** while working

- Using the **mouse** and **keyboard** conventions

- Instructions for **entering text**

Learning Outcomes

The main aim of this book is to enable you to benefit from the advanced features of Access.

On completion of all the lessons, you will be able to:

- Design **robust** and **efficient** relational databases
- **Import** and **export** data and manage **linked** tables
- Use **calculated fields** and **expressions** in queries, forms and reports
- Use **action queries** to modify data
- **Customise** and **improve** basic form and report designs
- Use **charts** to display data graphically
- Create **data access pages** for internet use
- Design and implement **macros**
- Use database **management** and **administration** tools

You can also use this book to prepare for **Microsoft Office User Specialist** (MOUS) certification at the **Expert** level. The basic lessons **together with** the "Going Further" sections have been prepared to include all the topics required by **MOUS Access 2000 Expert**.

For further information on MOUS, refer to the website:

www.mous.net

On completion of this course, you may wish to go on to learn about other Office and Windows applications. For details of other books in the Learn series, please refer to page 341.

Assumed Knowledge

This course is intended for users with some previous experience of Access. This could have been gained from the workplace, from a training course or from completing the companion Learn IT series course **MS Access 2000**.

You should know how to:

- **Start** and **exit** Access, get **help** and **manage files**
- Create basic **tables** using **data types** and **field properties**
- **Add** and **edit records** using a **datasheet** or **form**
- Create **queries**, **forms** and **reports**

Some understanding of relational database design and the form/report design worksurface would also be an advantage.

MS Office 2000

Not all features of Access discussed in this course are installed by default. The software may ask you to run Setup to install these features.

Some topics cover integration with MS Excel 2000. You will need this application installed to complete the practical examples in these sections. A basic understanding of how other Office software works would be an advantage.

MS Windows

This book can be used with PCs running MS Windows 95, Windows 98, Windows NT4 and Windows 2000. Access works in much the same way for each different version of Windows.

It is assumed that you know how to work with files and folders in Windows. If instructed to do something in Windows you do not understand, try running the Windows Tutorial (on the Windows CD) or referring to the online help.

The Data Disk

The CD-ROM attached to the back cover of this book contains sample data files for use during the lessons.

The data files for this course are stored in the folder **MS Access 2000 Expert**.

You should copy the files from the CD to your PC's **C:** drive (the hard disk). Do this now.

- Insert the CD into your CD drive
- Using **My Computer**, open the **MS Access 2000 Expert** folder on the CD
- Copy all the files
- Using **My Computer**, open the **My Documents** folder on your PC
- Paste the files into **My Documents**
- Put the CD somewhere safe so that you have a **backup copy** of the files

Note that the location of **My Documents** varies according to the version of Windows you have. If you are using Windows 98/2000, select the special **My Documents** icon on the **Desktop**. If you are using Windows 95/NT4.0, use **C:\My Documents**.

When the files are copied from the CD-ROM, they remain **Read-Only**.

- Select all the files in the **My Documents** folder
- From the **File** menu, select **Properties**

The **Properties** dialogue box is displayed.

- Click the **Read-only** check box to clear it
- Click **OK**

The data files are now ready to use.

Working Through the Lessons

Work through each lesson from start to finish taking things step-by-step. If you are completing the lessons at home or in the workplace, use each lesson as many times as you want, until **you** feel confident that you can move on.

If you are studying with a tutor, try working back through the lesson in your own time if you feel that a study session has moved to quickly for you.

There may be some skills covered in a lesson that you are already familiar with. If this is the case, you can jump to the next lesson. This is indicated at the beginning of each lesson.

Jump lesson...

> If you already know these basic features, find out how to get help by jumping to: GETTING ASSISTANCE on page 33 or learn the basics of EDITING DOCUMENTS on page 47.

To learn skills, a description of a topic is usually followed by hands-on examples. These are shown in this book as *Try*ITs. The **Actions** on the left are instructions for you to follow. The **Result** is what you will see on screen.

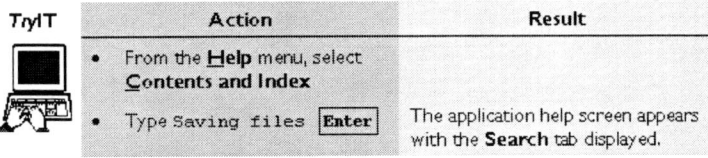

In some lessons, **Practice** topics ask you to complete similar tasks without giving you step-by-step instructions.

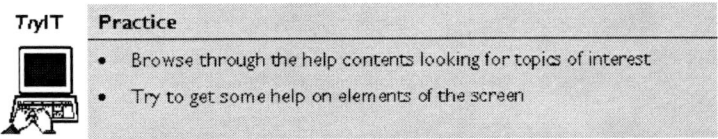

Review and Going Further

At the end of each lesson, a set of review questions help you consolidate all the skills you have learned. Working through the review questions ensures that you are properly prepared for the next lesson (The answers are given on the page following).

Following on from the review questions is a **Skills Summary**. This lists all the features you have learned, providing a springboard for the next lesson. Review your lesson objectives and check that you have mastered them.

Review objectives...

☐ **Start** and **exit** the application

☐ Identify different elements of the **screen**

☐ Create a basic **document**

At the end of *some* lessons is a **GOING FURTHER** section explaining more advanced features related to the topic. You can go back to complete **GOING FURTHER** sections when you have worked through the basic lessons.

Notes, Tips and Warnings

Notes and tips are given throughout each lesson.

Notes give additional information about the current topic. Always read the note before completing the task.

 Read this section before starting.

Note

Tips provide alternative ways of carrying out a task.

 As well as using the toolbar button or menu, you can get help by pressing **F1**.

Tip

You may also see the **Stop** sign . This warning sign means you must pay careful attention to the text before proceeding.

Index and Glossary

At the back of the book you will find an index to the topics and features covered in the course. Introduction courses also have a glossary of software terms and jargon.

Mouse Conventions

The **mouse pointer** is the term given to the symbol that appears when the mouse is pointing to a particular element. Typically it is a white arrow pointing to the left, although its shape varies depending on the action you are carrying out at the time.

Most mouse commands are issued using the **left** mouse button. When instructed to click with the mouse, you should click the **left** mouse button, unless you are explicitly told to **right-click**.

> If you have configured the mouse for **left-handed** use, you should reverse these instructions. When instructed to click, use the *right* mouse button; when instructed to right-click use the *left* mouse button.

Several other terms are used when providing mouse instructions. These are described in the following table:

Term	Action
Point	Move the mouse so that the mouse pointer is positioned on top of the item specified.
Click **Right-click**	Point to the item you want to click on then press-and-*release* the mouse button.
Click-and-drag	Use this to select text and groups of objects. Move the mouse pointer left/above of the relevant item(s) then press-and-*hold* the left mouse button. Holding the button down, move the mouse pointer across/down the item(s). Release the mouse button.
Double-click	Point to the item then press-and-release the left mouse button *twice* in quick succession (If you are not used to the mouse, double-clicking may require some practice).
Drag-and-Drop	Point to the item then click-and-*hold down* the left mouse button. Still holding the button down, **point** to another area of the screen then release the mouse button.

Keyboard Conventions

When you are instructed to press a key on the keyboard, the key is illustrated as shown in the following examples: F1 or Caps Lock.

If you are not familiar with a PC keyboard, use the table below to help recognise certain keys.

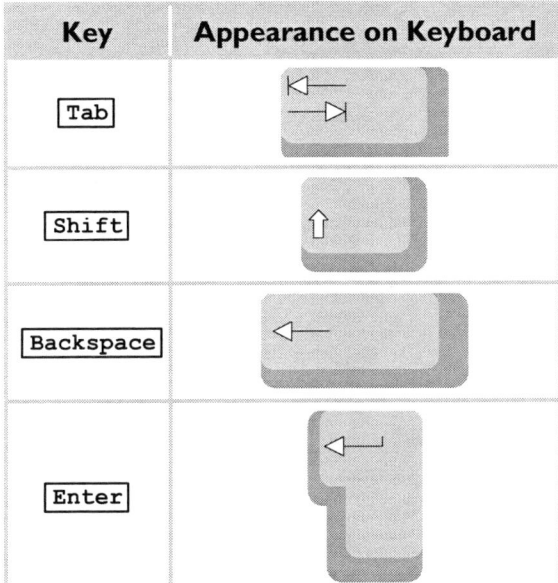

Key	Appearance on Keyboard
Tab	
Shift	
Backspace	
Enter	

Two keys with a plus sign (+) between them means you should press both keys together. So: Alt+F4 ...means "Hold down the Alt key while you press F4 then release both keys".

Two keys with a comma (,) between them means you should press one key after another. So: Alt,F means "Press-and-release the Alt key, then press-and-release the F key".

Instructions for entering text

When you are asked to type text, numbers or letters, the text appears in a different typeface from the instructions. For example:

- Type This text is in a different typeface

You would be expected to type "This text is in a different typeface".

Notes

Lesson 1: Database Development

Relational database design is a methodology that produces robust, efficient databases. This lesson reviews database design concepts.

Lesson objectives...

- ☐ Review the principles of **relational** database design
- ☐ Apply the theory of **normalisation** to database design
- ☐ Understand the importance of **documenting** database structure

Jump lesson...

If you already know how to normalise tables, or if you want to get started with some practical examples straight away, jump to DEFINING RELATIONSHIPS on page 25.

Designing a Relational Database

To create a relational database that meets the needs of the user, you must define the purpose or objective of the database. Only then can you decide what data needs to be stored. Once the requirements are outlined, you will then be able to create the table(s) and fields required.

The key to creating a fast, easy-to-use and efficient database lies in the design of tables and their relationships.

In a very simple database, every record is stored in a single table, which can lead to many fields being blank (data redundancy), and data in other fields being duplicated. A relational database splits large tables into smaller, more workable tables. This should eliminate duplication and wasted space. This process is referred to as **Normalisation**.

Generally speaking, tables should contain a **primary key**, which uniquely identifies each record in the table (that is, the primary key is not allowed to contain duplicate values).

Relationships are created between the normalised tables to link the data in each table as if it were still in one large table. The **Parent** table will usually contain a single record that is linked to several records in a **Child** table. To link the tables, an identical item of data is duplicated in each table. The duplicated field is usually the **primary** key, which becomes the **secondary** (or **foreign**) key in the child (or secondary) table.

The source of your data can affect the design process. As well as manually entering data into tables you have created, data may be imported directly from an existing database, spreadsheet or other type of data file. Imported tables and data can become part of your database.

Alternatively, the database may be linked to external data files, which remain in their original format and location, but are used as if they were part of your database. You will be able to change the data within these files but will not be able to amend the structure of them.

Ask yourself how long it will take to adapt existing data to fit the design of your database. You may be able to keep data in its existing form. On the other hand, some extra work put in at the beginning of the design process to normalise the existing data may avoid many hard-to-solve problems later on.

Normalisation of Data

One of the purposes and benefits of using a relational database is to cut down on duplication of data. This makes it easier to enter, search for, and use the data, and takes up less disk space. A **normalised** database is easier to maintain and can be modified more readily as requirements change. A large database will also run significantly faster when it is normalised.

As part of any database design, it is necessary to analyse the information you are going to store. Part of the analysis process is **Normalisation**.

Normalisation is the process of finding the best structure for the database. A series of rules, called **normal forms**, are applied to the data until it is in the best structure. The goal of normalisation is to ensure that:

- All data can be used efficiently
- The amount of redundant data in any table is minimised
- Modifications to a table are robust and consistent with the rest of the table structure

The theory of **normal forms** allows for five levels of table normalisation, however, the fourth and fifth normal forms are considered to be special cases. Ideally, you should aim to get all of the tables in the third normal form.

The second normal form builds on the first normal form, the third on the second, and so on.

You can analyse your tables in one of two ways:

- List all of the fields that you are using in the entire database in one large table. Modify the table to conform to each normal form, until you think that the table has been sufficiently **normalised**. You will generally be left with several additional tables, to which you should apply the same process.

- As you become more experienced, you should be able to work out the main database tables in advance, and group the fields by these major headings. This allows you to apply normal forms to smaller sets of data. Take care with this approach though - you may have a poorer understanding of how tables relate when it comes to aggregate the tables into a single relational structure.

First Normal Form

The **First Normal Form** (1NF) is the simplest. The rule is that fields in a table cannot contain a list of data and that a table cannot contain repeating fields.

An example of a repeating group would be, in a Customer database, adding each contact name as a new field (Contact1, Contact2...). A ContactName field is also an example of listing several pieces of information in a single field (first name and last name).

- To resolve the table to 1NF, it would be necessary to add a ContactID field and split the existing ContactName fields into two fields: FirstName and LastName.

Second Normal Form

The **Second Normal Form** (2NF) rule states that a table must be in 1NF and every non-key column must be dependent on the primary key.

To resolve a table to 2NF, the table must be **decomposed**:

- Identify the primary key for the table.

- Identify fields not dependent on the primary key. This group of fields should have its own choice for primary key. You may need to create more than one group.

Generally speaking, if creating a new record causes data to be repeated in the table, the fields that do not repeat belong in a new table.

> This is a guideline, not a rule. Obviously in some circumstances data will be repeated. For example, values in a Country field would repeat often but you would not *always* want to create a separate Country table.

- Create new tables based on the groups you identify. Each table should contain a primary key field. A copy of this field will remain in the original table in order to link the two.

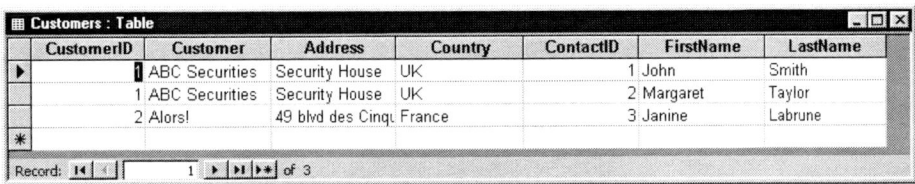

The table above is in 1NF, as there are no repeating fields and each cell contains only one data item. However, there is now no obvious candidate for a primary key. Each new contact requires duplicate information about the company they work for.

- ContactID, FirstName and LastName should be split to their own table (**Contacts**), leaving a copy of ContactID in the Customers table so that new contacts can still be added at the same company.

- Any duplicate records in the Customers table should be deleted, so that the table also contains a valid primary key.

Third Normal Form

A table is in the **Third Normal Form** if it is in 2NF (that is, all fields depend on the primary key) and the other fields do not depend on each other.

The table in the example above is not in 3NF. The Country field depends on the Address. The Country field could be removed into a **lookup** table (a table that only stores one set of values). However, as mentioned above, you may not want to create a separate Country table, especially if you do not want to use Country values in tables other than the Customers table.

Another example of one field depending on another is a calculated field, which should be removed to a query, not stored in a table.

Think of normalisation as a means whereby all fields in a table should relate to the primary key of that table, except for linking fields (foreign keys). Do not repeat fields and do not store more than one "piece" of data in a field.

De-normalisation

The effect of normalisation is to create many small tables containing just a few fields, which can in itself create unnecessary duplication of key fields. De-normalisation reverses the process until an acceptable level of duplication and redundancy is achieved.

Queries, Forms and Reports

Remember that as well as designing a data store, it is also important to work out how the data will be accessed and used.

You can set **field properties** for tables during the design process to improve query performance. You may also need to de-normalise a database to make queries run faster.

Users may require a range of forms for different purposes. For example, they may need different forms for adding and editing than for viewing data.

Finally, you need to establish a management strategy for the database, by resolving questions such as the following:

- Is the database to be shared by multiple users?
- What security is required to protect the data?
- What features will different users have access to?
- What backup strategy is in place?
- Who is responsible for the management of the database?

Documenting the Database

It is important to keep notes on design decisions, explaining why they were made. It is also important to comment database features, such as fields and queries. Most objects have space for you to add comments in the database file itself.

You may also want to adopt a naming system when creating objects in your database. This can be especially useful when naming controls on forms and reports. Most naming systems mean adding a three character prefix to the name.

The following tables illustrate a naming convention based on proposals by Microsoft and Greg Reddick. However, the naming convention has been updated to suggest names for new objects (such as Data Access Pages) that are not within the scope of the current recommendations.

Database Objects		
Object	Prefix	Example
Database	db	dbUniversal
Table	tbl	tblCustomer
Query	qry	qryUKCustomers
Form	frm	frmCustomerUpdate
Report	rpt	rpt2001Sales
Data Access Pages	dap	dapCustomerQuery

Lesson 1

Field Names

Field Data Type	Prefix	Example
Yes/No (boolean)	bln	blnDiscontinued
Currency	cur	curOrderAmount
Date/Time	dtm	dtmLastLogin
Number	num	numCustomerID
Text	chr txt	chrTelephoneNo txtContactFName
Memo	mem	memComments
AutoNumber	anm	anmProductID

Controls

Control Type	Prefix	Example
Check Box	chk	chkOnOff
Combo Box	cbo	cboCountry
Command Button	cmd	cmdCancel
SubForm	frm	frmMain
Image	img	imgCurrent
Label	lbl	lblCompanyName
Line	lin	linLeftBorder
List Box	lst	lstCountry
SubReport	rpt	rptUKOrders
Text Box	txt	txtContactName

Some of the above are "non-standard" in that they do not follow other widely recognised conventions. You should find a naming convention that you can use easily, rather than using a more complex "standard" convention.

Make sure that you document the convention that you use.

Database Terms

Database

A **database** is a collection of **objects** used for storing and managing information. Examples of databases are: a telephone directory, an encyclopaedia, a catalogue, a stock file and a customer record.

Object

An **object** is a database component such as a **table, query, form** or **report**.

Table

The data in a database is stored in **Tables**. Tables are the main elements of a database. In a relational database the data is held in several separate tables for compactness and ease of use. The tables are linked together by a key data field to allow cross-referencing of related data. Data in a table is shown as a datasheet (like a spreadsheet).

Each column in a table is a field. Each row in a table is a record.

Forms

Forms are a more user-friendly way of presenting data than tables. Several different forms can be created for different activities associated with a single table, such as adding new records, editing records and filtering records. Forms can also be used to display and edit data from several different tables at the same time. Forms based on queries have the flexibility of limiting the records and fields displayed to only those selected in the query.

Queries

Queries are a method of selecting and sorting data from tables to make it easier to work with. Data is presented in the same way as a table and in some queries records can be entered, edited, and deleted directly from the query datasheet. Several tables can be joined in a query to provide more flexibility when working with related data. Calculations can be performed to produce new fields. Queries can also be used to add, delete, and automatically update data.

Reports

Tables, queries and forms can be printed as seen on the screen, but **reports** allow the data to be presented in a more structured format. Reports based on queries print only the selected fields and records that the query produces. Reports can also include calculations and summaries of the data printed.

Macros

Macros are lists of stored commands that provide automation for frequent or complex activities. Macros can be triggered by a certain event, such as opening a form, moving into or out of a field, or clicking a command (macro) button. Access contains a list of macro instructions to select from, which require no programming ability to use.

Modules

Modules are lists of programming instructions created in Visual Basic. They duplicate and extend the function of macros and also run faster, but require some knowledge of programming to create. Modules are outside the scope of this book.

Data Access Pages

Data Access Pages are separate files stored outside of Access in HTML format, designed for an internet or intranet. However, when you create the file, Access automatically adds a shortcut to the file in the Database window.

Review Questions

(1) What is the first step in the design process?

(2) What is normalisation?

(3) When is a table in Second Normal Form?

(4) What are the basic steps to take when normalising a data store?

Answers on the next page.

Lesson 1

Review
Answers

(1) State the purpose of the database and identify requirements

(2) Normalisation is the process of finding the best structure for the database. A series of rules, called normal forms, are applied to the data until it is in the best structure

(3) To be in 2NF, a table must be in 1NF and every non-key column must be dependent on the primary key

(4) i) List all the fields to use in one large table
ii) Apply 1NF to the table by splitting fields that contain lists of data and removing repeating fields (this will usually require key-type fields to be added)
iii) Apply 2NF to the table by decomposing it into new tables related by foreign keys
iv) Apply 3NF to each table by removing calculated fields and splitting dependent fields into lookup tables

Skills Summary

Review

Congratulations on completing the first lesson. You should have a better understanding of database design theory and methods.

Review objectives...

- ☐ Review the principles of **relational** database design

- ☐ Apply the theory of **normalisation** to database design

- ☐ Understand the importance of **documenting** database structure

Notes

Lesson 2: Defining Relationships

This lesson deals with the importance of table relationships, the need to apply referential integrity where necessary and creating subdatasheets.

Lesson objectives...

- ☐ Understand different kinds of **table relationships**
- ☐ Create **relationships** between two tables
- ☐ Set **referential integrity** in a relationship
- ☐ Use the **Cascade Update** and **Cascade Delete** options
- ☐ Specify **join** properties for relationships
- ☐ Create a **subdatasheet**

Jump lesson...

If you know how to create table relationships and enforce referential integrity between tables, you can learn how to make tables more robust and efficient in WORKING WITH FIELD PROPERTIES on page 51. Alternatively, jump ahead to WORKING WITH EXTERNAL DATA on page 83 to find out about importing, linking and exporting data.

What are Table Relationships?

Once you have analysed the information you need to store and created the various tables in your database, along the lines of **Normalisation** discussed on page 13, you need a way for Access to bring the information together. This is accomplished by establishing **relationships** between the tables in the database.

A relationship is established by linking a common field (often with the same name) in both tables. For example, the **Orders** table contains the **CustomerID** field from the **Customers** table.

Two tables can only have one relationship. Defining a second relationship replaces the existing relationship. However, a table can be related to more than one other table. For example, the **Order Details** table is related to the **Orders** table and the **Products** table, through the **OrderID** and **ProductID** fields respectively.

There are three different types of relationship, as explained below.

One-to-Many relationships

One-to-Many relationships are by far the most common type of relationship. In a one-to-many relationship, a record in the first table (known as the **parent**) can have many matching records in the second table (the **child**). A record in the second table can have only one matching record in the first table.

Throughout the course you will be using a database for the fictitious company Universal Import Ltd, a small company that specialises in the import of foods from across the world. The company is developing a database to deal with the tracking of orders.

Many of the relationships in the sample database are one-to-many:

One	Many	Explanation
Customers	Orders	Each customer places more than one order
Orders	Order Details	Each order contains more than one type of item
Order Details	Products	Each product is on more than one order's item list

One-to-One relationship

In a **One-to-One** relationship, each record in the first table can have only one matching record in the second table, and vice versa. This means that the common fields are **both primary keys** (or at least, must both contain unique values).

This type of relationship is not used very often, as it is often simpler to store all the data in one table. This type of relationship could be used for a table with an extremely large number of fields or to separate confidential information from more public data.

A Many-to-Many relationship

A **Many-to-Many** relationship cannot be created directly since it requires **three** tables to operate. One example is the **Order Details** table, which has one-to-many relationships with both the **Orders** and the **Products** tables. This means that the Orders and Products tables have a many-to-many relationship (Products can belong to multiple orders and orders can contain multiple products).

Creating Relationships

Relationships are created and edited using the **Relationships** window.

When viewing the **Relationships** window, all tables and queries must be saved and closed.

To display the Relationships window

TryIT	Action	Result
	• Open the database **UNIVER_2** • On the **Standard** toolbar, click **Relationships**	The **Relationships** window is displayed.

The **Relationships** window contains list boxes representing the tables in your database. Each list box shows all the fields in the table.

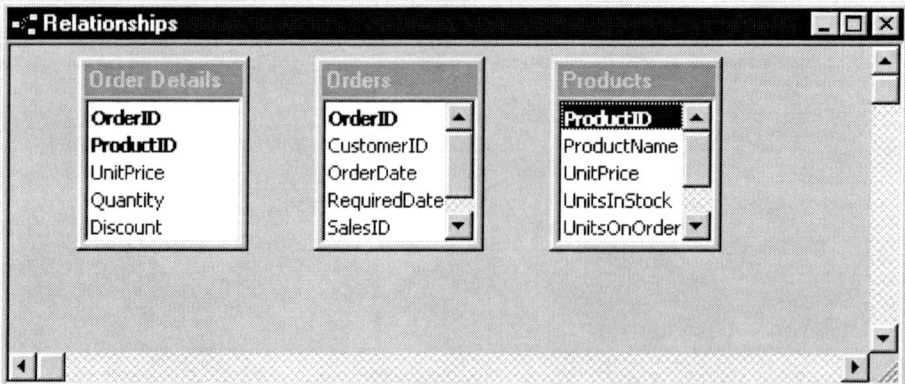

Relationships Window

 If relationships are already defined between the tables, they are displayed as thin lines linking the related fields.

To arrange tables in the relationship window

Moving the tables is simply a case of dragging the header bar of the appropriate table. This is very useful in a more complex design, where there are many more tables than in this simple example.

To add a table to the Relationships window

When a new table is added to the database, it will not automatically be added to the **Relationships** window. If you want to work on a table, you will have to add it manually to the window.

- On the **Standard** toolbar, click **Show Table**

OR

- From the **Relationships** menu, select **Show Table...**

The **Show Table** dialogue box is displayed.

Defining Relationships

- Select the table to use then click **Add**
- Add any more tables if you wish then click **Close**

In our practice example, the Customers table has not been added to the Relationships window.

TryIT 	Action	Result
	• On the **Standard** toolbar, click **Show Table**	The **Show Table** window is displayed.

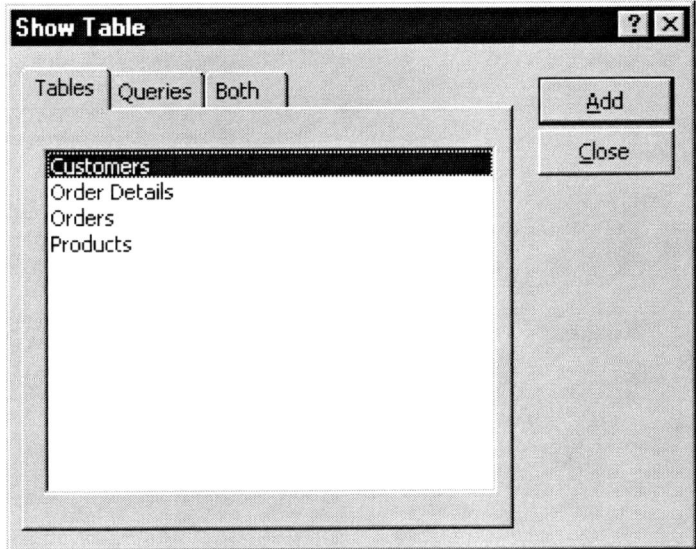
Show Table dialogue box

All available tables are displayed - including those (if any) that are already displayed in the Relationships window.

TryIT 	Action	Result
	• Select the **Customers** table and click **Add**	The **Customers** table is added to the **Relationships** window.
	• Click **Close** to close the dialogue box	The **Show Table** dialogue box is closed.

Lesson 2

To create a relationship

To create a relationship between tables, you drag the field that you want to relate from one table to the related field in the other table.

In most cases, you drag the **primary key** field (displayed in bold) from one table to a similar field (often with the same name) called the **foreign key** in the other table.

It is not necessary for the fields to have the same name, but they **must** use the same **data type**.

The only exception to this is an **AutoNumber** field. With an AutoNumber field, the field in the related table can be an AutoNumber or any other **numeric** type.

TryIT

Action	Result
• Drag the **CustomerID** field from the **Customers** table to the **CustomerID** field in the **Orders** table	The **Edit Relationships** dialogue box is displayed.

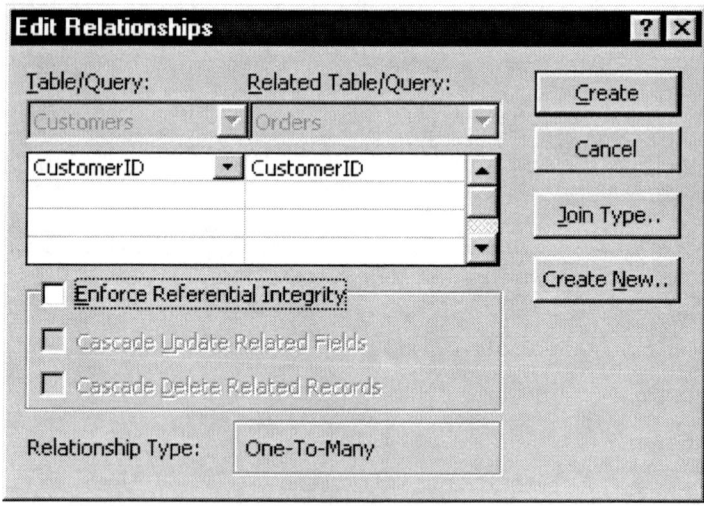

Edit Relationships dialogue box

• Click **C**reate	The **Relationships** window is displayed again. A thin line links the related fields.

Defining Relationships

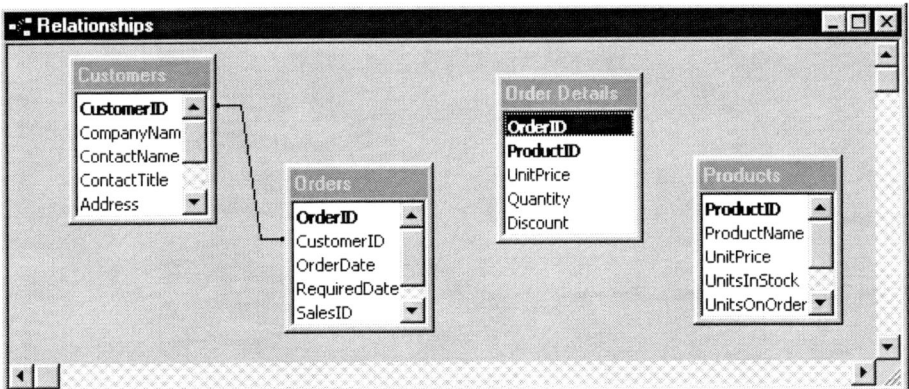

Relationships Window

 You can only define one relationship between two tables. If you define a second relationship, it replaces the existing one. You can remove a relationship by selecting the join line and pressing `Delete`.

 You can select multiple fields, and drag to create a relationship based on those multiple columns, or you can drag-and-drop a single field, then add the other fields in this dialogue box.

To save and close the Relationships window

You must save any changes to the Relationships window.

TryIT

Action	Result
• From the **File** menu, select **Save**	The **Relationships** layout is saved.
• From the **File** menu, select **Close** or click **Close** X to close the **Relationships** window	The **Relationships** window is closed and the **Database** window is displayed.

Referential Integrity

Once tables are linked, data accuracy becomes an important issue. **Referential integrity** means that you cannot enter a value in a foreign key field that does not have a corresponding value in the primary key field of the joined table.

One consequence of this is that you cannot delete records in the table with the primary key field (the **parent** table) if there are corresponding records in the foreign key table (the **child** table).

For example, you would not want to create an Order record for a customer who does not exist in the Customers table. Also you do not want to delete a customer while the customer still has outstanding orders.

Referential integrity is enforced by ticking the check box in the **Relationships** dialogue box.

You cannot define referential integrity with a **linked** table. Also cannot use **OLE**, **Memo Hyperlink** or **Yes/No** fields to create table relationships.

To edit a relationship and enforce referential integrity

TryIT	Action	Result
	• Close any tables you may have open	
	• On the **Standard** toolbar, click **Relationships**	The **Relationships** window is displayed.
	• Double-click the **join line** between the **Customers** table and the **Orders** table	The **Edit Relationships** dialogue box is displayed.
	• Click the **Enforce Referential Integrity** check box	

Defining Relationships

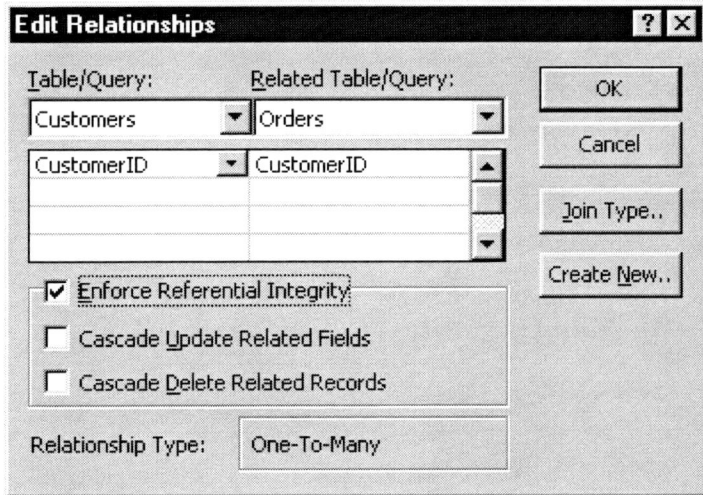
Edit Relationships dialogue box

• Click **OK**	The following message is displayed.

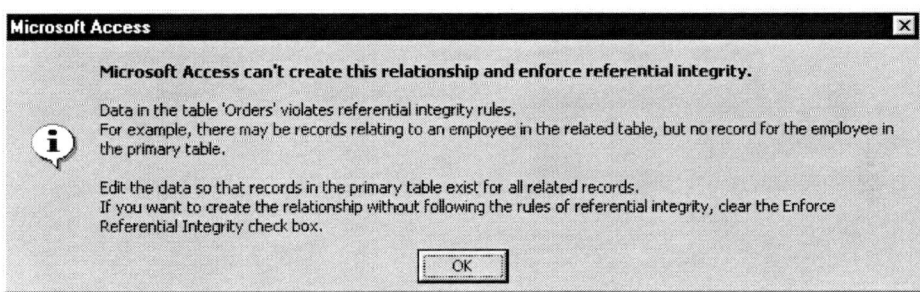
Error enforcing referential integrity

This is a common problem encountered when enforcing Referential Integrity on tables that contain existing or imported data. If you read the message, you should be able to work out that there is at least one child record in the **Orders** table that has no corresponding data in the parent **Customers** table.

• Click **OK** • Click **Cancel** to close the dialogue box then exit the **Relationships** window	The warning dialogue box is removed. The **Database** window is displayed.

Find Unmatched Query Wizard

In order to enforce referential integrity in this database, you need to clean up the existing data. A query that finds all **CustomerID** values in **Orders** that do not have a relevant **Customers** table entry will do this and fortunately, Access provides a wizard to perform this task - the **Find Unmatched Query Wizard**.

To use the Find Unmatched Query Wizard

TryIT	Action	Result
	• In the **Database** window, select the **Queries** object • Click **New**	The **New Query** dialogue box is displayed.

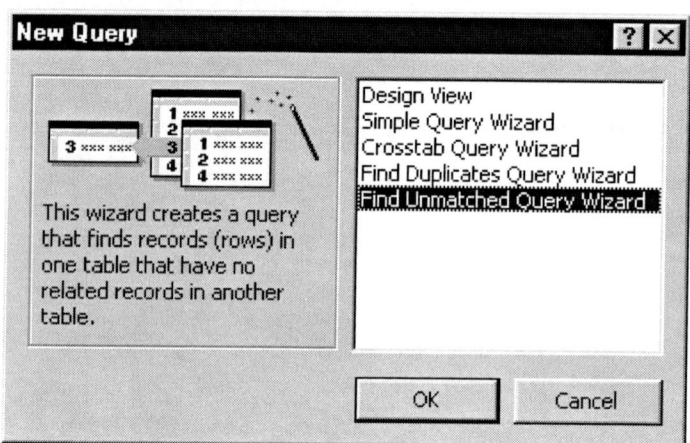

New Query dialogue box

	• Select **Find Unmatched Query Wizard** • Click **OK**	The **Find Unmatched Query Wizard** dialogue box is displayed.

Defining Relationships

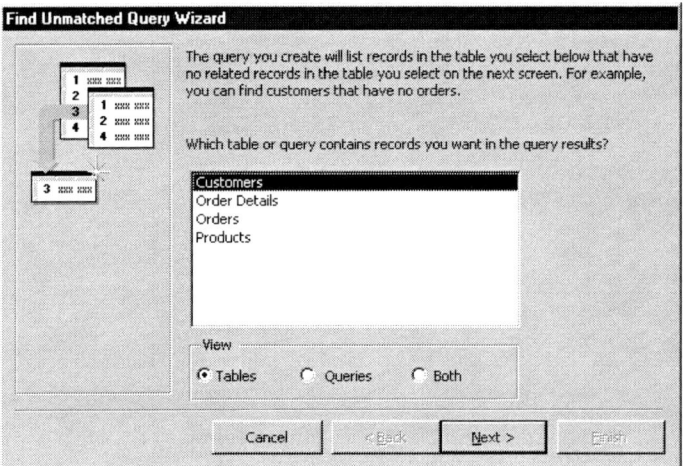

Find Unmatched Query Wizard - First screen

This first screen prompts you to select the table **in which** to find the unmatched records. In this example, we know that the Orders table has records with no customers, so this is the table we should pick.

- Select the **Orders** table then click **Next >**
- Select the **Customers** table then click **Next >**

The next page lets you select the table that provides the matches.

The next page asks you to select the field containing the values to check. Access has already identified the correct field (CustomerID).

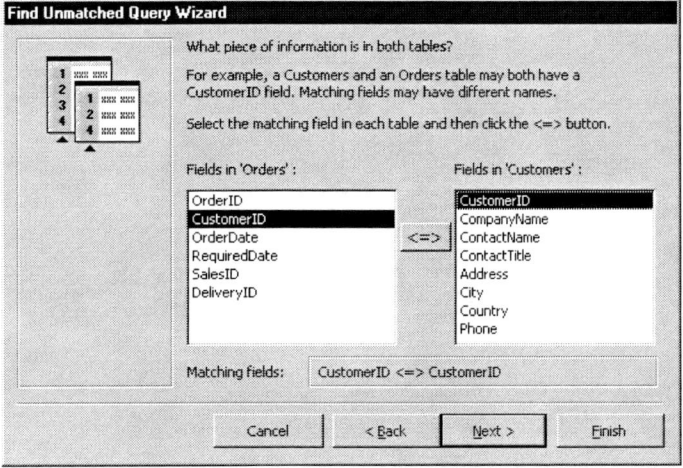

Find Unmatched Query Wizard - Third screen

Lesson 2

• Ensure that the **CustomerID** field is selected	This field needs to be the joining field in both tables.
• Click **Next >**	
• Select all the available fields for display in the query results	
• Click **Finish**	The query is created with the default name and the results displayed.

Find Unmatched Query results

It could be that the ANTON customer was deleted or that the CustomerID had been entered wrongly. Referential integrity makes these kinds of error impossible.

For this example, we will assume that the CustomerID in the Customers table has been changed by accident.

• Close the query	
• From the **Database** window, open the **Customers** table	
• Modify the **CustomerID** for **ANTAN** to **ANTON**	
• Close the **Customers** table	
• On the **Standard** toolbar, click **Relationships**	The **Relationships** window is displayed.
• Double-click the **join** line between the **Customers** table and the **Orders** table	The **Edit Relationships** dialogue box is displayed.

Defining Relationships

- Click the **Enforce Referential Integrity** check box
- Click **OK**

The **Relationships** window is redisplayed, showing the one-to-many relationship.

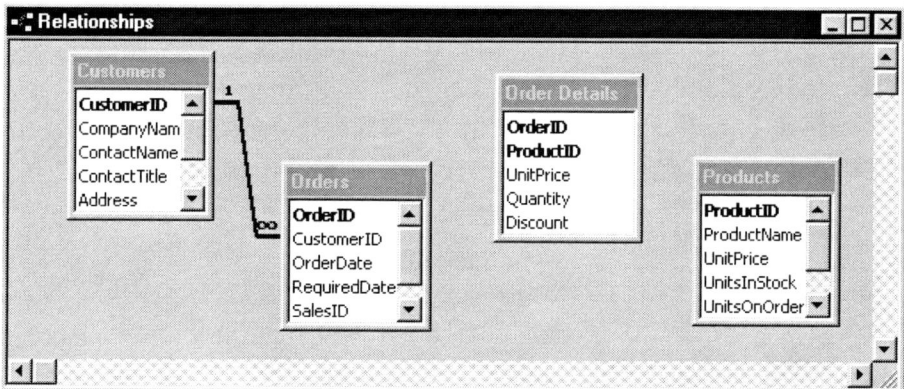

Relationships dialogue box

Access displays a "1" above the join line to show which table is on the "one" side of a one-to-many relationship and an infinity symbol ∞ to show which table is on the "many" side.

- From the **File** menu, select **Save**

The Relationships layout is saved.

Cascade Update and Delete

The **Cascade Update** and **Cascade Delete** options allow you to delete and amend existing records without manually editing or deleting any related records in child tables.

For relationships in which **referential integrity** is enforced, you can specify whether Access should automatically **cascade update** and **cascade delete** related records. If these options are set, delete and update operations in the parent table, normally prevented by referential integrity rules, are allowed. Access automatically "purges" records in the secondary table related to the one you want to modify or delete.

- If you select the **Cascade Update Related Fields** check box, when a primary key of a record in the primary table is changed, Access automatically updates the primary key to the new value in all related records.

- If you select **Cascade Delete Related Records** check box when defining a relationship, Access automatically deletes related records in the related table. For example, if a customer record is deleted, all associated orders records would also be deleted.

In many cases this will suit the function of the database. However, some care does need to be taken before setting these options. You should be aware that an on-screen warning is displayed when you manually delete or update a record that will affect related records:

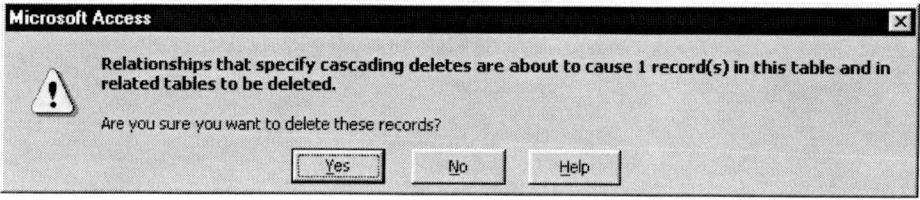

Cascade Deleting

However, if you use an action query to amend records (see page 101) no warning will be given.

To set the cascade delete/update option

The Relationships window should still be open.

TryIT

Action	Result
• Double-click the **join** line between the **Customers** table and the **Orders** table • Select the **Cascade Update Related Fields** box • Click **OK**	The **Edit Relationships** dialogue box is displayed.

This option means that the **CustomerID** field is changed in a customer's record, the change will automatically be made in all Orders records related to that customer.

TryIT

Practice
• Setup the following relationships between tables: • **ProductID** in **Products** to **ProductID** in **Order Details** • **OrderID** in **Orders** to **OrderID** in **Order Details** • Enforce referential integrity in both these relationships (You will find that you need to delete unmatched Order Details records) • Set **Cascade Update/Delete** options as appropriate (if at all) • Save your changes but keep the Relationships window open

You can print the Relationships layout by selecting **File**, **Print Relationships**. This creates a **report**, which can be printed as normal and also saved, if required.

Join Types

When you use a query, form or report to extract information from **multiple** tables, you can specify how Access **joins** these tables. The join affects which records are selected.

While it may seem that there is only one obvious way of joining the tables, there are in fact three. When you are joining two tables, consider that there may be records in one table that do not have related records in the other table. For example, you can add information about a customer who never places an order. This does not violate any rule of normalisation, but in a real-life situation you may want to include these records in your output.

Consider the **Orders** and **Order Details** tables:

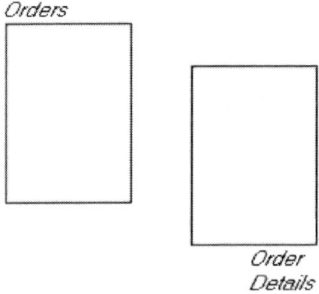

The default join type is an **Inner Join**, which only returns records where there are matching records in both tables. In this case, it means only returning records where there is an identical OrderID value in **both** tables.

The join type is independent of referential integrity considerations, so tables can contain records where there are no matching entries in the joined table.

The Inner Join can be best summarised by a diagram, where the grey area represents the records returned:

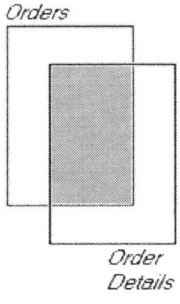

Inner Join

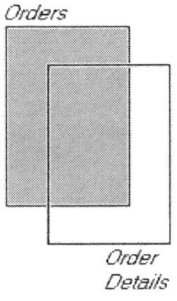

Left Outer Join

The second option is often called a **Left Outer Join**, since it returns **all** records from the left-hand table, along with matching records from the right-hand table. In the case of the example, this will return all records from the **Orders** table, even if they have no matching records in the **Order Details** table. Again, a diagram may make this more obvious.

Not surprisingly, the third option is a **Right Outer Join**, where all the records from the right-hand table are returned, along with matching records from the left-hand table.

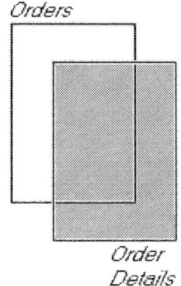

Right Outer Join

Table joins operate independently of table relationships. You do not need to create a permanent table relationship to use both tables in a query. However, when you do create a relationship, you can also change the default **Join Type**.

While this may seem unimportant at this stage, specifying the default join type for a set of related records from the start will speed up the creation of queries, multiple table forms and so on.

Lesson 2

To change the default join type

TryIT	Action	Result
	• Double-click the join line between the **Customers** and **Orders** tables	The **Edit Relationships** dialogue box is displayed.
	• Click the **Join Type...** button	The **Join Properties** dialogue box is displayed.

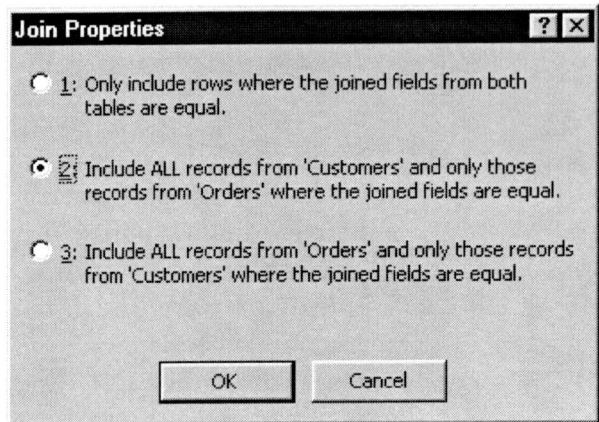

Join Properties dialogue box

	• Select the **2:** option button and click **OK** to exit both dialogue boxes	The join type is changed. Note that the relationship line now shows an arrow, indicating an outer join.

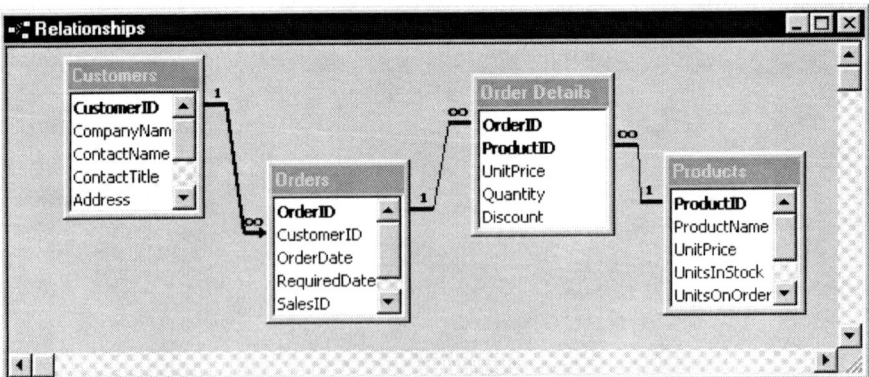

Relationship showing a left-outer join

To change the join type in a query

TryIT

Practice
• Create a new query in design view
• Add the **Customers** and **Orders** tables
• Add the **CompanyName** and **OrderID** fields then run the query
• How many records are returned? _____
• Switch back to design view and double-click the join line between the tables

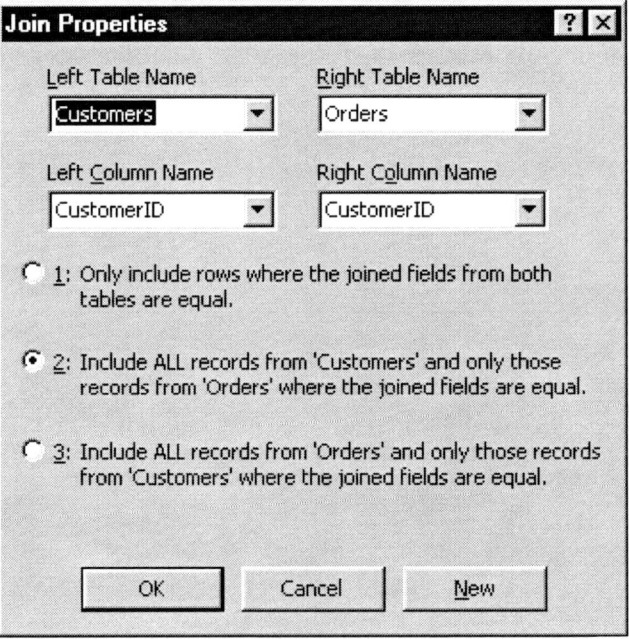

Join Properties

• Change the join to **1:** then re-run the query
• How many records are returned? _____
• Save and close the query

Changing the join type in a query **only affects that query**. The default join type remains the same. You can remove a join in a query by selecting the join line and pressing `Delete`.

Lesson 2

Subdatasheets

In a table that has a one-to-many relationship (for example the Customers and Orders tables), Access allows you to view the related records (Orders) from the primary table (Customers). You can view and edit the related data in tables, queries, or subform datasheets. For related tables, Access automatically creates a **subdatasheet**

You can nest up to eight levels of a subdatasheet within a subdatasheet, but each datasheet can only have one nested datasheet.

By default, Access creates multiple table datasheet views when you add relationships to the table. If you have only one child relationship, it is automatically set as the subdatasheet. If there are two child tables, you are presented with a dialogue box to make a (wide ranging) selection for the subdatasheet.

To view multi-table datasheet view

TryIT	Action	Result
	• From the **Database window**, open the **Customers** table	
	• Click the **expand indicator** (plus sign) next to the first record	This expands the subdatasheet related to that record.
	• Click the **collapse indicator** (minus sign) next to the first record	This collapses (or closes) the subdatasheet related to that record.

	CustomerID	CompanyNam	ContactName	ContactTitle	Address
▶ +	ALFKI	Alfreds Futterki	Maria Andson	Sales Represer	Obere Str. 57
−	ANATR	Ana Trujillo Em	Ana Trujillo	Owner	Avda. de la Cor

	Order ID	Order Date	Required Date	SalesID	DeliveryID
	10308	15 April 1998	13 May 1998	1	3
	10625	i March 1999	02 April 1999	6	3
	10759	25 June 1999	23 July 1999	2	3
	10926	October 1999	29 October 1999	6	1
*	:oNumber)			0	0

| + | ANTON | Glorious Foods | Jill Goody | Proprietor | 15 Golden Squa |

Subdatasheet

To create a subdatasheet

For any related tables, Access automatically creates the subdatasheets. However, you can also add a subdatasheet to any table, query or form.

TryIT	Action	Result
	• From the **Database** window, **O**pen the **Orders** table	
	• From the **Insert** menu, select **S**ubdatasheet...	The **Insert Subdatasheet** dialogue box is displayed.

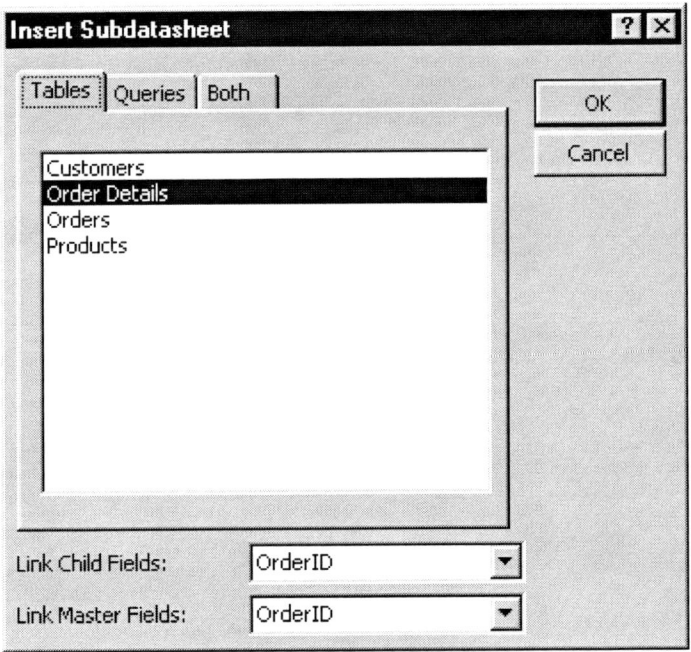

Insert Subdatasheet dialogue box

 Access will attempt to guess the appropriate object, based on the table relationships.

Lesson 2

- Select the **Order Details** table
- Leave the **Link Child Fields:** and **Link Master Fields:** as they are — Sometimes it may be necessary to modify these links, but they are correct for this exercise.
- Click **OK**
- Click **Yes** to create relationships — The **Orders** table is displayed with an extra column on the left with plus (+) signs.

- Click the **expand indicator** (plus sign) next to the Customer VINET — This expands the subdatasheet related to that record.
- Click the **collapse indicator** (minus sign) — This collapses (or closes) the subdatasheet related to that record.
- Click the **Close** button (X) to close the table window — The **Database** window is displayed.

Review Questions

(1) How do you create relationships in Access?

(2) What is referential integrity?

(3) In what situations is it not possible to define referential integrity?

(4) What is the effect of Cascade options?

(5) What is the difference between a join and a relationship?

(6) What is the effect of the join type?

(7) What is a subdatasheet?

Answers on the next page.

Lesson 2

Review
Answers

(1) i) From the Database window, click the Relationships button on the toolbar
ii) Add the relevant tables to the window
iii) Drag the field from the primary table to the foreign key field in the secondary table
iv) Save and close the window

(2) Referential integrity prevents you entering a value in a foreign key in a secondary table that does not have a matching entry in the primary key field of the primary table

(3) i) Using a field from a linked table
ii) Using an OLE, Memo, Hyperlink or Yes/No field
iii) If existing data is invalid

(4) Cascade Update or Delete allows you to change values in a primary key field after referential integrity has been enforced because foreign key records will be updated or deleted automatically

(5) i) A join applies only to the query in which is it created
ii) Relationships are permanent and can be used repeatedly in different situations

(6) The join type affects which records are selected in a query. By default only records with matching values in the joined field are selected (inner-join) but this can be changed to select all records from either table regardless (outer-join)

(7) A subdatasheet is a view from the primary table of related records in a secondary table, and is automatically created by Access where tables are related in a one-to-many relationship

Review

Skills Summary

Congratulations on successfully completing LESSON 2. You now know how to define table relationships.

Review objectives...

- ☐ Understand different kinds of **table relationships**

- ☐ Create **relationships** between two tables

- ☐ Set **referential integrity** in a relationship

- ☐ Use the **Cascade Update** and **Cascade Delete** options

- ☐ Specify **join** properties for relationships

- ☐ Create a **subdatasheet**

Notes

Working with Field Properties

Lesson 3

Maintaining accurate information in a database is a critical part of its management. The objective of this lesson is to show you a variety of ways in which field properties can be used to create more robust tables.

Lesson objectives...

- [ ] Use **field properties**
- [ ] Understand the different **field sizes** and **data types**
- [ ] Create a **validation rule**
- [ ] Create a **validation message** for the rule
- [ ] Create an **input mask**
- [ ] Use **lookup** fields
- [ ] Create an **index**

Jump lesson...

If you know how to use field properties effectively jump ahead to WORKING WITH EXTERNAL DATA on page 83 to find out about importing, linking and exporting data.

Lesson 3

Creating a Robust Database

When creating a database, it is important to ensure that the database is structured in such a way as to allow as little human error as possible when keying in data. Common errors are numbers that are too large or small, dates that are too early or late, duplicate records, or coded values that are not entered in a consistent format - all of which makes searching for data difficult and reports inaccurate.

Many problems can be solved by use of **field properties**. Field properties define how data will be entered, stored and displayed. For example, the **Indexed** property can be set to prevent a user typing a duplicate value into a field, or the **Validation Rule** property can be used to check that data entry matches a set of criteria.

Properties set in tables are carried through to queries and forms. Therefore, it is preferable to define data validation and restriction by setting a field's data type or properties when designing the table in the first place. Whenever that field is used in a form, the field's properties will also apply to data entry performed using the form.

Setting Field Properties

You set a field's properties in **Table Design** view, by selecting the field in the upper portion of the window and then selecting the appropriate property in the lower portion of the window.

Press [F6] to switch between the upper and lower panes of the **Design** window.

The **General** tab allows you to set properties such as size, format, caption and so on. The **Lookup** tab lets you create a list of values on a field or displays the details created by the **Lookup Wizard**.

Data Type and Field Size

Smaller fields take up less space and make the database faster. However, if a field is too small to hold data it will cause enormous problems to users. If possible, test the database with a wide range of records before delivering it to users.

You can specify the length of **Text** and **Number** data types.

Text

Text can be from 0 to 255 characters. The default length is 50 characters, but it is worth changing this where possible to optimise the performance of the database.

Numbers

The range of available field sizes for number data types is set out below.

Number	Description	Storage Size
Byte	0 - 255 (no fractions)	1 byte
Integer	-32,768 to 32,767 (no fractions)	2 bytes
Long Integer	-2,147,483,648 to 2,147,483,647 (no fractions)	4 bytes
Single	A 4 byte floating point number	4 bytes
Double	An 8 byte floating point number	8 bytes
Decimal	A 16 byte integer	16 bytes
Replication ID	A 16 byte field used to create a Globally unique identifier (GUID)	16 bytes

Long Integer is the default setting. Neither of the integers can store decimal point values. If you want to store monetary values, use the **Currency** data type, which can store up to 4 decimal places.

Lesson 3

Validation Rules

Access automatically validates the contents of a field, depending on a field's data type. For example, Access does not allow text in a date field or a numeric field.

A **Validation Rule** sets restrictions or conditions on what can be entered into a field. The validation rule is checked when you move to a different field. If the data entered in the field breaks the rule, Access displays a message telling you what is allowed.

Validation rules can be set for a table, field, a record or a control on a form.

Validation examples

Validation rules are **expressions**. Below are some examples of commonly used operators. For further information about expressions, lookup "What is an expression?" in the online help.

Expression	Meaning
>=Date()	A date that is either today's date or some date in the future.
BETWEEN 10 AND 100	A value between 10 and 100.
"UK" OR "USA"	Match UK or USA
LIKE "K???"	Value must be four letters beginning with K.
"M" OR "F"	Entry must be **M** or **F**.

To create a validation rule

TryIT

Action	Result
• Open the database **UNIVER_3**	
• Open the **Order Details** table in design view	The **Order Details** table is displayed.

Working with Field Properties

Action	Result
• Select the **Quantity** field • In the **Field Properties** pane, select **Validation Rule** • Type >0	The lower half of the window displays properties for the Quantity field. The rule means that only figures greater than zero can be entered.

Validation Text

You can add **Validation Text** to the field properties, which displays a warning message if the user enters data that breaks the rule.

To create validation text

TryIT

Action	Result
• In the **Field Properties** pane of the **Quantity** field, select **Validation Text** • Type Quantity must be greater than zero	 The message is displayed in the **Validation Text** field.

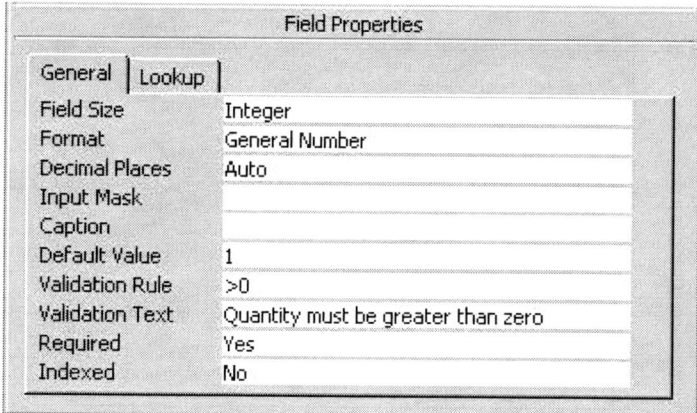

Field Properties panel

• On the **Standard** toolbar, click **Save**	The message below is displayed.

LearnIT MS Access 2000 Expert — Page 55

Lesson 3

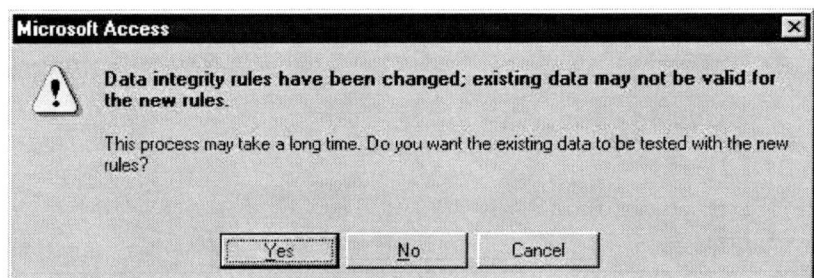
Warning message

• Click **Yes**	The **Validation Text** is saved.

To test the validation rule and text

TryIT	Action	Result
	• Click the **View** button on the toolbar to switch to **Datasheet** view	
	• Click into the **Quantity** field of one of the records	A new blank row is displayed.
	• Type 0 and press `Tab`	The **Validation Text** message below is displayed.

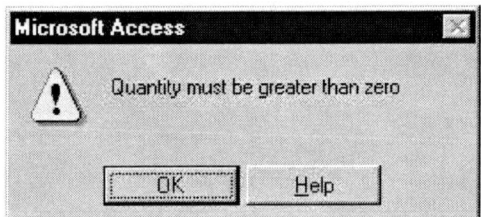
Validation Text message

• Click **OK**	The cursor remains in the field.
• Press `Esc` to exit the record	The original value is restored.
• Close the table	

Table Level Validation

Field level validation is limited in that you cannot validate changes to the selected field against values in other fields in the table.

However, Access also lets you perform **table level validation**. With table level validation, Access checks the statement that you enter when you move off the record, rather than the field. You can only have one validation expression at the table level, but this may be as complex as necessary.

To create a table-level validation statement

- Open the table in **Design** view
- On the **Standard** toolbar, click **Properties**

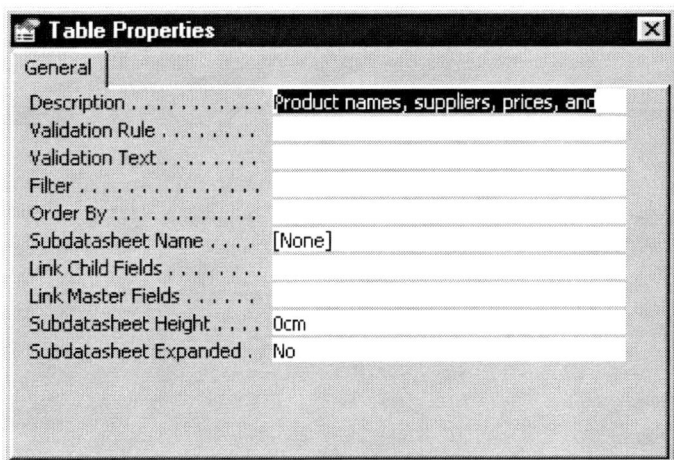

Table Properties dialogue box

At table level validation, the **Validation Rule** and **Validation Text** fields work in the same way as those at field level, except that you must always specify the field for which you are performing a validation.

Click the **Ellipses** button to launch the Expression Builder and create complex validation rules. You can learn more about the Expression Builder on page 254.

Input Masks

Another method of controlling data entry is to create an **input mask** to restrict the kind of values that can be entered in the field.

An input mask is a specific format for fields (in tables and queries), and text boxes and combo boxes (in forms) to format data and provide some control over what values can be entered. An input mask consists of literal characters (such as spaces, dots, dashes, and parentheses) that separate blanks to fill in.

An input mask not only formats an entry but applies strict rules as to the number and type of characters that can be entered. Some of the mask characters apply to the entire field, and some to the character position at a particular position in the field.

Input Mask codes

Mask	Use
0	Any digit (required)
9	Any digit (not required)
#	Any digit, + or - sign or space
L	Letter (required)
?	Letter (not required)
A	Letter or digit (required)
a	Letter or digit (not required)
&	Any character or space (required)
C	Any character or space (not required)
. : ; - /	Decimal point, date and time separators
<	Convert characters to lower case
>	Convert characters to UPPER case
!	Causes the mask to fill from right to left
\	Next character shown as literal

Working with Field Properties

To create an Input Mask

TryIT	Action	Result
	• Open the **Customers** table in design view • Select the **CustomerID** field • In the **Field Properties** pane, select **Input Mask** • Type >LLLLL	This limits the field to 5 letters and sets them to display in upper case.

Field Properties panel

	• From the **File** menu, select **Save**	The **Input Mask** field is saved.
	• Click the **View** button on the toolbar to switch to **Datasheet** view	The datasheet is displayed.
	• Add a new record to test your Input Mask is working	
	• Type a b c	
	• Press Tab	The following error message is displayed.

Lesson 3

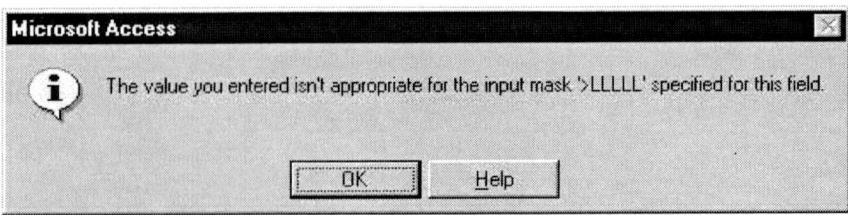

Input Mask error message

• Click **OK**	You are returned to the record.
• Type two more characters	
• Press `Tab`	This time no error message is displayed.

 The characters you typed are automatically converted to upper case.

Format Property

The **Format** property determines how data is displayed and printed after it is saved (unlike an input mask, which formats the user's data entry as it is typed).

The Format property **overrides** the Input Mask property if both are set (For example, if the input mask forces upper case characters and the format property lower case characters, the field will display and print lower case characters).

Many data types have several predefined formats, which will suit most uses. You can also enter custom format codes. For more information about creating custom formats, lookup "Format Property" in the online help.

Lookup Fields

Lookup fields are used to show "pick-lists" of information from related tables. The list is displayed in a drop-down list box (or combo box) on forms and datasheets. This makes data entry much more accurate, and in most cases much easier.

Using the Lookup Wizard, you can create a field that displays one of two kinds of lists to make data entry simpler:

- A lookup list that displays values from an existing table or query

- A value list that displays a set of values saved in the field definition itself

> Once you have created a lookup field at the table level, if you add the field to a form, Access automatically copies the definition to the form. However, if you change the definition of the value list field in the table after adding it to a form, those changes will not be reflected in that form. To correct this, delete the field from the form and then add it again.

Creating a Lookup List

To create a Lookup field in the Orders table to the Customers table

TryIT	Action	Result
	• Open the **Orders** table in design view • Click the drop-down arrow in the **Data Type** column for the **CustomerID** field	**Design** view is displayed.

Lesson 3

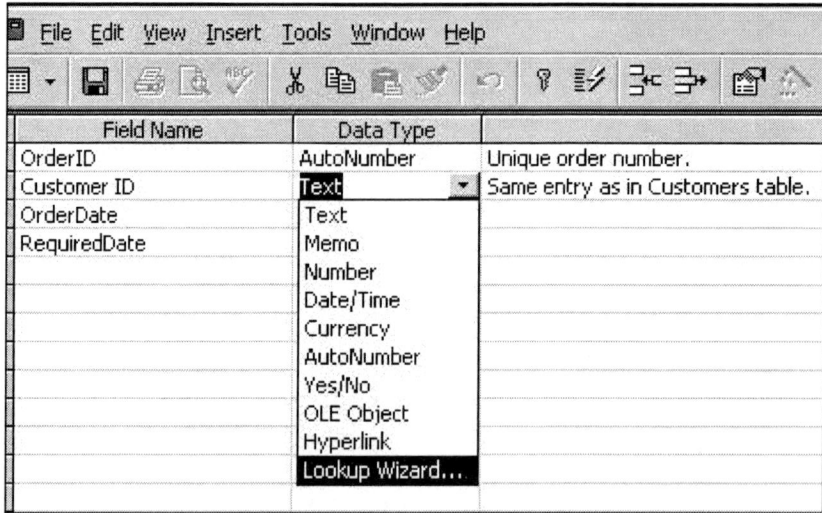

Data Type drop-down list

- Select **Lookup Wizard...**
- Click the option button **I want the lookup column to look up the values in a table or query**

The Lookup Wizard starts.

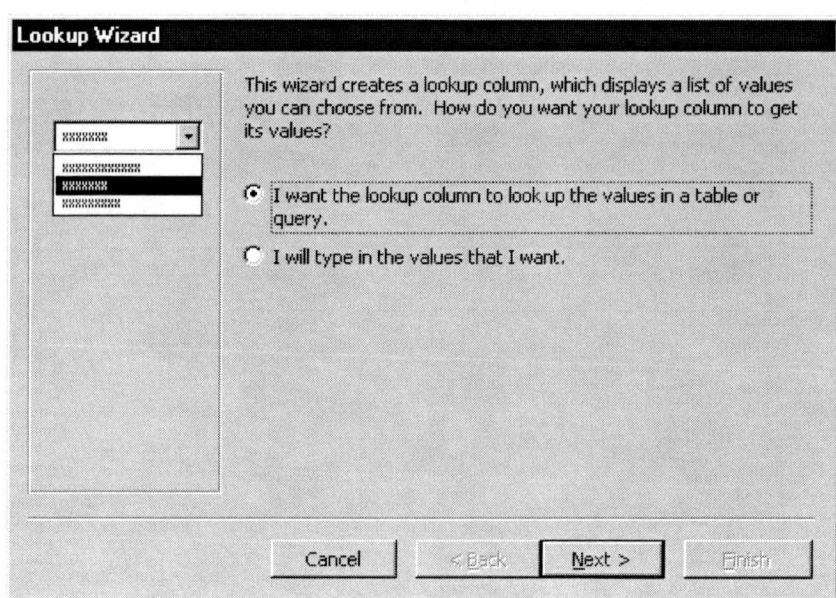

Lookup Wizard - first screen

Working with Field Properties

- Click **Next >** | The next Lookup Wizard dialogue box is displayed. This page lets you choose which table (or query) to select the lookup values from.

You can create lookup lists from tables or queries, or a combination of both.

- Select the **Customers** table
- Click **Next >** | The next step of the Lookup Wizard is displayed.

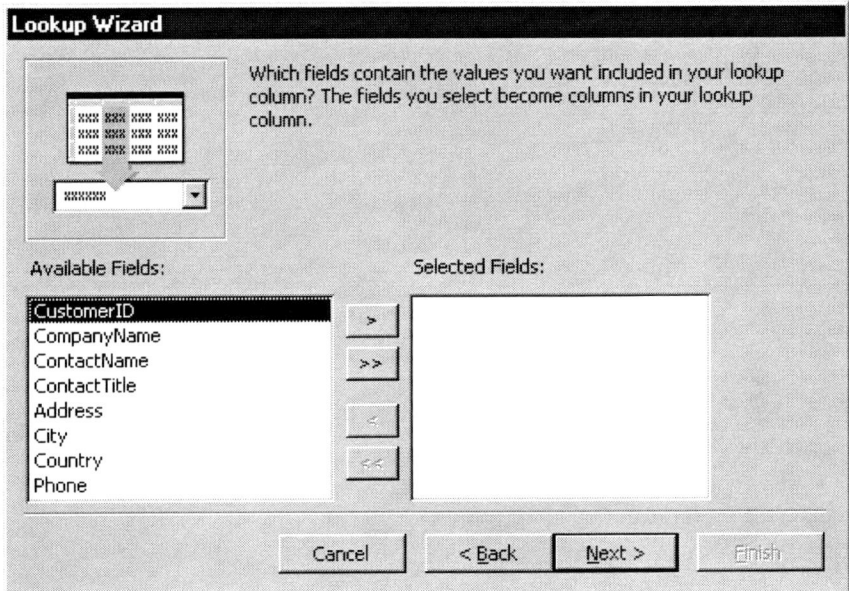

Lookup Wizard - third screen

Lookups typically consist of two columns - a value to store (usually a key field) and a value to display to the user.

- From the **Available Fields** list select the **CustomerID** field | The **CustomerID** field contains the values you want to include in your lookup column.
- Click the **Select** button | The **CustomerID** field is moved to the **Selected Fields**.

Lesson 3

- Move the **CompanyName** field to **Selected Fields** also

    The **Company Name** will also appear in the lookup field to assist the user in choosing.

- Click **Next >**

    The Lookup Wizard moves to the next step.

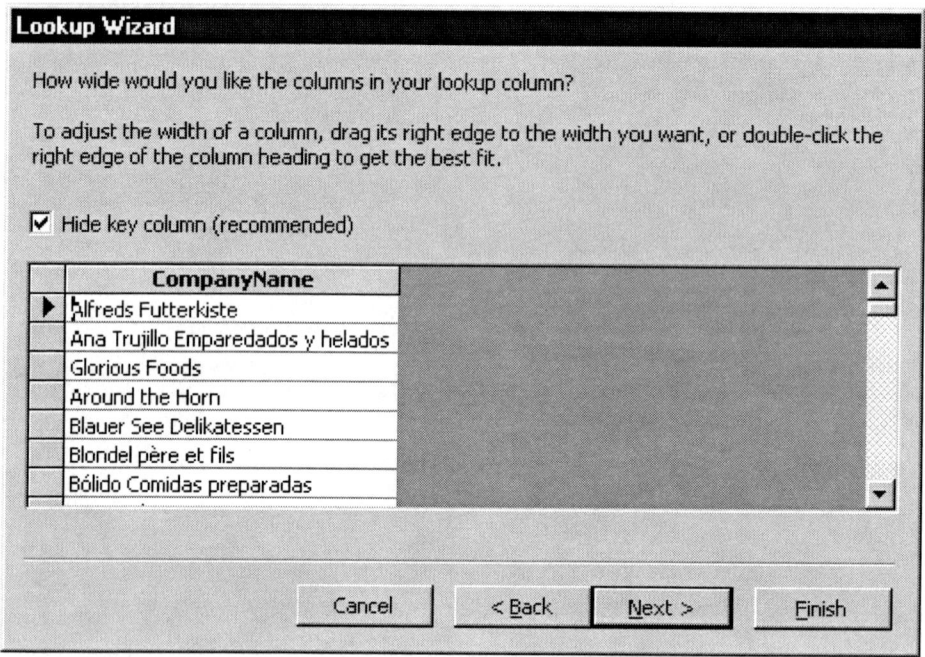

Lookup Wizard - fourth screen

The key column (**CustomerID** here) is usually hidden because it does not present any meaningful information to the user. You can scroll down the column to check that all your current data is visible, and make the column wider if necessary.

- Click-and-drag the right edge of the column to adjust the column size to the best fit

- Click **Next >**

    The Lookup Wizard displays the final dialogue box, prompting you for a label for the field.

Working with Field Properties

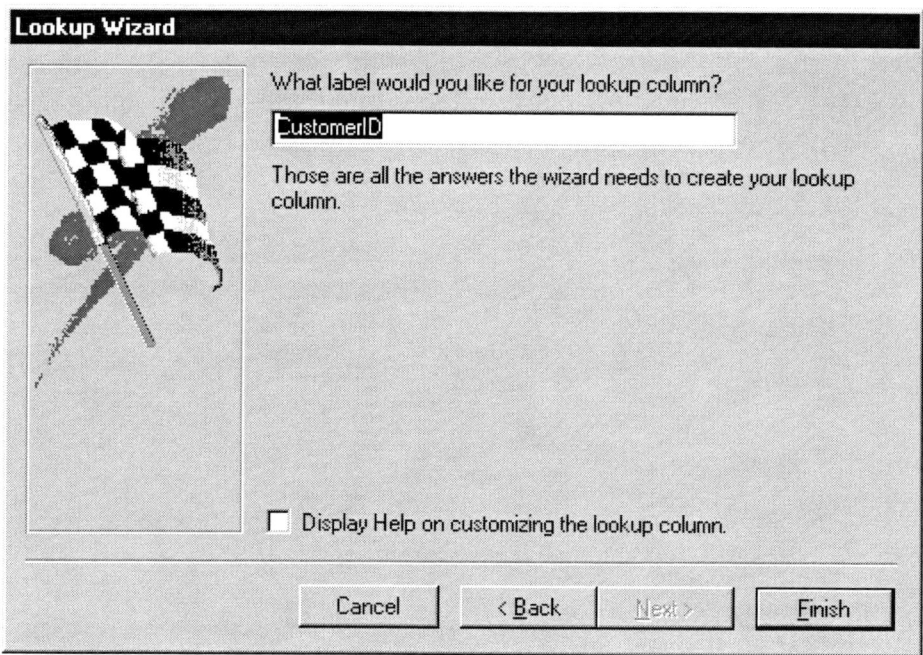

Lookup Wizard - fifth screen

- Leave the title set to **CustomerID**
- Click **Finish**   Access prompts you to save changes to the table.

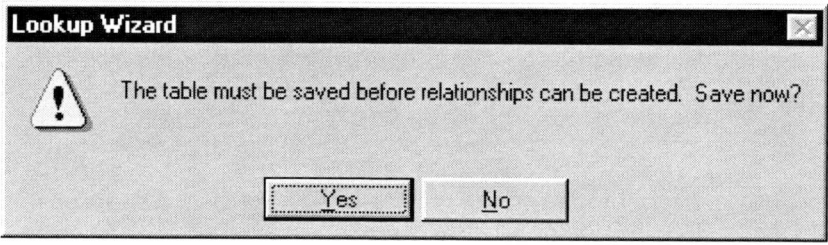

- Click **Yes**   The Lookup Wizard creates a relationship between the **Customers** and **Orders** tables.

Lesson 3

To view and edit the Lookup properties

Properties for lookup fields are stored under the **Lookup** tab in table design view.

TryIT

Action	Result
• In the **Field Properties** pane, select the **Lookup** tab	The **Lookup properties** are displayed.

```
General  Lookup
Display Control      Combo Box
Row Source Type      Table/Query
Row Source           SELECT DISTINCTROW [Customers].[Cus
Bound Column         1
Column Count         2
Column Heads         No
Column Widths        0cm;4.604cm
List Rows            8
List Width           4.603cm
Limit To List        Yes
```

Lookup field properties

The **Row Source** property shows the SQL (Structured Query Language) expression that returns values from the **Customers** table.

The shortcut key to see the full properties of the Row Source is `Shift` + `F2`.

The other crucial lookup property is **Limit To List**. When set to **Yes**, this ensures that a user can only select valid primary key values. If you enter text that does not match a listed item, Access does not accept it and the user must retype the entry, select a listed item, or press `Esc` (or click the **Undo** button).

To test the lookup field

- Click the **View** button 　　　　　　　**Datasheet** view is displayed.
- In the **Customer** field, type an incorrect customer name
- Press `Tab`　　　　　　　　　　　　　When you move from the field, Access displays the following error message.

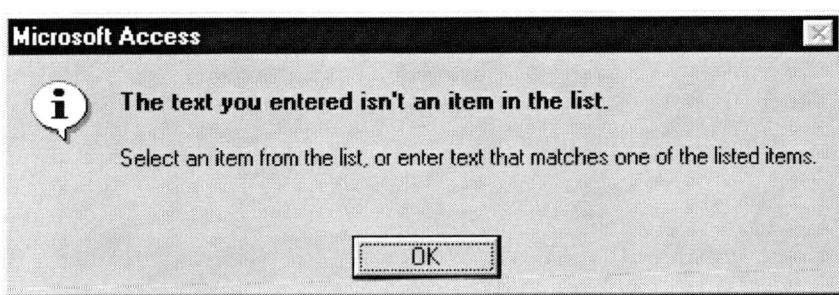

Lookup field error message

- Click **OK**　　　　　　　　　　　　You are returned to the **Orders** table.
- Click **Undo**　　　　　　　　　　　This cancels the incorrect **CustomerID**.
- Click the **Close** button to close the table window　　　　　　　The table is closed.

Refer to the **GOING FURTHER** section to learn how to create a lookup from a list of values (page 76).

Indexes

An index in a database works just like an index in a book. It makes commonly used data easy to find.

The more you include in your tables, the more you need indexes to help Access search your data efficiently. Indexing generally speeds up searches (or queries) on large tables, but can slow up the process of adding, deleting or changing data.

The following fields could be used for indexes:

- Fields containing Text, Date/Time, Number or Currency data
- Fields by which you are going to regularly search for data, especially ranges of data
- Primary key fields
- Foreign key fields
- Fields that you will use to sort information when you return the data

However, also consider the following:

- Avoid using too many indexes, since this will slow updates
- Do not create indexes where there are not many unique values

Another consideration is the number of fields that you include in a particular index. Access allows you to create indexes based on multiple fields, which is useful when searching for information in a particular order. As an example, you may often search a Customers table by Country then City fields. Creating an index based on these two fields will allow Access to search for the appropriate information more quickly, and/or order the results using the index.

A multiple column index based on Country then City is only useful to queries that require the information in that order. For instance, a query that sorts output in City then Country order would not use the index.

To create an index

TryIT	Action	Result
	• From the **Database** window, select the **Customers** table	
	• Click **Design**	The **Customers** table is displayed in Design view.
	• Select the **Country** field	
	• Select the **Indexed** property drop-down list	
	• Select **Yes (Duplicates OK)**	The Country will now be indexed allowing duplicates.

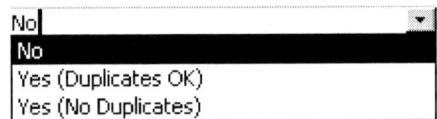

Options available for Indexed property

> The **Yes (No Duplicates)** option allows you to create a **unique** index - you will only be able to add a value into the field if it does not already exist in that field for another record. This property is one of the means by which Access enforces a specified primary key.

To view all indexes for a table

Indexes may also be administered at table level using the **Indexes** dialogue box. This lists all the indexes for the currently selected table, and allows you to specify multiple-column indexes.

■ On the **Standard** toolbar, click **Indexes**

OR

■ From the **View** menu, select **Indexes...**

The **Indexes** dialogue box is displayed.

■ To add an index, enter a suitable name and pick the field to be indexed then set other options (Sort Order, Primary Key, Unique...)

- To create a multiple field index, add fields below the first field without entering an index name - you can add up to 10 fields

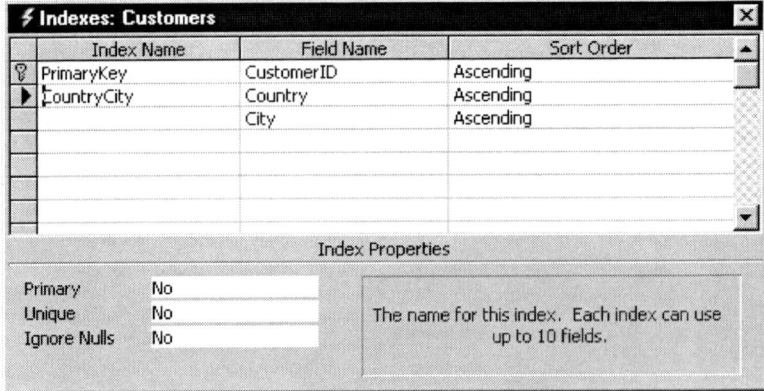

Indexes dialogue box showing a multiple field index

Other Useful Fields

Name	Description
Caption	You can add a caption to a field, which Access displays automatically when you create forms and reports using that field.
Default Value	Set a default value for a field, which Access will use when you add a new record. For example, it might be useful to add a default value for the current date: =Date() to a date field.
Required	The Required property means that records cannot be accepted without data in that field. A field without any data has a value of null. If the Required property is set to Yes, null values are not allowed. For example, it would be sensible to make the UnitPrice field required, as a product should always have a price.
Allow Zero Length	Specifically for Text, Memo and Hyperlink fields, when set to "Yes", this property allows the user to enter zero-length strings (" "). By default, empty quotation marks count as data. Therefore the field containing the zero-length string is not empty (Null). A common query can be to find all those records with a particular empty field.

Review Questions

(1) What is a validation rule?

(2) What validation rule checks that a date entry is not in the past?

(3) How do you create a validation error message?

(4) What is an input mask?

(5) What is the difference between an input mask and the format property?

(6) What is a lookup field?

(7) Why use an index?

(8) Why should you restrict the number of fields that are indexed and describe some fields that are suitable for indexing?

(9) What is a required field?

Answers on the next page.

Lesson 3

Review Answers

(1) A validation rule is an expression that limits data entry in a field or control. If the value the user attempts to enter breaks the rule, a message appears. The user cannot exit the field until valid data is entered (or the record is abandoned)

(2) >=Date()

(3) By specifying a message in the validation text property of the field or control

(4) An input mask is a specific format to provide some control over the data that can be entered for a particular field or control. An input mask consists of literal display characters (such as parentheses, periods (full stops) or hyphens) that specify where data can be entered and the number or type of characters that are allowed

(5) The format property controls how data is displayed in datasheets, queries, forms and reports. It does not affect how data is entered

(6) A lookup field provides a list of entries for the user to select from rather than having to type the values (which can lead to inaccuracies). A Lookup list that displays values from an existing table or query. A value list that displays a fixed set of values that you enter when you create the field

(7) Indexes can improve the performance of queries

(8) Indexes can slow down adding and editing records so only relevant fields should be indexed. These could include:
i) Fields with data type Text, Number, Currency or Date/Time
ii) Primary and foreign key fields
iii) Fields that will regularly provide query criteria and sorting

(9) The required property of a field determines whether a field can be left blank. If the required property is set to Yes, the user must enter a value in the field

Lesson 3

Skills Summary — Review

Congratulations on successfully completing LESSON 3. Now you are more familiar with some of the field properties and know how to make your database information more reliable.

Review objectives...

- ☐ Use **field properties**
- ☐ Understand the different **field sizes** and **data types**
- ☐ Create a **validation rule**
- ☐ Create a **validation message** for the rule
- ☐ Create an **input mask**
- ☐ Use **lookup** fields
- ☐ Create an **index**

Going Further

 Going Further

Using the Input Mask Wizard

Access provides the **Input Mask Wizard** with ten sample masks, to which you may add your own, such as postcode and telephone number. It is possible to edit the built-in masks, or create your own.

 The **Input Mask Wizard** is available only for text and date fields. If you want to create an input mask for numeric fields, you must enter the formatting symbols yourself.

To use the Input Mask Wizard

- Display the table in design view
- Click anywhere in the field to which to add the input mask
- From the list of **General** properties, select **Input Mask**
- Click the **Build** button at the end of the field

The **Input Mask Wizard** dialogue box is displayed.

- Select an input mask from the list
- In the **Try It:** box, enter a sample value (if the value you enter is invalid for that position in the input mask, your computer will bleep)
- Click **Edit List** to change or add input masks
- Click **Next >** to change the input mask or placeholder character
- Click **Cancel** to return to the table without making any changes

OR

- Click **Finish** to insert the mask into the field property

Creating a Lookup List from a Fixed Set of Values

If your lookup list is short and does not often change, it is probably easier to type in the values.

When you select this option, the list is stored as a property of the field itself.

To create a Lookup list

- Open the relevant table in design view
- Click the drop-down arrow in the **Field Type** for the field and select the **Lookup Wizard**
- Click the option button **I will type in the values I want** and click **Next >**

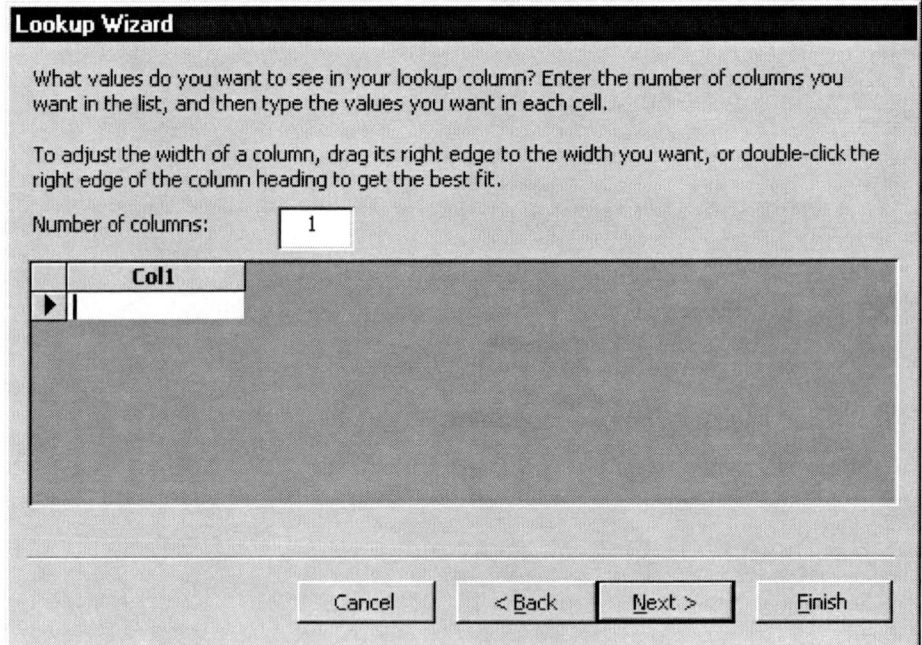

Lookup Wizard - creating a fixed list

- Click in the first row and type your list, pressing Tab after each line to move to the next row

The figures are added to **Col1**.

- Click **Next >**
- In the **What label** box, amend the title if necessary then click **Finish**

Design view is redisplayed

- To view the Lookup details, select the **Lookup** tab in the **Field Properties** pane

The values are displayed in the **Row Source** field.

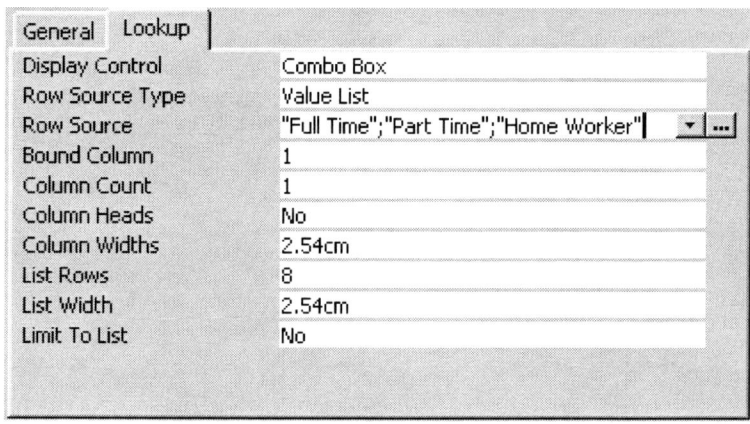

Fixed list lookup

- You can edit the list by typing new values
- Save changes to the table

Modifying Tables and Fields

You can add, remove and rename fields from a table at any time. If you take care when designing your tables, you should not need to make these changes later on. As well as revising the structure of fields, you can change the data type and any associated field properties.

If you do need to make changes to fields, be aware of the following:

- Deleting a field deletes any data stored in that field as well.
- You will need to repeat any changes made to the field in the table in any forms, reports or queries using the field also. For example, if you delete a field in a table, Access will not delete the field control from a form based on the table, you must do so yourself.

To insert a field

- Click the row selector (the grey box to the left of the field name) for the field that you want to see **underneath** the inserted field then press `Insert`

OR

- Right-click the row below where you want to insert a field then from the shortcut menu, select **Insert Rows**

To delete a field

- Click the row selector to highlight the entire field then press `Delete`

OR

- Right-click the field to delete and from the shortcut menu, select **Delete Rows**

A dialogue box is displayed to confirm this action.

To change the field name

- Click into the **Field Name** column and overtype the existing name with the one you want

To change the data type

- Click into the **Data Type** column and select a new type from the drop-down list

- On the **Standard** toolbar, click **Save**

Access tries to convert any existing data to the new data type. If for some reason the data cannot be stored in the new data type a warning will be displayed when you try to save the table.

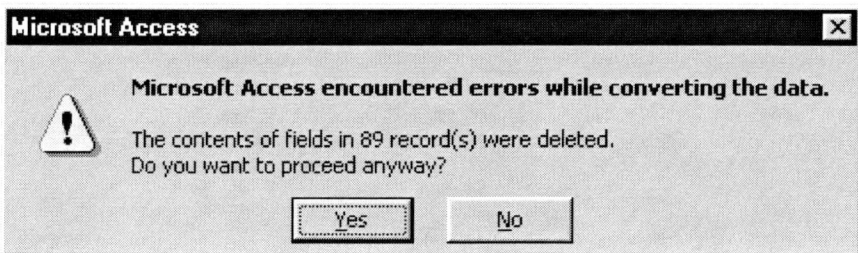

Invalid data type warning message

- Click **Yes** to keep the new data type

 This operation deletes any existing data. You cannot recover the data and the operation cannot be undone.

To change the field size

- Click into the field then alter properties in the lower panel
- On the **Standard** toolbar, click **Save** 💾

If you selected a smaller field size than before, Access warns you that existing data in the field may be lost.

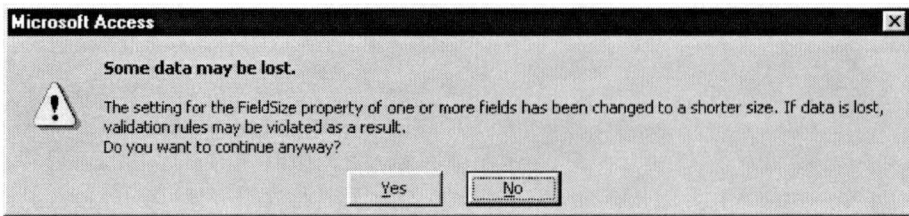
Field size warning message

- If you click **Y**es the field size will be changed and any data that does not fit will be cut from the field
- If you click **N**o, the field size will remain the same

To change other field properties

- Click into the field then alter properties in the lower panel
- On the **Standard** toolbar, click **Save** 💾

Access can test existing data to see if it conforms to the new field property rules. For example, if you set the **Required** property to **Yes**, Access will check to see if the field in any of the existing records is blank.

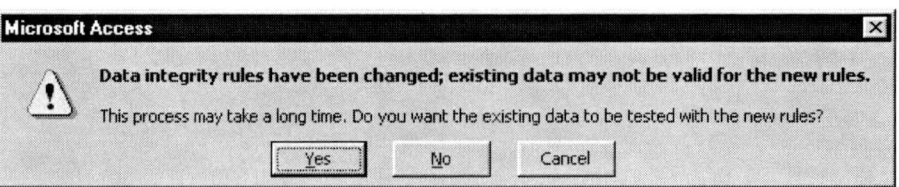

- Click **Y**es to check the data

Going Further

If Access comes across invalid data, it displays another message:

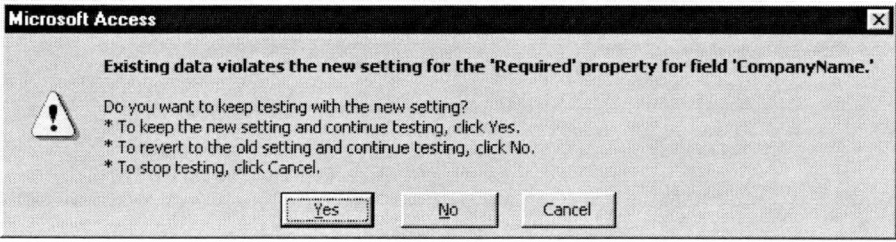

- Click **Yes** to continue

OR

- Click **No** to abandon the changes you made

Access does not tell you **which** records are invalid, but you can open the table and sort the records to display blank fields.

Some changes cannot be made at all without changing the existing data first. For example, you cannot set the **Indexed (No duplicates)** property on a field if existing data contains duplicates!

Lesson 3

Notes

Lesson 4: Working with External Data

This lesson shows you how to work with data created in external applications, such as a separate Access database or using Microsoft Excel.

Lesson objectives...

- ☐ **Import** data from an Excel spreadsheet
- ☐ **Link** data from an Access database
- ☐ Use the **Linked Table Manager**
- ☐ **Export** data to an Excel spreadsheet

Jump lesson...

If you know how to import, export and link data, learn how to create action queries in MANIPULATING DATA WITH QUERIES on page 99.

Using External Data in Access

In most businesses, data is frequently stored in a variety of formats (for example, in a different type of database or spreadsheet). Access can accommodate this problem by being able to incorporate data from many different software packages.

Data can be **imported** directly into Access to form part of the current database. The data is in effect copied into the Access table.

Data can also be **linked** to the database and used as if it were part of the database. A **link** is a connection between the file in which the data was created, called the **source**, and the place to which the file has been linked, called the **destination**. Linked data always remains in its source file, but can be edited using Access. Any changes to the data using either the source or the destination are updated in both.

Data can be imported or linked from a variety of sources including:

- Spreadsheet files, such as Microsoft Excel or Lotus 1-2-3 (one worksheet from within a workbook).

- A text file, such as you might create in Microsoft Word or a text editor.

- A file in another database format, such as FoxPro or Paradox.

In this lesson we will look at importing data to and from MS Excel. However, the procedures used can generally be applied to any type of data.

Importing Data

The import procedure is handled by a wizard. Certain options will vary depending on the type of file being imported.

During the import process, you will be allowed to either create a new table in your database, or to import data into an existing table.

If you are importing data into an existing table, the data will only be imported successfully if the **source** table has column names identical to each field in the **target** table, and if the order of columns is the same in both source and target tables.

Working with External Data

To import data from an Excel spreadsheet

We are going to add some data about Universal Import employees to the database. This information is already stored in an Excel worksheet and can be imported.

TryIT 	Action	Result
	• Open the database **UNIVER_4** • From the **File** menu, select **Get External Data** • From the submenu, select **Import...**	The **Import** dialogue box is displayed.

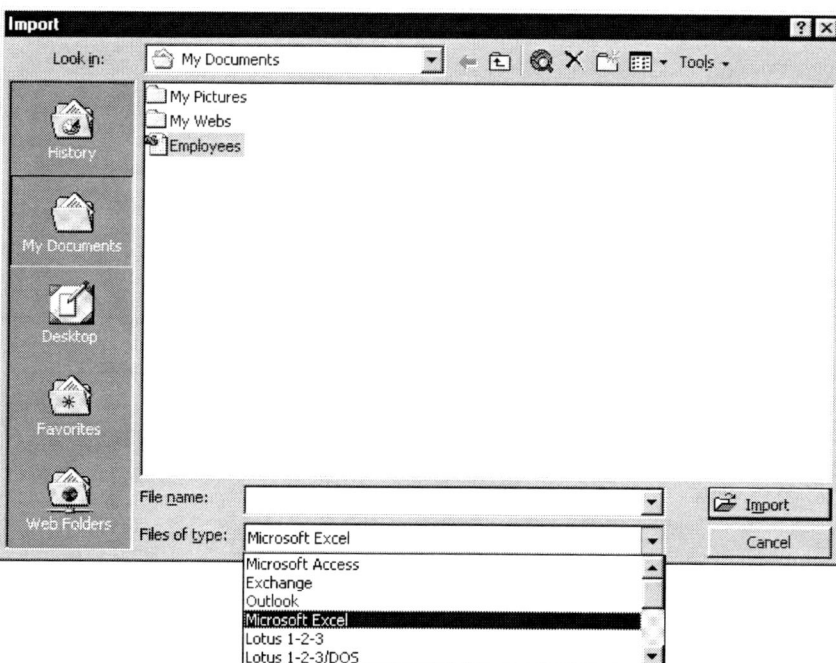

Import dialogue box

- From the **Files of type:** box, select **Microsoft Excel**
- From the file list select **EMPLOYEES.XLS**
- Click **Import**

The **Import Spreadsheet Wizard** starts.

Lesson 4

To complete the Import Spreadsheet Wizard

The exact choices to make when importing data will depend on the format of the data (spreadsheet, text file, database and so on).

The **Import Wizard** guides you through each step of the process.

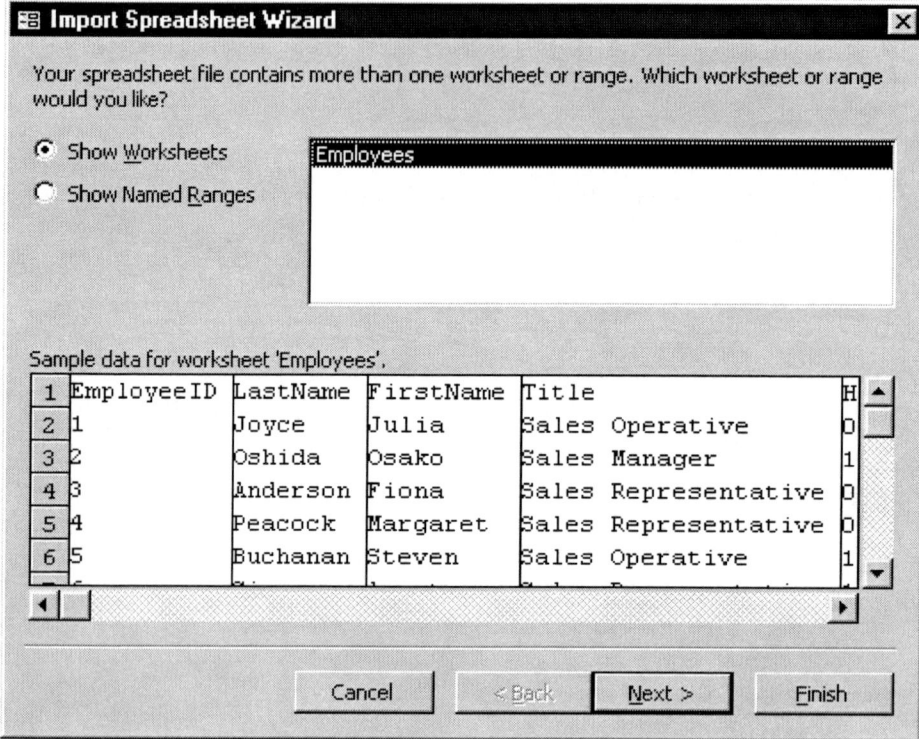

Import Spreadsheet Wizard

As there is only one worksheet in the EMPLOYEES workbook, the wizard has automatically selected it for import.

If you are **linking** to data in **part** of a worksheet, use Excel to **name** the range of cells. Then select **Show Named Ranges** to import just the data you want (as opposed to the entire worksheet).

Working with External Data

TryIT	Action	Result
	• In the **Import Spreadsheet Wizard**, leave the default options as they are	
	• Click **Next >**	The wizard moves to the next step.
	• Click the **First Row Contains Column Headings** check box	Column headings are shown as grey buttons.
	• Click **Next >**	The **Where to store your data?** dialogue box is displayed.

 If the data is to be **appended** to an existing table (added to the records already there), select the table name from the drop-down list in the **Existing Table:** field.

	• Click the **In a New Table** option button	
	• Click **Next >**	The **Field Options** dialogue box is displayed.

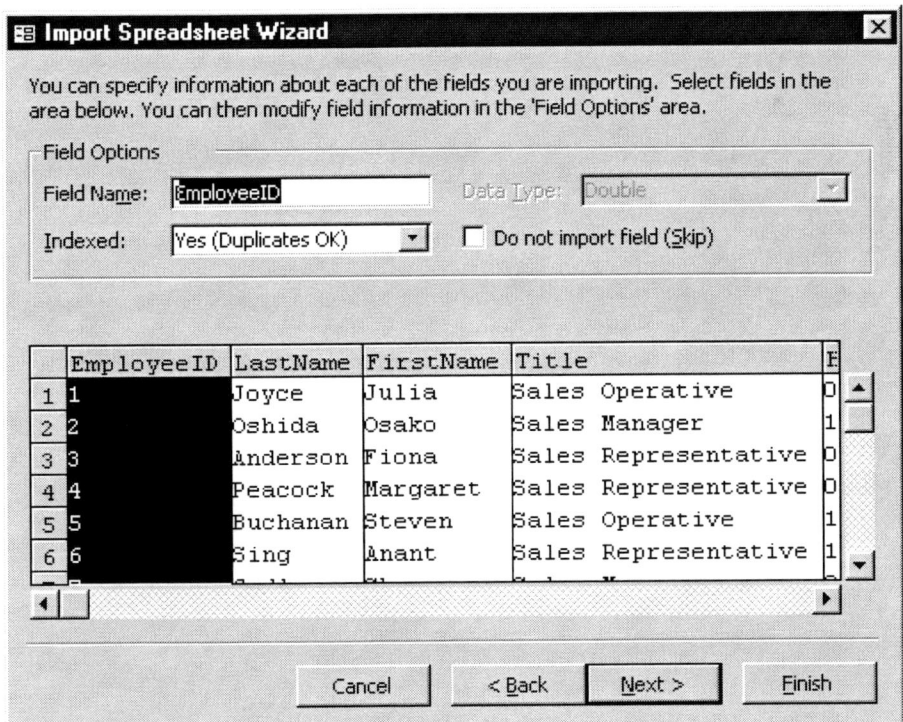

Lesson 4

This dialogue box allows you to modify field names if necessary, and to specify whether fields are indexed.

You do not need to make any changes to the suggestions made by Access.

- Click **Next >**
  The Import Spreadsheet Wizard moves onto the next step, prompting you for a primary key.

- Select the **Choose my own Primary Key** option

- Select **EmployeeID** from the drop-down list
  The primary key is set as **EmployeeID**.

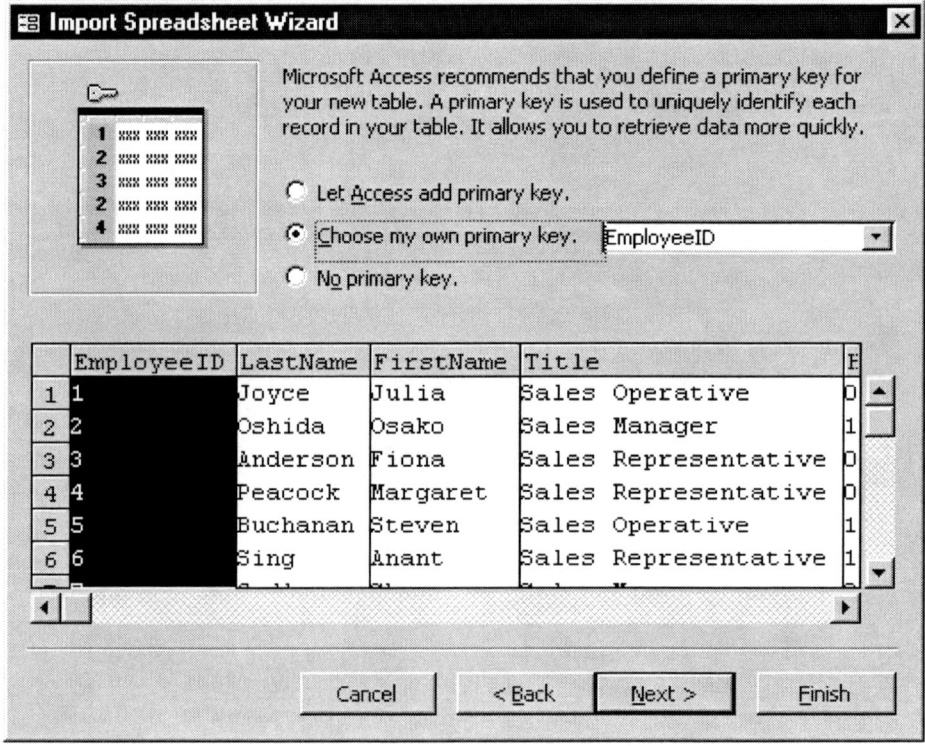

Import Spreadsheet Wizard

- Click **Next >**

  The last dialogue box of the **Import Spreadsheet Wizard** is displayed.

- In the **Import to Table** box, leave **Employees** as the title

- Click **Finish**

  A message box is displayed confirming the import.

- Click **OK**

It is necessary to check the field lengths and data types of tables imported from Excel. The default field length of text fields during conversion is 255 characters.

Also check any date fields carefully, especially if they use 2-digit year formats (dd/mm/yy).

Linking Data

Linking data enables you to **read**, and in most cases **update**, data in the external data source, without importing it into your database.

This can be enormously useful if you have information such as names and addresses that need to be available in more than one database.

The external data source's format is not altered. Therefore you can continue to use the file with the program in which it was originally created, but you can also add, delete, or edit its data using Access.

Linking a table saves disk space because there is only one table rather than multiple tables with duplicate data. Linking data also saves time because it is unnecessary to update the same information in more than one table.

However, Access performs better when working with its own files within the current database.

Lesson 4

To link data from a separate Access database

TryIT	Action	Result
	• In the **UNIVER_4** database, from the **File** menu, select **Get External Data**	
	• From the submenu, select **Link Tables...**	The **Link** dialogue box is displayed.
	• Select the **SUPPLIERS** database	
	• Click the **Link** button	The **Link Tables** dialogue box is displayed.

Link Tables dialogue box

	• From the **Tables** tab, select **Suppliers**	
	• Click **OK**	The **Suppliers** table is now linked into the database. Note the arrow next to the table icon, indicating a linked data source.

Suppliers
Linked table icon

When linking to files other than Access databases, select the data format from the **Files of type:** list box.

The Linked Table Manager

The **Linked Table Manager** allows you to monitor the file location of any external data tables. If the file is moved, you can update the file location here, without re-linking the data table.

To use Linked Table Manager

- From the **Tools** menu, select **Database Utilities** then **Linked Table Manager...**

The **Linked Table Manager** opens a dialogue box that displays all the linked tables in the database.

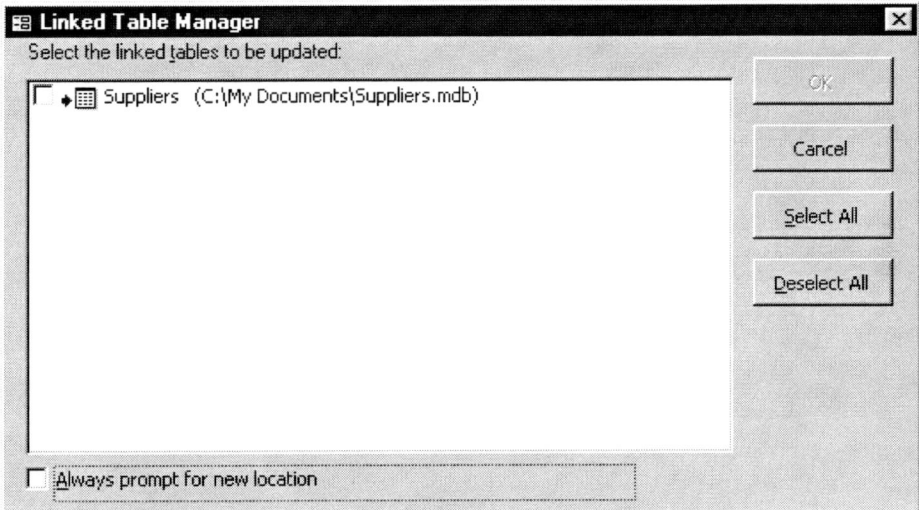

Linked Table Manager

- Select the table that needs to be verified and updated
- Click **OK**

If any table has been moved to a different location, the Linked Table Manager prompts you with a dialogue box, so that you can specify the new file location.

Lesson 4

Exporting Database Records

Data created in Access can be exported to a variety of different formats used by other applications or to another Access database.

You can save a copy of tables, forms, queries and reports within the current database or in another Access database and you can export the output from tables, queries and reports to different data formats.

You can also export to HTML files, which you can then use as part of a world wide website (see page 214).

To export records to Excel

TryIT	Action	Result
	• From the **Tables** tab, select the **Customers** table • From the **File** menu, select **Export...**	The **Export Table** dialogue box is displayed.

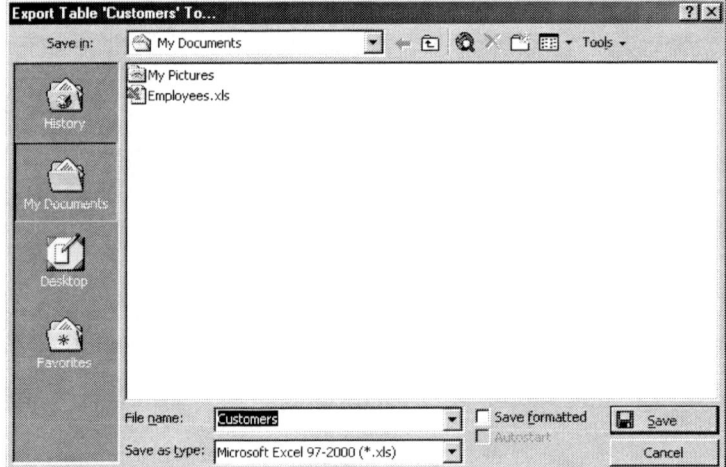

Export dialogue box

	Action	Result
	• From the **Save as type** box, select **Microsoft Excel 97-2000** • Leave the file name as `Customers` • Click the **Save** button	The **Customers** table is exported to Excel.

Working with External Data

To export records using drag-and-drop

Another technique for exporting records to Excel is to use **drag-and-drop**.

To use this technique, it is necessary to have both Access and Excel open at the same time and to have the applications tiled vertically on the screen.

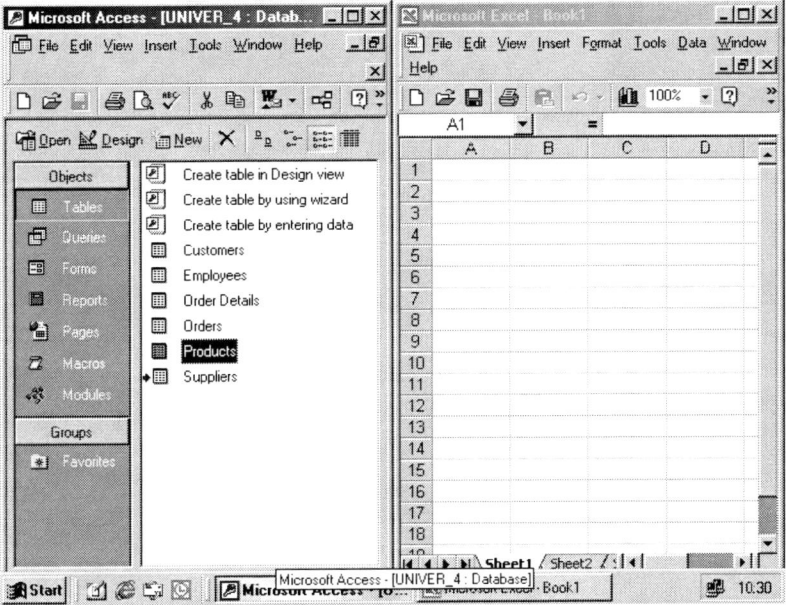

Application windows tiled

TryIT

Action	Result
• Start MS Excel	A blank workbook is displayed on the screen.
• Right-click the Windows Taskbar and select **Tile Windows Vertically**	Both windows are arranged together on-screen.
• From the **Database** window, select the **Products** table	
• Click-and-drag the table across to the Excel workbook	
• Position the cursor in **Cell A1**	The data contained in the **Products** table is displayed in the Excel workbook.
• Release the mouse button	

LearnIT MS Access 2000 Expert — Page 93

Lesson 4

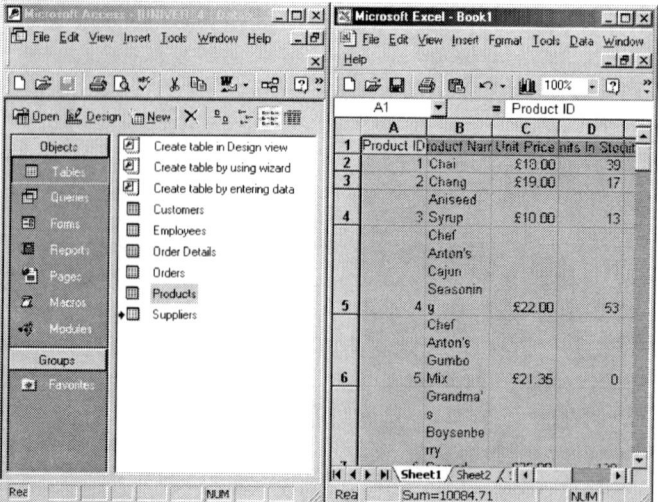

If you prefer to work with maximised windows, you can also drag the data over the destination application's (Excel for example) **Taskbar** icon. This makes the workbook the active window and you can drop data as normal.

- In Excel, from the **File** menu, select **Save**

- In the **File name** box, type
  `Products`

- Click **Save**

  The Products table is now saved as an Excel spreadsheet.

- From the **File** menu, select **Exit**

  Excel is closed.

- Close the database

You can export a variety of database objects in one step using the **Office Links** button. You can open reports and datasheets in MS Word for further **editing** and **printing**, **merge** records with form letters in Word or export the output of an object to an **Excel** worksheet. Simply select the object from the **Database** window then choose the appropriate command from the list button.

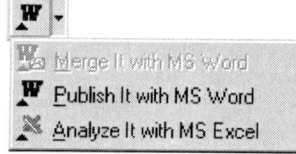

Office Links button

Review Questions

(1) Identify the differences between Importing and Linking.

(2) How do you import data?

(3) How do you link data?

(4) What does the Linked Table Manager do?

(5) Name two methods of exporting data to an Excel spreadsheet.

Answers on the next page.

Lesson 4

Review Answers

(1) i) Imported data is copied from the source application into Access
ii) Linked data always remains in its source application
iii) Linked data can be edited in Access but the structure of linked data cannot be modified in Access
iv) The design of imported data tables can be changed

(2) i) From the File menu, select Get External Data
ii) From the submenu, select Import
iii) The Import Wizard guides you through the rest of the steps

(3) i) From the File menu, select Get External Data
ii) From the submenu, select Link Tables
iii) The Import Wizard guides you through the rest of the steps

(4) The Linked Table Manager updates the file location if a database is moved to a different folder

(5) i) From the File menu, select Export then Save it to an External File or Database and select File Type: Microsoft Excel
ii) Drag-and-drop the table from Access to an open worksheet

Skills Summary

Review

Congratulations on successfully completing LESSON 4. You now know how to import and export data in Access.

Review objectives...

- ☐ **Import** data from an Excel spreadsheet

- ☐ **Link** data from an Access database

- ☐ Use the **Linked Table Manager**

- ☐ **Export** data to an Excel spreadsheet

Notes

Lesson 5 — Manipulating Data with Queries

In this lesson you will learn to use different types of query to manipulate and analyse data.

Lesson objectives...

- [ ] Create **action** queries
- [ ] Create a **summary** query
- [ ] Use **expressions** in **calculated fields**
- [ ] **Combine** queries
- [ ] **Filter** query results
- [ ] Create a **parameter** query
- [ ] Create a **crosstab** query

Jump lesson...

If you can use advanced query features, learn how to design complex forms, reports and charts by jumping to BUILDING AND MODIFYING FORMS on page 139 or REPORTS AND CHARTS on page 177.

The Different Types of Queries

There are several types of queries that help you retrieve information.

Select queries

You should already have plenty of experience with **select** queries, the most common type of query. A select query selects and sorts records from multiple tables based on criteria. You can use select queries to analyse data or as the basis for forms and reports.

Summary queries

A **summary** query groups data by particular fields and performs summary calculations on other fields (for example, to show the total or average value of a row).

Crosstab queries

A **crosstab** query also displays summarised values (sums, counts and averages) from one field in a table, but groups them by one set of fields listed down the left side of the datasheet and **another** set of fields listed across the top.

Action queries

An **action** query performs operations on the records that match your criteria.

- **Delete** queries delete matching records
- **Update** queries make changes to matching records
- **Append** queries add new records to the end of a table
- **Make-table** queries create new tables based on matching records

Parameter queries

A **Parameter** query prompts you for a single piece of information to use as selection criteria in the query.

Action Queries

Action queries perform an action on the selected records, such as copying, amending or deleting them. Action queries can be used for regular functions such as archiving data, or occasional operations such as splitting tables.

Query Type	Description
Make Table	Creates a new table and copies the selected records into it.
Append	Adds the selected records to the end of an existing table.
Update	Changes the values in one or more fields to new values for all records that match the criteria.
Delete	Deletes the selected records.

Planning an Action Query

Before you start to design and use Action Queries, you must be aware of the damage that can be done to a database by the incorrect or inappropriate use of these tools.

Access's single level of undo means that any operation that modifies, inserts or deletes more than one record in a database table **cannot be undone**. Although this will be stressed again throughout this section, you should take the following precautions before running action queries:

- Backup your database before designing any action query (see page 281)

- If your query operates on a filtered set of records, design it as a simple select query first - this prevents you from mistakenly deleting records if the query is not quite right

- If the query modifies information in fields, again write a simple select query with the modification statement as a calculated expression, to ensure that the calculation results are as expected

Lesson 5

- If the query is particularly complex, put some test data in a sample table and test the query against it, in order to test that all of the conditions of your query work under all circumstances

Make-Table Queries

A **Make-Table** query creates a new table and copies the selected records into it. This can be used for splitting up existing tables into smaller tables, or creating temporary tables to work with a selected group of data.

For example, it could be useful to extract all European contacts from the **Customers** table and save them in a new table using **Make Table** and **Append Table** queries.

To create a make-table query

TryIT	Action	Result
	• Open the database **UNIVER_5**	
	• From the **Database** window, select the **Queries** object	
	• Double-click **Create query in Design view**	The **Show Table** dialogue box is displayed with the Query Design window behind it.
	• From the **Show Table** dialogue box, add the **Customers** table	The **Customers** table is displayed in the upper pane of the Query window.
	• Click **C**lose	
	• Double-click the title bar of the **Customers** table	All the fields are selected.
	• Position the mouse anywhere in the highlighted selected fields	
	• Drag them to the **Query** grid	All fields are added to the Query grid.

Manipulating Data with Queries

- Click the **Criteria** row in the **Country** column on the query grid
- Type `France`
- Press `Enter`

Note that the word **France** is automatically enclosed with quotation marks - "France".

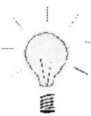

The quotation marks indicate text. There are no quotation marks if criteria are numbers.

- Click the **Sort** drop-down list box in the **CompanyName** field
- Select **Ascending** order

The records are sorted in alphabetical order by Company.

- From the **File** menu, select **Save**
- Type `EuroList`
- Click **OK**

The query is saved.

- Click the **Run** button to check the results
- Switch back to design view
- From the **Query** menu, select **Make-Table Query...**

The query returns 11 French customers.

The **Make-Table** dialogue box is displayed.

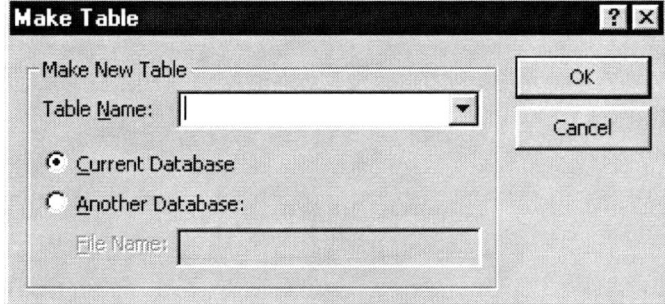

Make Table dialogue box

LearnIT MS Access 2000 Expert — *Page 103*

Lesson 5

You can save the results of the query in a table in the current database or into a different database.

- Leave the **Current Database** option selected
- In the **Table Name:** box, type `European Customers`
- Click **OK**
- From the **File** menu, select **Save**

The new query definition is saved.

- Click the **Run** button
- Click **Yes**

The message below is displayed.

A new table is created and the selected records copied to it.

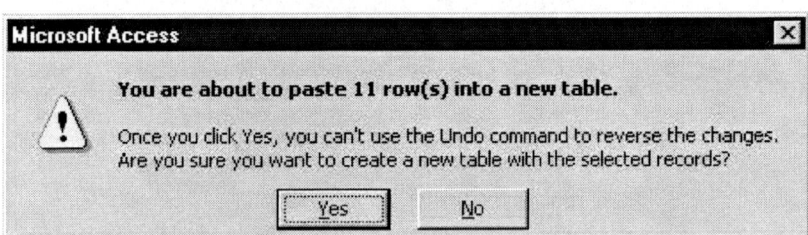

Make-Table query warning message

Running the query again will delete the existing table and create a new one.

Make-Table queries (and in fact all action queries) have distinctive icons, to differentiate them from normal select queries. Also whenever you run an action query, a warning message is displayed, allowing you to cancel.

EuroList
Make-Table Query icon

Append Queries

An **Append** query copies selected records to the end of an existing table.

Although we have created a table for European Customers, at this stage we only have French customers in our table. To add details of further European customers, it is now necessary to create an Append query to add the new records onto the end of the existing European Customers table.

To create an append query

TryIT	Action	Result
	• Change the criteria in the **Country** field to `Germany` • From the **Query** menu, select **Append Query...** • Leave the table name as **European Customers** • Click **OK**	The **Append** dialogue box is displayed.
	• From the **File** menu, select **Save** • Click the **Run** button ❗ • Click **Yes** to append rows	A warning message is displayed. The selected records for Germany are copied to the table.

TryIT	Practice
	• You can now continue adding the European countries to the European Customers table, by modifying the **Append** table for each country • When you have finished, close the query without saving the changes

Lesson 5

Delete Queries

A **Delete** query deletes the selected records from a table. This can be used for regularly deleting redundant records, or for deleting records after they are copied to another table with Make-Table or Append queries.

To create a delete query

A query for finding discontinued products in the **Products** table already exists, and now we need to delete these products.

TryIT	Action	Result
	• From the **Database** window, select **Queries** • Select the **Discontinued Products** query • From the **File** menu, select **Save As...**	The **Save As** dialogue box is displayed.

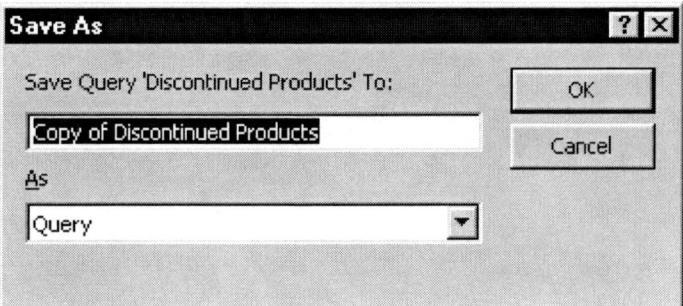

Save As dialogue box

	• In the top text box, type `Delete Discontinued Products` • Leave the **As** text box as **Query** • Click **OK**	A copy of the **Discontinued Products** query is saved with a different name.

Manipulating Data with Queries

- With **Delete Discontinued Products** selected, click **D**esign [Design]

    The query is opened in design view.

- From the **Q**uery menu, select **D**elete Query

    The **Sort** and **Show** lines are replaced by the **Delete** line on the query grid.

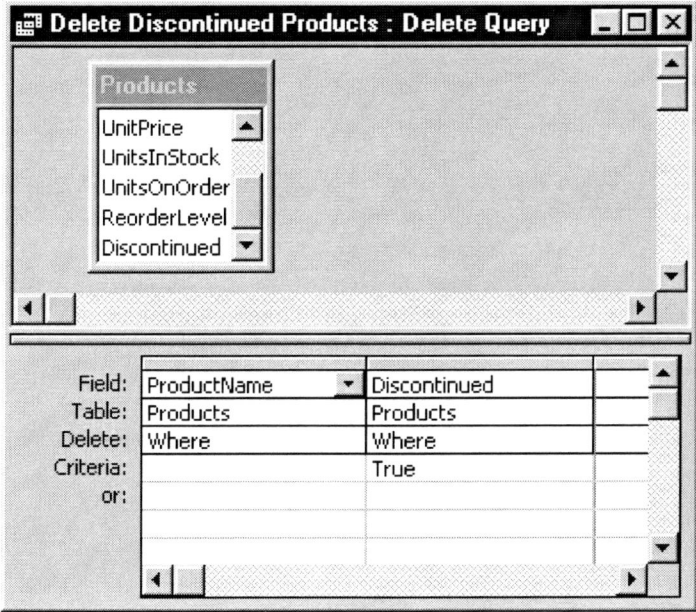

Delete Query

- Click the **Run** button

    A warning message is displayed.

- Click **Y**es

    The **Discontinued** products are deleted from the table.

- From the **F**ile menu, select **S**ave

    The query is saved.

- Close the query window

Because the **Cascade Delete** option (see page 38) was set for the Product table's relationship, records in the Order Details table were also deleted by this query, though no warning of this is given. If **Cascade Delete** were **not** set, the delete query would fail to delete any records.

Lesson 5

Update Queries

An **Update** query allows you to make changes to values in one or more fields for selected records. A good example for use of an update query would be to implement salary or price increases.

To create an update query

This exercise will increase the price of all stock by 5%.

TryIT	Action	Result
	• Create a new query in design view, adding the **Products** table to the query	The new query is displayed in design view.
	• Add the **ProductName** and **UnitPrice** fields to the query grid	
	• From the **Query** menu, select **Update Query**	The **Sort** and **Show** lines are replaced by the **Update To:** line on the query grid.
	• In the **Update** row of the **UnitPrice** field, enter the following calculation	When the query is run, this will add 5% to the unit price of all stock.
	`[UnitPrice] + [UnitPrice] * .05`	

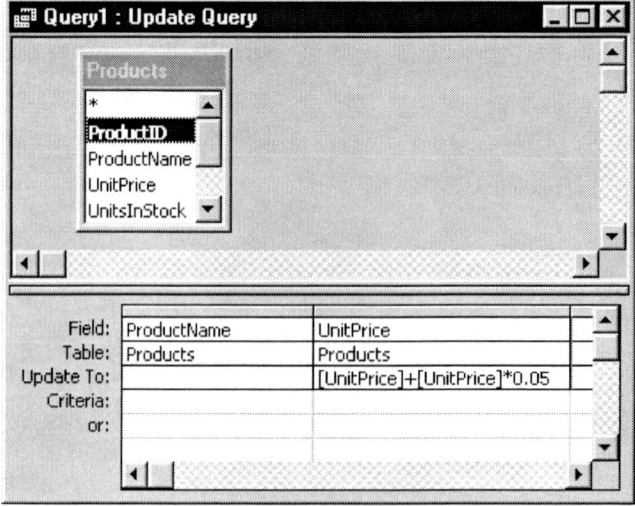

Manipulating Data with Queries

The square brackets in the calculation indicate field names. Brackets automatically appear around a single word field, but if the field name contains a space, you must type the brackets.

If you want to see the full expression, press `Shift`+`F2` to open the **Zoom** box.

The Zoom box is available in queries, table Design view, property sheets, the macro window and datasheet view.

Alternatively you can drag the column border to make the field wider.

- Run the query ![!] | The following message is displayed.

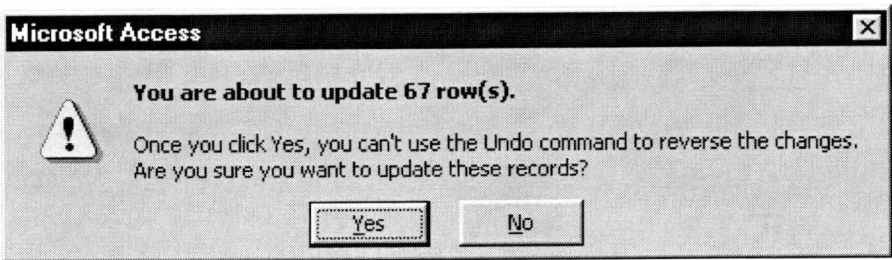
Update query warning message

- Click **Y**es | The **UnitPrice** in the **Products** table is updated.
- From the **F**ile menu, select **S**ave
- Type 5%PriceIncrease
- Press `Enter` | The query is saved.
- Close the query

Running the query again with the same criteria will add a further 5% of the value to the unit price of each item.

Creating Summary Queries

By default, a query will return a set of selected rows from the source table(s) of the database. However, queries also allow you to produce summary data from the source data, as the basis for reports and internet pages.

While the Query Wizard provides a limited means of summarising information, you can modify existing queries to provide more complex information.

The following aggregate expressions are available when creating summary queries.

Expression	Result
SUM	A total of the numeric values from the selected field.
AVG	An average of the numeric values from the selected field.
MIN	The minimum value from the selected numeric or text field.
MAX	The minimum value from the selected numeric or text field.
COUNT	A count of the non-NULL entries in the selected field. If you want to count all of the records returned by a query, use COUNT(*).
STDEV	Standard deviation of the numeric values from the selected field.
VAR	Variance of the numeric values from the selected field.
FIRST	The first record returned by the query, according to the query SORT order.
LAST	The last record returned by the query, according to the query SORT order.
EXPRESSION	Returns a value calculated using more than one summary function.
WHERE	Allows you to supply additional criteria to filter the expression.

Manipulating Data with Queries

To create a summary query

- On the **Standard** toolbar, click **Totals** Σ

OR

- From the **View** menu, select **Totals**

A new **Total:** row is displayed in the query design window.

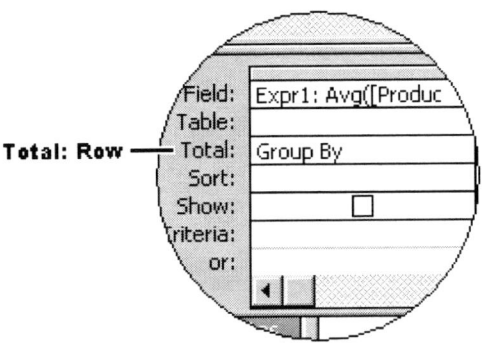

Total: row displayed in query design window

- In the **Total:** row, select an **aggregate** expression appropriate to the field

Grouping in Queries

The default value for the **Total:** row is **Group By**, which requires a little explanation. A query containing solely aggregate functions outlined in the table on page 110 will return a single record containing summary information calculated from all of the input records.

However, if you include any fields whose **Total:** property is set to **Group By**, then the calculated results will contain one row for each unique value in the **Grouped By** field.

For example, if you created a query for the sum of product sales, you would return a single row containing summary information for all sales. Including the **Country** field with the **Total:** value set to **Group By** will return a sum of sales for each country in the table.

Lesson 5

This facility makes queries an extremely powerful method of generating summary information to feed into reports, especially when you consider that **Group By** can be nested up to ten levels deep.

To use grouping in a query

TryIT 	Action	Result
	• Create a new query in design view	
	• Add the **Customers**, **Orders** and **Order Details** tables	
	• From the **Customers** table, add the **Country** field to the query grid	
	• From the **Orders** table, add the **OrderID** field to the grid	
	• On the **Standard** toolbar, click **Totals** Σ	The **Total:** line is added to the query grid. The **Group By** expression is selected by default.
	• In the **Total:** row for the **OrderID** field, select **Count**	This expression will return the number of orders.
	• In the **Sort** row, select **Descending**	The country with the most orders will top the list.
	• Save the query as **Orders By Country** then run ! it	

To group by multiple fields

Group By criteria are evaluated in the order that they are positioned on the query design grid.

TryIT 	Practice
	• Add the **City** field to the design grid, after the **Country** field
	• Remove the Sort option from the **OrderID** field
	• Run the query and note the differences
	• Close the query without saving changes

Using Calculated Fields in a Query

As well as using fields as the basis for a query, you can also create expressions using anything from simple mathematical operators to complex built-in functions.

For example, for an order it is necessary to calculate the line total for each item (the unit cost of the product multiplied by the quantity ordered less and customer discount).

Calculation expressions can be placed in queries, forms or reports and are used when it is necessary to perform a calculation on your data. However, the advantage of creating the calculated field in a query is that multiple forms and reports can use the calculated field as a control.

When you display the results of a calculation in a field, the results are not stored in the underlying table. Instead, Access reruns the calculation each time you run the query so that the results are always based on the most current data in the database.

This is often a better solution than storing certain data in a field. For example, you should store someone's date of birth (which never changes) rather than their age (which changes every year) in a table field, as the person's age can always be calculated from the date of birth.

Calculations

To create a calculation you build up an **expression**. An expression is a combination of symbols - identifiers, operators, and values - that produce a result.

You create a calculated field by entering an expression into an empty field cell in the query grid.

Examples of characters used in an expression are

- Mathematical operators such as: +, -, *, /, ^, (,)
- Field names, which must be in square brackets: [Product Name]
- Functions such as: Date(), Now()

When Access performs calculations containing a number of mathematical operators, it uses a set of rules to dictate which operators are evaluated in which order. The order of precedence is:

- Exponential
- Multiplication
- Division
- Addition
- Subtraction

These words form the acronym EMDAS. Remember this as "Eeks - My Dear Aunt Sally!"

Guidelines for entering expressions in queries

Item	Action	Example
Title	The field heading for the calculated column. Follow with a colon (:)	Value:
Identifier	Enclose field names and control names in brackets. Use a period (.) to separate a table name from a field.	[Order Date] [OrderDetails].[Order Date]
Date	Surround dates with a hash sign (#).	#21/01/1999#
Text	If the text is more than one word, enclose it in quotation marks.	UK, "United Kingdom"

For identifiers, it is only necessary to include the table name if the same field name occurs in two or more tables used in the query.

To use a calculated expression

In this exercise, we will adapt the **Orders by Country** query to show total order values as well as numbers.

TryIT	Action	Result
	• Open the **Orders By Country** query in design view • Save it as **Order Values By Country** • In the blank column after the **OrderID** field, enter the following calculated expression `Value: [UnitPrice]*[Quantity]*(1-[Discount])` • In the **Total:** row for the **Value** calculated field, select the aggregate function **Sum**	A copy of the query is saved with a new name. This expression calculates the net value of an order. The query will sum the result of the calculation for each row (each **Country** in this case) returned.
	• Select the **Value** field • On the **Standard** toolbar, click **Properties** • In the **Format** box, select **Currency** • Sort the results by **Value** in **Descending** order • Save the query then run ! it	The **Properties** sheet is displayed. The output of the calculated field will be formatted as currency. The country placing the most valuable orders will top the list.

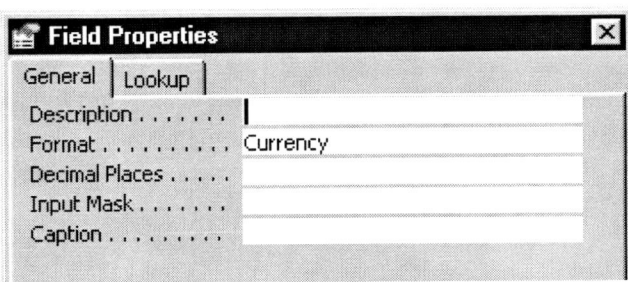

Field Properties

Lesson 5

Combining Queries

Up until now, you have probably used tables as the source of data for your queries. However, it is possible, and often easier, to use the output from one query as the data for another query.

The next exercise is to produce a query displaying the Employees' sales by country using a calculation.

To do this, we can create two queries. The first needs to calculate the order subtotals from the Order Details table. This is a good example of an "all purpose" query that will find many future applications within the database.

The second query then uses the output from the subtotals query to show which employees have been pulling in the best orders.

To create the subtotals query

TryIT	Action	Result
	• Close the **Order Values By Country** query • Create a new query in design view, adding the **Order Details** table only • Add the **OrderID** field to the **Query by Example** grid • In the next column, carefully type the following (all on one line) `Subtotal: ([UnitPrice]*[Quantity]* (1-[Discount])/100)*100`	This calculates the discount from any given UnitPrice.
	• On the **Standard** toolbar, click **Totals** Σ • In the **Total:** row for the **Subtotal** field, select **Sum**	The **Total:** line is added to the query grid. The **Group By** expression is selected by default.

Manipulating Data with Queries

- On the **Standard** toolbar, click **Properties** 📄 — The **Properties** sheet is displayed.

- In the **Format** box, select **Currency** — The output of the calculated field will be formatted as currency.

- Save the query as **Orders Subtotals**

- Run the query to check the results then close it

Now we need to create the second query that combines the Orders Subtotals query and information from the Employees and the Orders tables.

To create the combining query

TryIT

Action	Result
• From the **Queries** object, select **Create query in Design view**	The **Show Table** dialogue box is displayed.
• From the **Tables** tab, add the **Employees** and **Orders** table to the grid	The **Employees** and **Orders** tables are added to the Query by Design grid.
• From the **Queries** tab, add the **Orders Subtotals** query	The **Orders Subtotals** query is added to the Query by Design grid.
• Click **C**lose	The **Show Table** dialogue box is closed.

At this stage no relationship has been created between the Employees and the Orders tables. A **join** can be created as part of the query definition. However, it is important to remember that when you create a join line in a query, the join applies to that query only. If you want to use the same two tables in another query, you will need to join them again in the new query.

Refer back to page 40 for more information about table joins.

Lesson 5

To create a join between tables

TryIT	Action	Result
	• Click-and-drag the **EmployeeID** field from the **Employees** table to the **SalesID** field in the **Orders** table	The join line indicates a relationship between the two fields that associates the data.

Now add the relevant fields to the query grid.

	• From the **Employees** table, add the **Country**, **LastName** and **FirstName** fields to the **Query** grid	The **Country**, **LastName** and **FirstName** fields are added to the Query grid.
	• From the **Orders** table, add **OrderDate** and **OrderID**	The **OrderDate** and **OrderID** fields are added.
	• From the **Order Subtotals** query, add **Subtotal**	The **Subtotal** field is added.

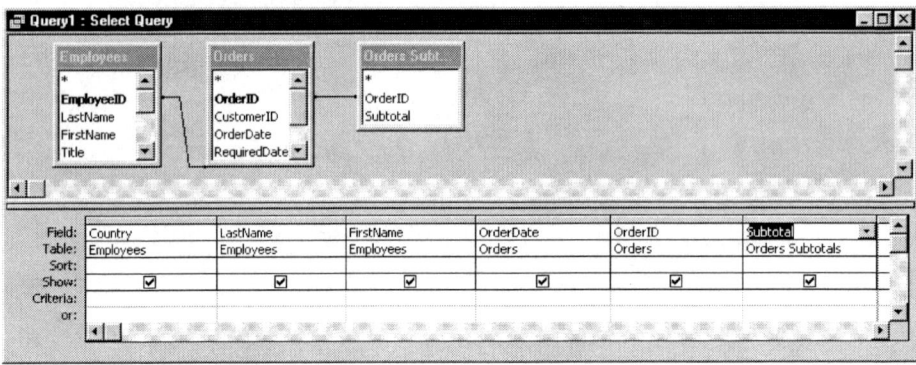

	• From the **File** menu, select **Save**	
	• Save as Employees Sales By Country	
	• From the **Query** menu, select **Run**	The query results are displayed.

Filtering Query Results

Instead of displaying all the records in a table or query, you can use a filter to show only the records you want to see. This allows you to limit the number of records that are visible to a manageable sub-set of the records. Unlike queries, however, filters are temporary and are not stored in the database, unless they are subsequently saved as a query.

Now that the query is created, there are several methods of filtering the query records.

To filter by selection

The simplest way of filtering the display of records in a table or query is to use **Filter by Selection** which only displays records that have the same value in that field.

*Try*IT	Action	Result
	• Ensure the query is displayed in **Datasheet** view	
	• Click in the **LastName** field for Julia Joyce	Julia Joyce will be your selected filter criteria.
	• On the **Standard** toolbar, click **Filter by Selection** (OR from the **Records** menu, select **F**ilter, then choose **Filter by Selection**)	The datasheet is refreshed to display only Julia Joyce's records. You should get at least one record - the one that you selected for the filter.

 If you select part of a field, then the filter will be based on that partial selection. For example, if you pick 'F' in the third position of a field and filter this by example, then the results will be exactly that - fields that have an 'F' in the third position of that field.

Lesson 5

You can further limit the records that are displayed by adding to the Filter by Selection. If you select another field from this filter-limited list, and select Filter by Selection once more, the records displayed will match both criteria.

It follows that you can add successive filters by example, until the requirements match the criteria that you require.

To re-display all records

Once a filter is in place, you may want to re-display all records from the table. Access allows you to toggle the display of records between all records and the filter that you have created.

*Try*IT	Action	Result
	• On the **Standard** toolbar, click the **Apply Filter** button ▽	The **Apply Filter** button toggles between the filtered records and all records.

To filter by form

*Try*IT	Action	Result
	• On the **Standard** toolbar, click **Filter by Form** 🗇 (**OR** from the **Records** menu, select **Filter** then **Filter by Form**)	The **Filter by Form** presents an empty datasheet record into which you add your criteria.

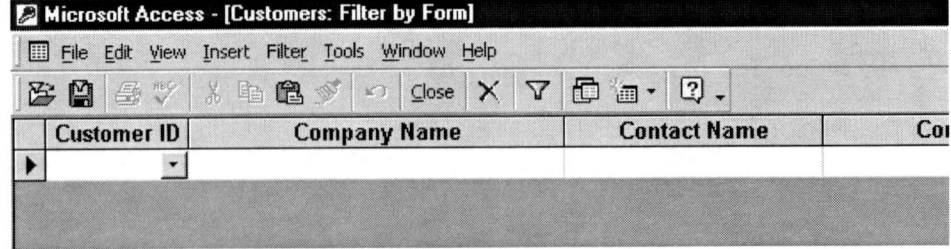

Part of a sample Filter by Form screen

Manipulating Data with Queries

- Type the filter selection criteria into the appropriate field(s)

- If you want to edit existing filter criteria, select the appropriate field and press F2

   The field is expanded to allow you to see the whole criteria.

- Click ▽ to toggle between filtered records and all records

   The **Apply Filter** button toggles between the filtered records and all records.

To specify multiple filter criteria

If you add entries to more than one field in the criteria row of the **Filter by Form**, this is known as an **AND** filter - in other words, all of the criteria that you add must be true for the record to be displayed in the filtered query results.

To expand the filter to include more records, you can create an **OR** filter by specifying criteria on the subsequent OR criteria row.

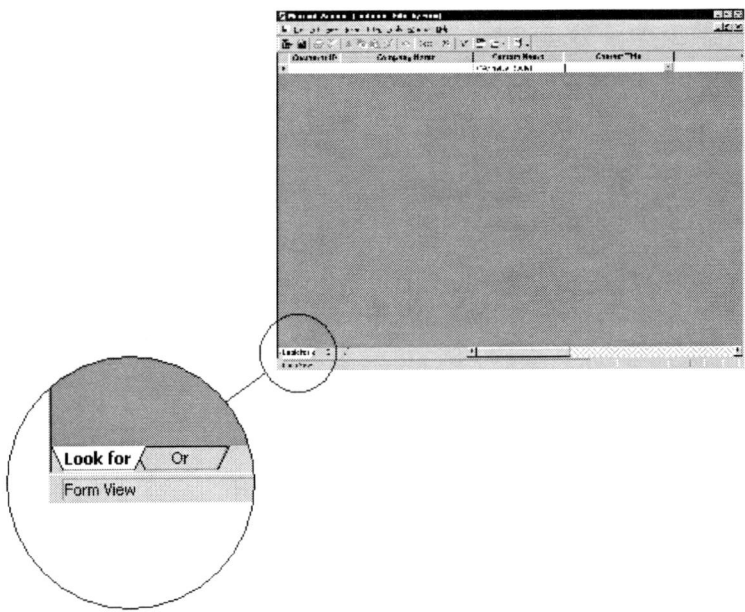

Using the Or tab to add criteria to the Filter by Form

To add OR criteria for multiple fields

TryIT

Action	Result
• Select the **OR** tab at the bottom-left corner of the window	A new empty **Filter by Criteria** row is displayed.
• From **LastName**'s drop-down list, select **Buchanan**	
• Click the **Apply Filter** button ▽	Steven Buchanan's records are added to the filtered records.
• Remove the filter	

Remember: by placing multiple criteria on one line, you want to use an **AND** set of criteria. By placing multiple criteria on multiple rows, you want an **OR** extraction.

Parameter Queries

While filters provide a means of displaying a static subset of query results, there may be occasions where the filtering that you wish to apply relies on data that does not remain static. In this case, you can create a **parameter** query.

For example, it may be that you are searching for information at or around a given date, but you are not quite sure of the exact date. A parameter query can be set up so that you type in a start date and an end date, which then allows you to search over a period of time. Another example is searching for the sales figures of a specific employee.

Each time that you run this query, Access will ask you for a parameter for one or more fields, which it will evaluate against an expression that you have created in the query.

To add a parameter to a query

To add a parameter to a field, you must provide a **prompt**, which will be displayed in the dialogue box used to supply the parameter when the query is run.

TryIT	Action	Result
	• Click the **View** button on the toolbar to switch to **Design** view • Click in the **Criteria** row of the **LastName** column • Type [Enter the employee's last name] • Press `Enter`	**Design** view is displayed. The text is added to the **LastName** criteria row.

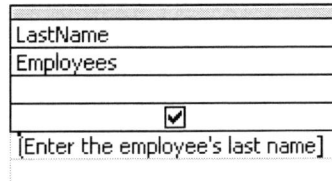

 It is important to include the square brackets for parameter prompts. If you do not add them, Access will treat the prompt text as sample data for the criteria.

The prompt text must be different from the field name and cannot contain the period (.) character.

	• Run the query	The parameter prompt is displayed.

Lesson 5

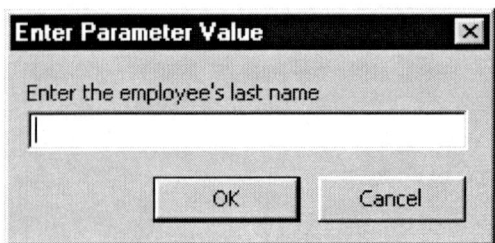

Parameter dialogue box

- Type the last name of an employee (Sing)
- Click **OK**

The results of your query are displayed

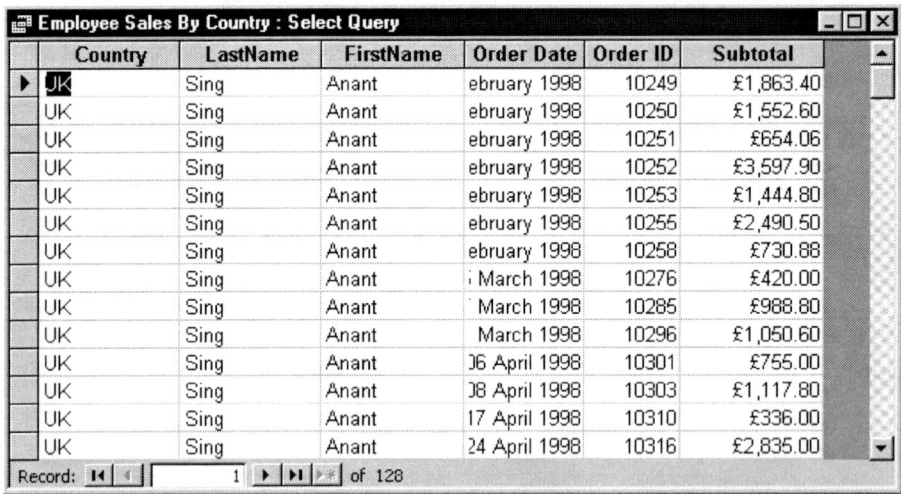

Parameter query results

To specify multiple criteria for a single field

It is possible to use the Boolean operators **AND, OR, NOT, BETWEEN** and **LIKE** to create multiple criteria for a single query field.

For example, to allow you to specify a range of prices to be included in a particular query, you could enter the following criteria:

```
BETWEEN [Lower Stock Price] AND [Upper Stock Price]
```

Concatenation

Concatenation means joining together text. You can combine the text output of two or more fields along with any standard text you want to use.

The **&** operator is used to concatenate text. As usual, field names should be enclosed in square brackets and text by quotation marks.

To use concatenation

We will modify the previous query to see the total sales by employee.

TryIT	Action	Result
	• Open the **Employee Sales by Country** query in design view • Create a new calculated field to the right of **Country** (Use **I**nsert, **C**olumns) `Name: [FirstName] & " " & [LastName]`	
	• Delete the **FirstName**, **LastName**, **OrderDate** and **OrderID** fields from the query grid • On the **Standard** toolbar, click **Totals** Σ	A new **Total:** row is displayed in the query design window.
	• Choose **Sum** for the **Subtotal** field • Run the query ! • Save the query as `Employees' Sales` • Close the query	To see the results. The query is saved to a new name.

Crosstab Queries

Summary queries can aggregate and group information in "one-dimension" only. For example, consider a query that shows which products customers have been buying.

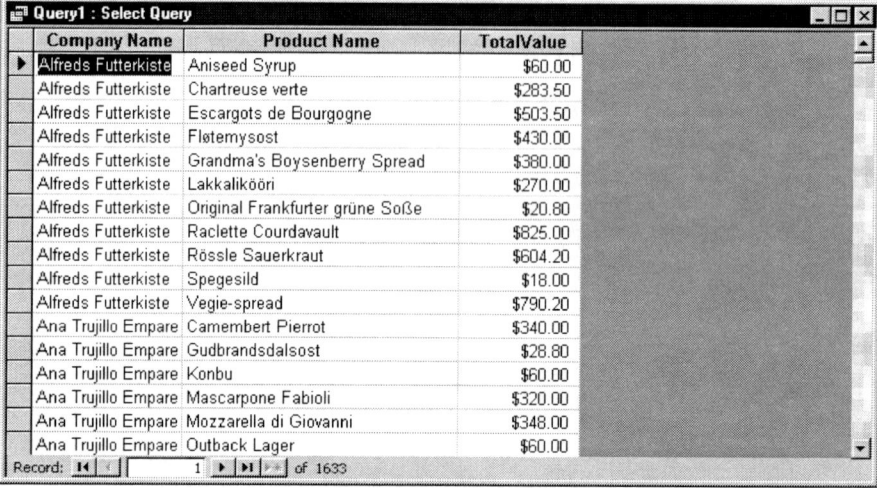

Product sales by customer

This query is adequate for its purpose. You can easily see which products a customer is buying. However, it is not so easy to see which customers are buying which products. It is not easy to read down the Product Name column to pick out customers who have ordered "Aniseed Syrup" for example, much less compare how much Aniseed Syrup they bought compared to other customers.

One possibility is to create a filter or criteria to show each product one-by-one. However, it is also possible to create a special kind of query that answers both questions: "Which products are given customers buying?" and "Which products are bought by which customers?"

Manipulating Data with Queries

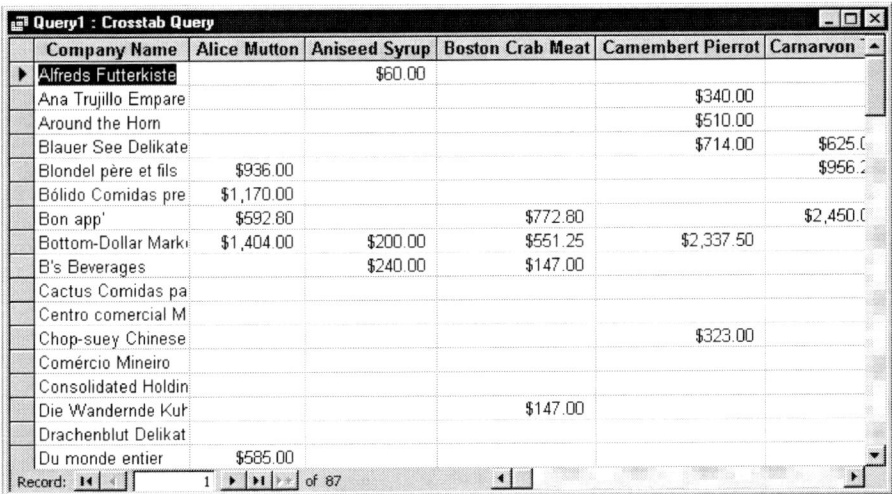

Crosstab query

This type of query is called a **crosstab query**. A crosstab query displays summary data vertically **and** horizontally, using **two** sets of headings.

The above example shows that you can see (by reading across a row) which products any given customer buys, **and** (by reading down a column) which products are popular with which customers.

To create a crosstab query

- Ensure that all the fields you want to include in the crosstab are in **one** table or query - you cannot create a crosstab from multiple tables/queries
- Create a query containing the following three fields:

The field that you want to display for each **row** of the crosstab

The field that you want to display for each **column** of the crosstab

The field for which you want to display summary information

- Display the query in design view

- On the **Standard** toolbar, click the down arrow on the **Query Type** button and select **Crosstab Query**

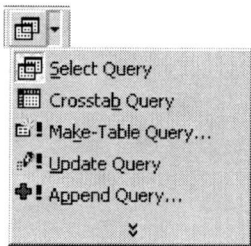

OR

- From the **Query** menu, select **Crosstab Query**

When you change the type of query to a crosstab query, an additional **Crosstab:** property row is added to the design window. Also, if this is not a Summary query, the **Total:** row is also added to the window.

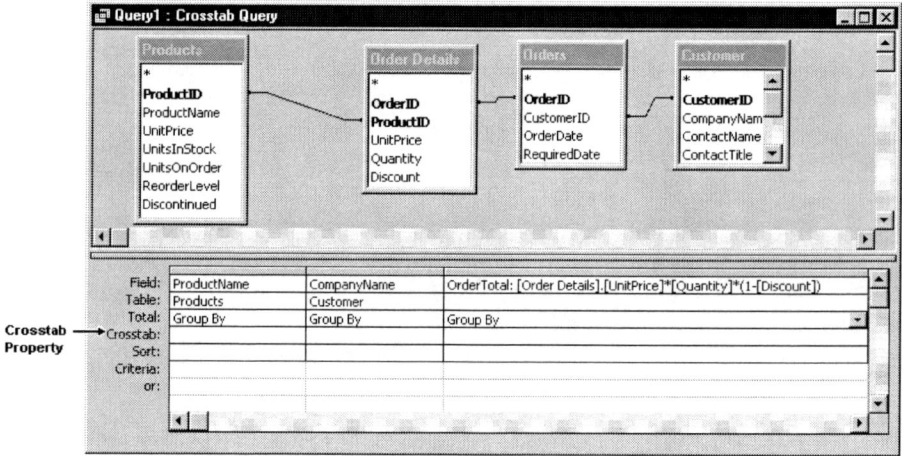

Crosstab property of a crosstab query

- Select the **Crosstab:** property of the first field

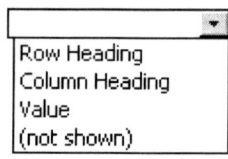

Crosstab: options

- Each of the three first options must be assigned to one field in the query grid - that is, at least one field must be the row heading, another the column heading and the third the value

There can be up to three row headings but only one column heading and one value.

- The fourth option (**not shown**) is for any other fields that are included in the query but not required in the output

Fields set to **Row Heading** and **Column Heading** must have a **Total:** setting of **Group By**, and the **Value** field must have the **Total:** property set to the aggregate value (**SUM**, **AVG** and so on) that you have chosen to display in the intersecting cells.

- Set the appropriate **Total:** settings

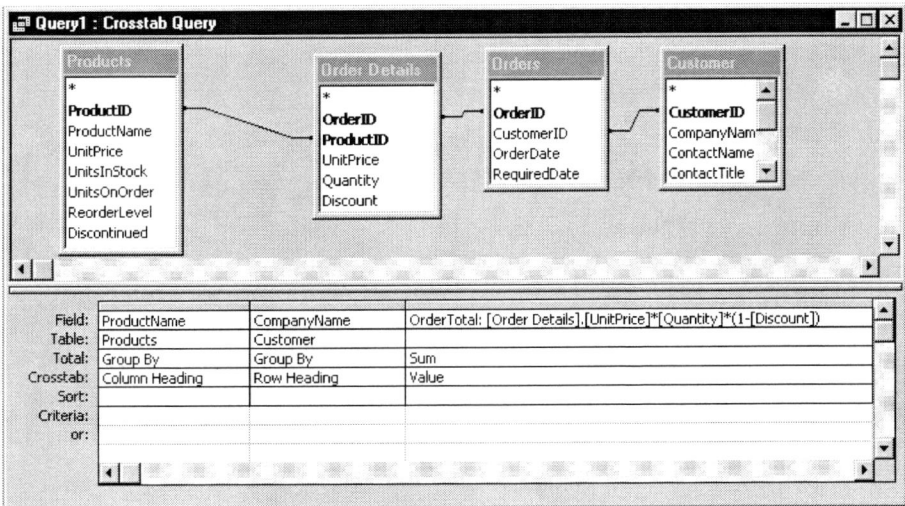

Sample settings for a crosstab query

- Save and run the query

Lesson 5

In this exercise, we will create the crosstab query discussed above, to show customers' product ordering habits. However, rather than designing the query from scratch, for this exercise, we will use the **Crosstab Query Wizard** to help define the query.

As the information we want to include is in different tables, the first step is to create a select query to combine the fields we want in one location.

TryIT	Action	Result
	• Create a new query in design view • Add the **Products**, **Orders**, **Order Details** and **Customers** tables to the query • From the **Products** table, add the **ProductName** field • From the **Customers** table, add the **CompanyName** field • Create a calculated field as below and format it as **Currency** `LineTotal: [Order Details].[UnitPrice]*[Quantity]* (1-[Discount])` • Save the query as **CustOrders** and close it	

Now that the source query is ready, we can create the crosstab.

	Action	Result
	• In the **Database** window, select the Queries object and click 🗐 New	The **New Query** dialogue box is displayed.
	• Select **Crosstab Query Wizard** and click **OK**	The **Crosstab Query Wizard** starts.
	• In the **View** panel, select **Queries**	
	• Select the **CustOrders** query	

Manipulating Data with Queries

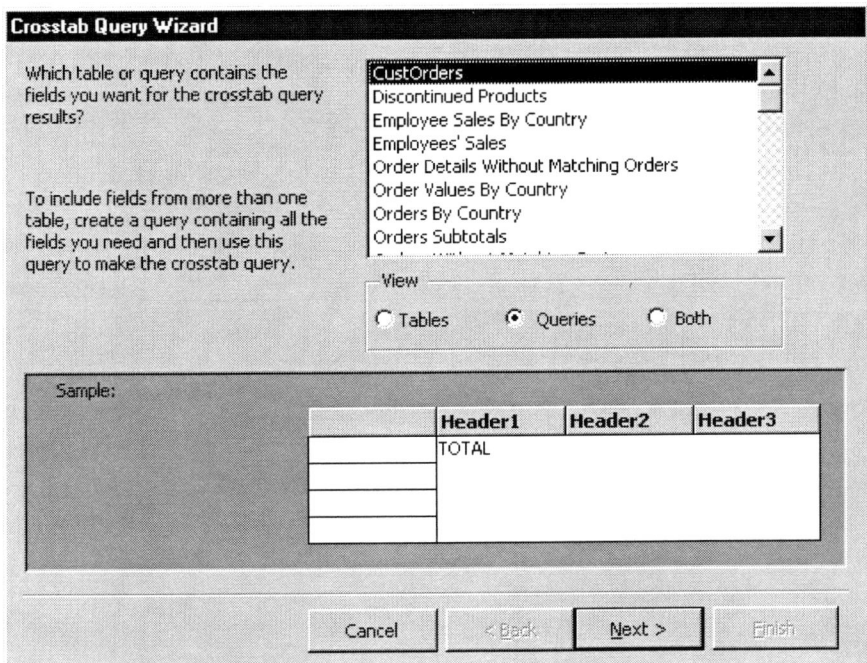

- Click **Next >**
- Select the **CompanyName** field for the row headings

The next screen of the **Crosstab Query Wizard** is displayed.

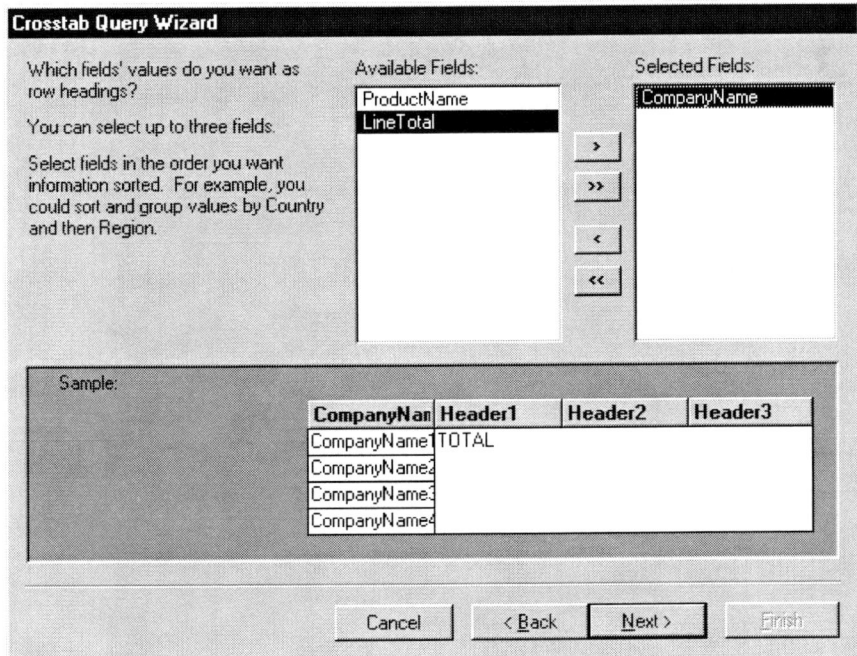

Lesson 5

- Click **Next >**
- Select the **ProductName** field for the column headings
- Click **Next >**

The next screen of the **Crosstab Query Wizard** is displayed.

The next screen lets you choose an aggregate function for the value field.

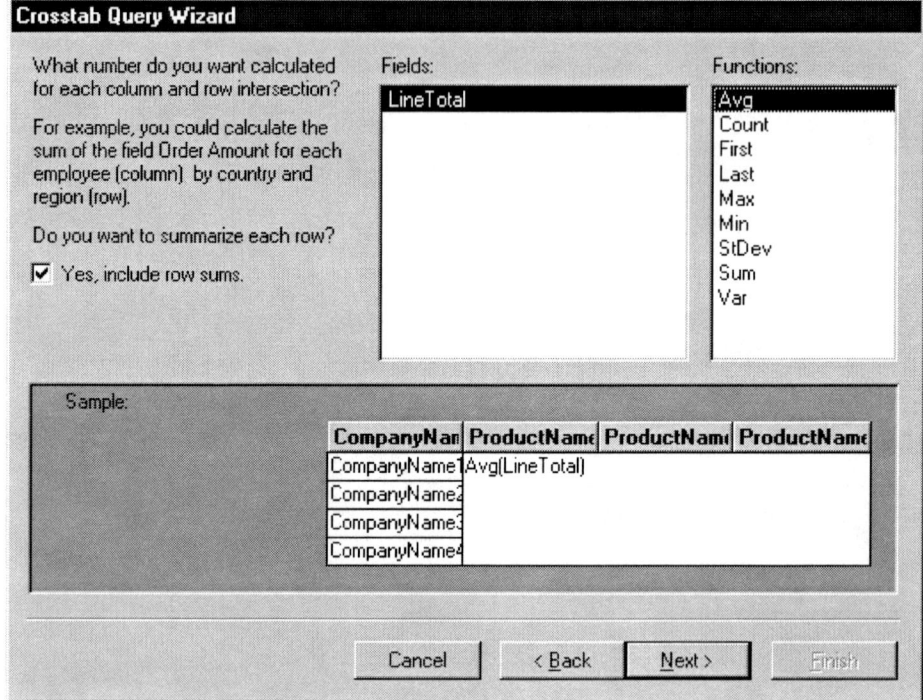

- Select the **SUM** function and click **Next >**
- Accept the default name by clicking **Finish**
- Open the query in design view and apply the **Currency** format to the calculated fields
- Save changes to the query and run it again
- Close the database

The final screen of the **Crosstab Query Wizard** is displayed.

The query results are displayed.

Review Questions

(1) Name five different query types.

(2) Identify the different action queries.

(3) What should you do before running an action query?

(4) How do you create a summary query?

(5) Name two ways of filtering records.

(6) Explain the difference between AND and OR in queries or filters.

(7) What is concatenation?

(8) What is a parameter query and how do you create one?

(9) What is a crosstab query?

Answers on the next page.

Lesson 5

Review Answers

(1) i) Select query
    ii) Summary query
    iii) Crosstab query
    iv) Action query
    v) Parameter query

(2) i) Delete query
    ii) Update query
    iii) Make-Table query
    iv) Append query

(3) i) Check the query results by running it as a select query
    ii) Backup the database

(4) i) From the Standard toolbar, select the Totals button OR
    ii) From the View menu, select Totals

(5) i) Filter by Selection
    ii) Filter by Form

(6) i) AND criteria (all entered on the same row) must ALL be met for the record to be included
    ii) Any of OR criteria (entered on different rows) must be met for the record to be included

(7) Concatenation means joining text together (using the & operator)

(8) A parameter query prompts the user to enter the criteria to run the query. To create a parameter query, add text to a field's criteria row and surround the text in square brackets

(9) A crosstab query displays summary data vertically and horizontally, using two sets of headings

Skills Summary

Review

Congratulations on successfully completing LESSON 5. You can now create a wide range of queries to perform a variety of tasks in your database.

Review objectives...

- ☐ Create **action** queries

- ☐ Create a **summary** query

- ☐ Use **expressions** in **calculated fields**

- ☐ **Combine** queries

- ☐ **Filter** query results

- ☐ Create a **parameter** query

- ☐ Create a **crosstab** query

Notes

Going Further

Between...And

Using the **Between...And** operator, you can search for data that falls between two dates. You can use it in a parameter query too

To use the Between...And operator

- Click the **View** button on the toolbar to switch to **Design** view
- Click in the **Criteria** row of the field
- Type `Between [Start date] And [End Date]`
- Press `Enter`

The text is added to the field's criteria row

- Run the query

The first **parameter prompt** is displayed

- Type the start date of your search
- Click **OK**

The second parameter prompt is displayed.

- Type the end date of your search
- Click **OK**

The results of your query are displayed.

Country	Empl	LastName	FirstName	Order Date	Order ID	Subtotal
UK	4	Peacock	Margaret	26 February 1998	10267	£3,536.60
USA	3	Anderson	Fiona	27 February 1998	10268	£1,101.20
UK	5	Buchanan	Steven	28 February 1998	10269	£642.20
UK	4	Peacock	Margaret	28 February 1998	10270	£1,376.00
USA	2	Oshida	Osako	28 February 1998	10271	£48.00
USA	2	Oshida	Osako	28 February 1998	10272	£1,456.00

Lesson 5

To use wildcards in parameters

You may use the **LIKE** wildcard * to create partial parameters that will work on part of the associated field. For example, in a field that displays names, the following locates fields where the beginning of the field matches the supplied parameter:

```
LIKE [Name begins with] & "*"
```

Display Only the Top Values

Use the **Top Values** property to limit a query to the top set of values specified in the criteria.

- Open the query in design view
- On the **Standard** toolbar, click the **Top Values** drop-down arrow

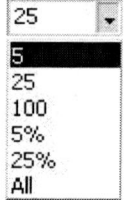

Top Values list box

- Select a value
- Run the query to see the result

Lesson 6 — Building and Modifying Forms

In this lesson you will learn how to customise forms.

Lesson objectives...

- ☐ Modify a form in **design** view using form **sections** and **controls**
- ☐ View a form's **properties**
- ☐ Add a **graphic** to a form
- ☐ Create a **calculated** control
- ☐ Create **multi-table** forms

Jump lesson...

If you can already customise forms, you may want to learn to apply the same techniques to REPORTS AND CHARTS on page 177 or you can learn how to create data access pages in PUBLISHING DATA ON THE INTERNET on page 209.

Using Advanced Form Features

Forms are an essential element of any database. As users' main interface to the database, a well designed form can increase their productivity when updating records and help to minimise data entry errors.

The following features can be used to extend basic forms created with the Forms Wizard.

Custom controls

The appearance of basic controls can be improved using the formatting tools and Property Sheet. You can also adjust the behaviour of controls.

Controls can be added to forms to serve a variety of purposes. You may want to display additional database fields, perform a calculation, add graphics objects or create a macro command button to automate some feature.

Multiple table forms

Multiple table forms can be used to view and work on two or more related tables at once; viewing a single record from the parent table will display all the related records from the child table(s).

Sections

Additional sections can be used to improve the appearance of forms on-screen and in print.

Switchboard forms

A **Switchboard** provides a user-friendly interface to your database, hiding unnecessary features of Access that users adding and editing records do not need.

Form Design Worksurface

Forms and reports are both customised in design view using very similar tools:

Worksurface

The **worksurface** is the area on which you layout the form/report. The worksurface is divided into different **sections**.

Controls

Controls display data and graphics. The **Toolbox** and **Field List** let you add controls.

Property Sheet

The **Property Sheet** lets you change the formatting of form/report **sections** and **controls**. You can also adjust some properties directly using the **Formatting** toolbar.

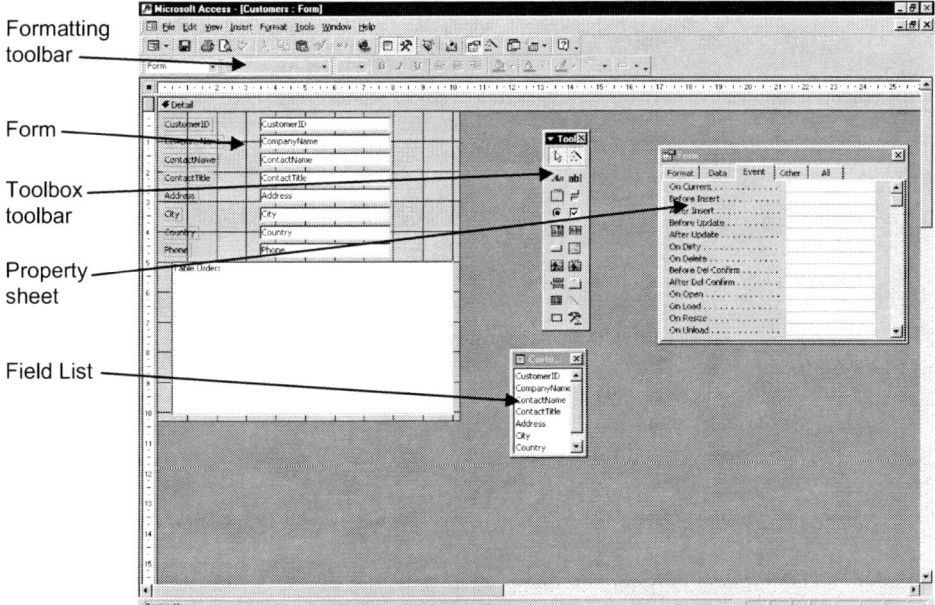

Form Design Worksurface

Form Sections

A form consists of several **sections**. Here is a blank form displaying all the available form sections:

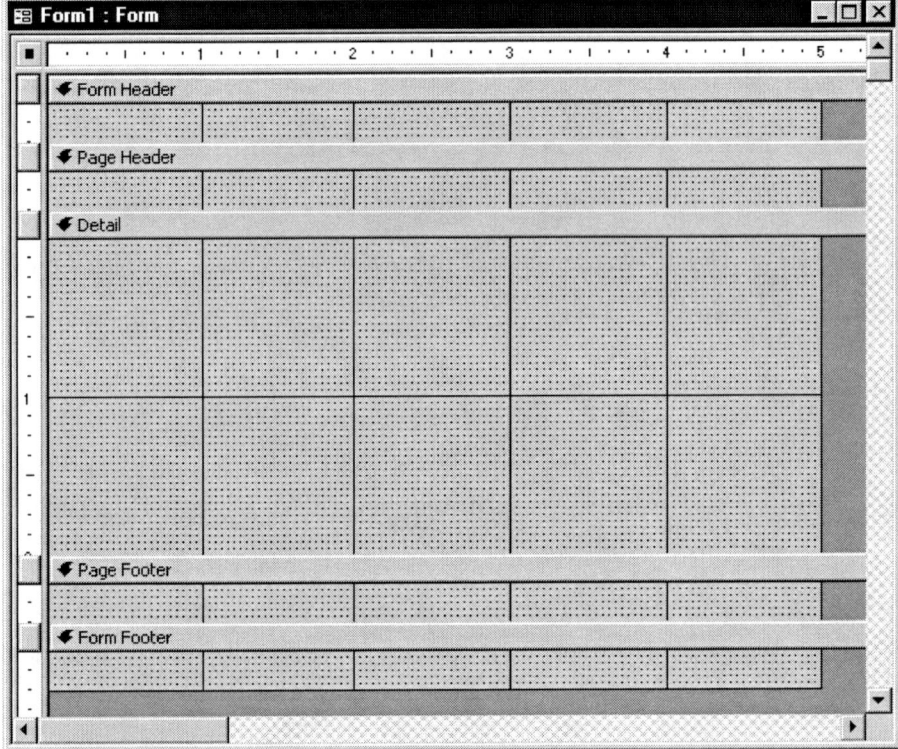

Form sections

Detail section

Each form must contain a detail section, which will contain fields from the currently selected record in the table or query that underlies the form.

Form Header / Form Footer sections

These sections are optional but if selected, the form header and/or footer will **always** be visible at the top and bottom of the form, no matter how large the detail section is.

Page Header/Page Footer sections

The main use for forms is for data entry and editing. However, it is also possible to print a form, which is where the **page header/footer** comes in.

The **page header** and **page footer** sections are never displayed as part of the form when it is on-screen, but are used when the form is printed. This is necessary because the **form header** and **form footer** sections only appear once when printed.

- The **form header** section is printed before the first form on the printout
- The **form footer** section is printed after the last form on the printout

In contrast to this, the **page header** and **page footer** sections will be printed at the top and bottom of the printed page, so making a multiple page printout much more readable.

If you are not planning to print your forms, you can ignore the **page header** and **page footer** sections.

To show/hide the form header and form footer sections

The header and footers are not always displayed by default.

- From the **View** menu, select **Form Header/Footer**

The menu option is a toggle - to hide the sections again, simply select the menu option again.

If you hide a section, Access will delete any controls on that section. You will receive a warning dialogue box to that effect:

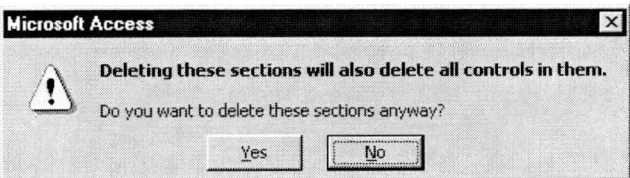

Lesson 6

Resizing Form Sections

You can resize the height of form sections to make more or less space. You can also change the width of the whole form.

To change the height of a form section or the width of the form

- Point the mouse to the border of the form section you want to change (see graphic below)

You will see the mouse pointer change to a re-size pointer ✢.

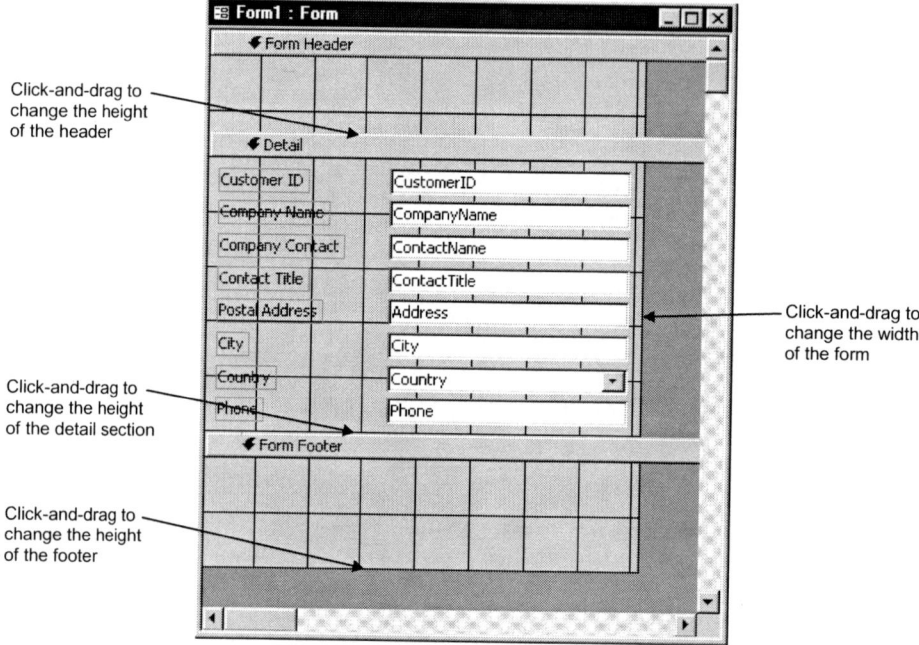

- To change the width of the form, click-and-drag the right-hand border - you cannot change the width of individual sections

 Access will only let you reduce the size of a section to the edge of the lowest/right-most control in the section.

 You may find it useful to have the ruler visible when working. To do this, from the **View** menu, select **Ruler**.

Form Controls

Controls are the means by which you present data and other information on a form. Every object on a form is a control of one type or another, be it a combo box, logo or line. Controls are added from the **Toolbox** toolbar and from the **Field List**.

There are two basic types of control:

Bound controls

Bound controls display dynamic information on a form.

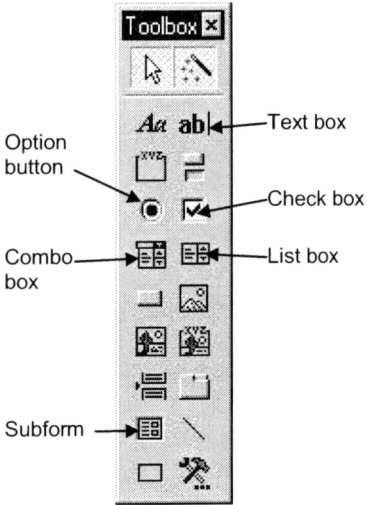

When you use the Form Wizard or AutoForm to create a form, it automatically creates bound controls for each field you add to the form.

The control is bound to a field of the currently selected record in the underlying data source. As the record changes, so the bound control is updated with the field information for the new record. When the user enters or edits data in the control, the data source is updated.

It is also possible to add controls directly from the underlying tables or queries using drag-and-drop. When you open a form in design view for the first time, Access also displays the **Field List** dialogue box.

Field list dialogue box

Unbound controls

Unbound controls tend to contain information that is **static** with respect to the underlying data source, such as labels, company logos, lines and boxes.

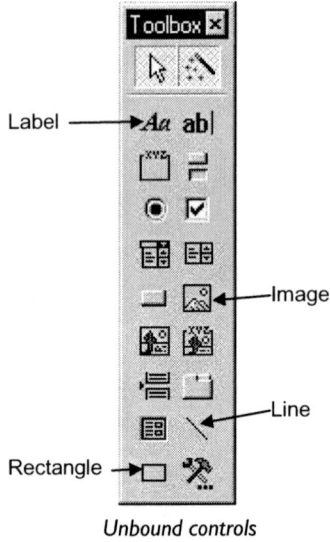

Unbound controls

To add a control

- To add a control to a form, click the appropriate control button on the Toolbox

The Toolbox toolbar also contains a useful tool called the **Control Wizard** tool. As its name implies, if the Control Wizard is selected, it provides additional wizard dialogue boxes (where appropriate) in order to allow you to set the properties of the control as you add it to the form.

If the toolbox is not visible, click the **Toolbox** button on the **Standard** toolbar.

Selecting Controls

Before you can perform actions on controls, such as moving or sizing them, you need to select the controls. The control is divided into two parts: the field name and the data entry box.

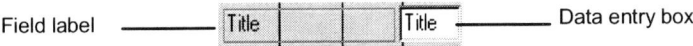

Field label ——— Title | Title ——— Data entry box

When a control is selected, handles (black squares) appear around the control:

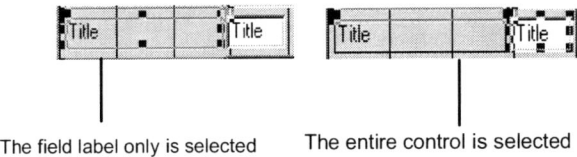

The field label only is selected   The entire control is selected

- To select the field label only, click somewhere on the field label
- To select the entire control, click somewhere on the data entry box
- To select multiple controls, hold down the `Shift` key and click on the desired controls
- To select all controls, from the **Edit** menu, choose **Select All**

When you move your mouse pointer around the edge of the field, you will notice that the pointer changes to several different shapes. The following table lists each shape that you will see and the operation that it performs.

Pointer	Operation
✋	Move both field and label
☝	Move either field or label
↕	Size the field horizontally
↔	Size the field vertically
↖	Size the field both horizontally and vertically

Lesson 6

If you want to re-size the label, simply click it, The sizing handles will appear around the label instead of the control. To move the control, point anywhere on the control, except the handles.

To resize multiple controls

If you want to size multiple controls so that they have the same dimensions, Access provides menu options to accomplish this quickly and easily.

- Select the controls then from the **Format** menu, select **Size**

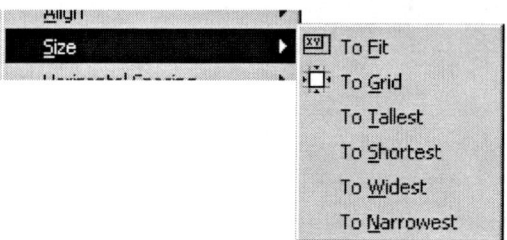

The **To Fit** option sizes the controls so that expected data that will be displayed in them.

To Grid "snaps" the object borders to an invisible grid, making it easier to line up controls.

The last four options should be self-explanatory.

- Select the appropriate sizing option

To align controls

When you have multiple controls on a form, it can often become fiddly and time consuming to align the controls on the form. Access provides a series of alignment controls to help this process.

- Select the controls that you wish to align

You can select a whole row or column of controls by dragging inside the rulers of the form design view. Note that if you are dragging inside the horizontal ruler at the top of the form, controls in all sections will be selected.

Building and Modifying Forms

- From the **Format** menu, select **Align**

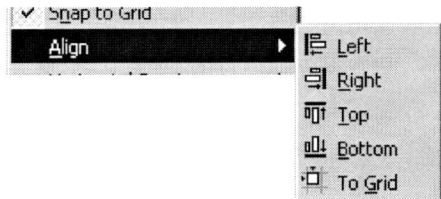

The first four options allow you to align the selected controls to one of the four sides of the control. The basic rule of alignment is that the controls are aligned to the furthest edge of all of the selected controls in the direction of alignment.

For example, if you choose several controls to align top, the controls will be aligned to the top of the top-most control.

Another rule of formatting is that controls aligned using Align will not overlap. If you have two controls which overlap in the direction in which you are trying to align them, then the controls will be aligned "as near as possible" without overlapping.

- Select an appropriate option from the **Align** submenu

To space controls

With multiple controls, another layout requirement is to be able to set equal spacing between groups of three or more controls. Access provides horizontal and vertical spacing tools in order to help you achieve this aim.

 While some spacing options will work with two objects, they are only effective when three or more controls are selected on-screen.

- From the **Format** menu, select either **Vertical Spacing** or **Horizontal Spacing**

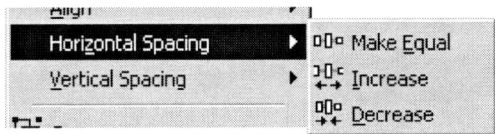

Lesson 6

The three options allow you to either make the spacing between objects the same or increase/decrease the spacing between them.

- Select the appropriate spacing option

If two or more controls are aligned in the direction that you are spacing them, they will be treated as a single unit. For example if, out of a group of controls two are aligned to top, then they will be treated as a single control for the purpose of spacing.

To create and customise a form

As our database does not yet have a form for the Employees table, we will create one using **AutoForm** then modify it in design view.

This is a very common technique: to use AutoForm or the wizard to create the basic form layout and then to modify it in design view. Creating a form from scratch in design view is usually time consuming and counter-productive.

TryIT

Action	Result
• Open the **UNIVER_6** database	
• Select the **Tables** object	
• Select the **Employees** table	
• Click the **AutoForm** button on the toolbar	**AutoForm** creates a form for the Employees table.
• Save the form as Employees	The **Employees** form is saved.

Form Properties

Everything on a form has properties, including the form itself. There are several ways to select the form:

- On the **Formatting** toolbar, select **Form** from the **Object** drop-down list

OR

- Click the dark grey area of the window

OR

- Click the grey box to the left of the ruler bar (Select **V**iew, **R**uler to see the rulers)

TryIT 	Action	Result
	• Open the **Employees** form in design view	
	• If the Property Sheet is not displayed, on the **Standard** toolbar, click **Properties**	
	• Click the **Object** list box on the left-hand side of the **Formatting** toolbar and select **Form**	The property sheet for the form is displayed as shown below.

On the **Format** tab, you can choose what elements of the form window to display (scroll bars, window control icons, record selectors) and whether to allow adding, editing and deleting of records (**Data** tab).

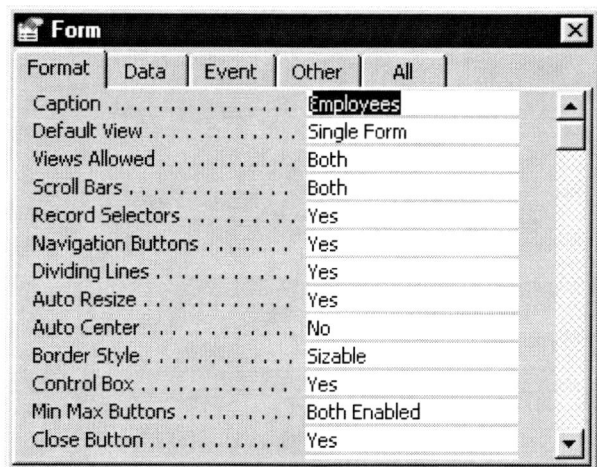

Form Properties dialogue box

Form Header

To add a heading that appears on every record in a form, it is necessary to use the form header.

To create a form header

TryIT	Action	Result
	• From the **View** menu, click **Form Header/Footer**	The **Form Header/Footer** sections are displayed.
	• On the **Toolbox**, click the **Label** control *Aa*	A crosshair symbol and the letter A appear on the mouse pointer.
	• Click-and-drag to create the label in the header section	
	• Type `Universal Import Ltd` then press `Enter`	The label is created.

The Formatting Toolbar

When you work in design mode, a **Formatting** toolbar is displayed below the **Standard** toolbar. This lets you set control properties, such as font type, size and colour and text alignment quickly. Any changes you make with the Formatting toolbar are automatically updated to the **Properties Sheet**.

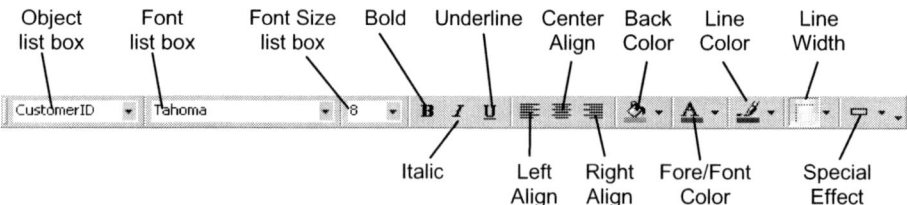

Formatting toolbar

Choosing fonts to use on a form

Different **font typefaces** are available for you to use on forms. Note that some fonts are not suitable for use on forms, as they are hard to read on-screen. Most on-screen forms use a **sans serif** font, such as **MS Sans Serif** or **Tahoma**. Sans serif fonts are quite plain (they do not have curly ends) which make them easier to read on-screen.

Note that not all fonts are available on all systems. If a font you choose for the form is not available, the default system font will be used instead, which may spoil the layout of your form and make it difficult to read.

As well as changing the typeface of text, you can change its size. Size is measured in **points**. A character that is 72pts is 1 inch (2.54cm) high. Most forms will use font sizes of between 10-12 points.

To change the format properties of controls

TryIT	Action	Result
	• With the header label still selected, click the **Center** button ≡	The text is centred within the control.
	• With the control still selected, click the **Bold** button B	The text is emboldened.
	• Make sure the title control is selected	
	• From the **Font** box, select **Arial**	The **Arial** font is applied to the text.
	• From the **Size** box, select **14**	The size of the text is changed to **14**.
	• From the **Font/Fore Colour** drop-down list, select **red**	The text is changed to **red**.
	• Move the control towards the centre horizontally in the header	The heading is now in the centre of the header.
	• Resize the text label to fit the larger text	

Lesson 6

Deleting Controls

To delete a control

TryIT	Action	Result
	• Select the **EmployeeID** control • Press the `Delete` key on the keyboard	The **EmployeeID** control is deleted.

Undo

If you accidentally delete a control, you can **undo** the deletion as follows:

To undo a deletion

TryIT	Action	Result
	• From the **Edit** menu, select **Undo Delete**	The deletion is undone and the **EmployeeID** control is restored.

Remember that you only have one level of undo - if you delete an object then do something else (move a field, for example), you will not be able to undo the deletion of the object.

	• From the **File** menu, select **Save**	The form is saved.
	• Click the **View** button on the toolbar to switch to **Form** view	Form view is displayed.

Adding a Graphic to a Form

Another important unbound control is the **Image** control. This allows you to add graphics such as company logos. Logos provide a more consistent and professional identity to the application.

> Most image formats are supported. If your chosen format does not seem to be available, you have probably not installed the associated graphics filter from your Office 2000 installation files. You will need to run setup and add the appropriate filter.

To add an image control to a form

TryIT	Action	Result
	• Click the **View** button on the toolbar to switch to **Design** view	Design view is displayed.
	• On the **Toolbox**, click the **Image Control** button	The mouse pointer changes to a cross with the **Image** tool attached.
	• Click to the right of the title in the Header section	The **Insert Picture** dialogue box is displayed.
	• Select **UILOGO.GIF** • Click **OK**	The image is inserted on the form.

To resize a graphic object

TryIT

Action	Result
• Select one of the corner **sizing handles**	The cursor should change to a double-headed arrow.
• Drag the sizing handle towards the centre of the image	The picture is reduced in size.
• In the Property Sheet **Format** tab, select **Size Mode**	
• Click the drop-down arrow and select **Zoom**	The picture is resized as necessary without distorting the proportions of the object.

The **Size Mode** property:

Clip (Default) displays the object at actual size.

Stretch sizes the object to fill the control. This setting may distort the proportions of the object.

Zoom displays the entire object, resizing it as necessary without distorting the proportions of the object.

• Adjust the form design to match the screenshot below then save

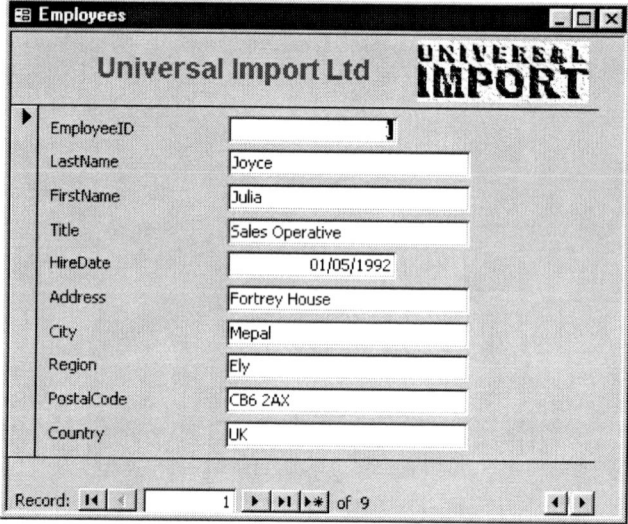

Creating a Calculated Control

Calculated controls are based on **expressions**. Simple expressions can be entered manually into the Control Source or complex expressions can be built up using the **Expression Builder**. Expressions can contain the following contents.

Item	Action
=	Denotes a calculated expression. Must be placed at the start of the calculation.
[UnitPrice]	Field name.
+ - / * ^ ( )	Arithmetic symbols - Add, Subtract, Divide, Multiply, Exponential, Enclosed.
SUM(field) MAX(field) DATE() PAGE()	Function keywords. Functions such as SUM and MAX require a field name between the brackets, others such as DATE and PAGE require empty brackets.
20	Number. Any number positive or negative can be used as part of a calculation. The way the result is stored depends on the way the data type properties are set in the table.
" "	String. Literal text enclosed in quotes. Can be joined to text from fields.
&	Concatenation symbol to join fields or strings together.

Lesson 6

Example calculations

Calculation	Action
= [UnitPrice] * [Quantity]	Calculate order value.
= [UnitPrice] * [Quantity] * [Discount]	Calculate discount value.
= [UnitPrice] * 1.05	Increase unit price by 5%.
= [ReorderLevel] + 10	Add 10 to reorder level.
= [City] & ", " & [Country]	Join City and Country fields together separated by a comma and a space.
= SUM ([Quantity])	Total quantity ordered.
= MAX ([Quantity])	Highest quantity ordered.
= Date()	Display today's date.
= Now()	Display the date and time.

To add a calculated control to a form

In this exercise, we will add a control to the form that displays how many years each employee has been with the company.

TryIT	Action	Result
	• Open the **Employees** form in design view	The **Employees** form is displayed in **Design** view.
	• Add a **Text Box** control abl to the form to the right of the **HireDate** field	The control and its label are added to the form.
	• Delete the label part of the control	

Building and Modifying Forms

- Select the text box
- In the Property Sheet, on the **Data** tab, select the **Control Source** property
- Type the following expression

  `=DateDiff("yyyy", [HireDate],Now()) & " years"`

- From the **File** menu, select **Save**
  The form is saved.

- Click the **View** button on the toolbar to switch to **Form** view
  Form view is displayed.

- Check through the records to ensure that the calculated control has worked

- Tidy up the size and positioning of the new control

Because the control is calculated, the user cannot edit it, but the default appearance of the text box control makes it look as though it is a normal field. Setting the **Enabled** property to **No** will make it obvious that the control cannot be selected and changed.

- Select the text box
- In the Property Sheet, on the **Data** tab, select the **Enabled** property
- Select **No**
- View the form again
  The control is greyed-out.
- Save and close the form

Multi-Table Forms

When a form uses information from more than one table, it is useful to create a main form with a **subform**. The main form displays data from the "one" side of the relationship and the subform displays data from the "many" side.

For example, the main form displays a single record at a time from the parent table (Customers), while the subform usually displays several related records in a datasheet style from the child table (Orders).

This makes viewing data in related tables easier. When data is entered using multiple forms, the data is saved back to the related underlying tables.

A main form can have any number of subforms if you place each subform on the main form. You can also nest up to two levels of subforms. This means you can have a subform within a main form, and you can have another subform within that subform.

For example, you could have a main form that displays customers, a subform that displays their orders, and another subform that displays the order details.

To create a mainform/subform using the wizard

This exercise creates a main form from the Orders table and a subform from the Order Details table.

TryIT	Action	Result
	• Start a new form using the **Form Wizard**	The first step of the **Form Wizard** is displayed.
	• From the **Tables/Queries** drop-down list, select **Table:Orders**	
	• Move the **OrderID**, **CustomerID**, **OrderDate** and **RequiredDate** fields to the **Selected Fields** list	Fields from the first table are added.

Building and Modifying Forms

- From the **Tables/Queries** drop-down list select **Table:Order Details**

- Move the **ProductID**, **UnitPrice**, **Quantity** and **Discount** to the **Selected Fields** list

- Click **Next >**

The **ProductID**, **UnitPrice**, **Quantity** and **Discount** fields are moved to the **Selected Fields** list.

The **Form Wizard** moves on to the next step, prompting you to select the main form.

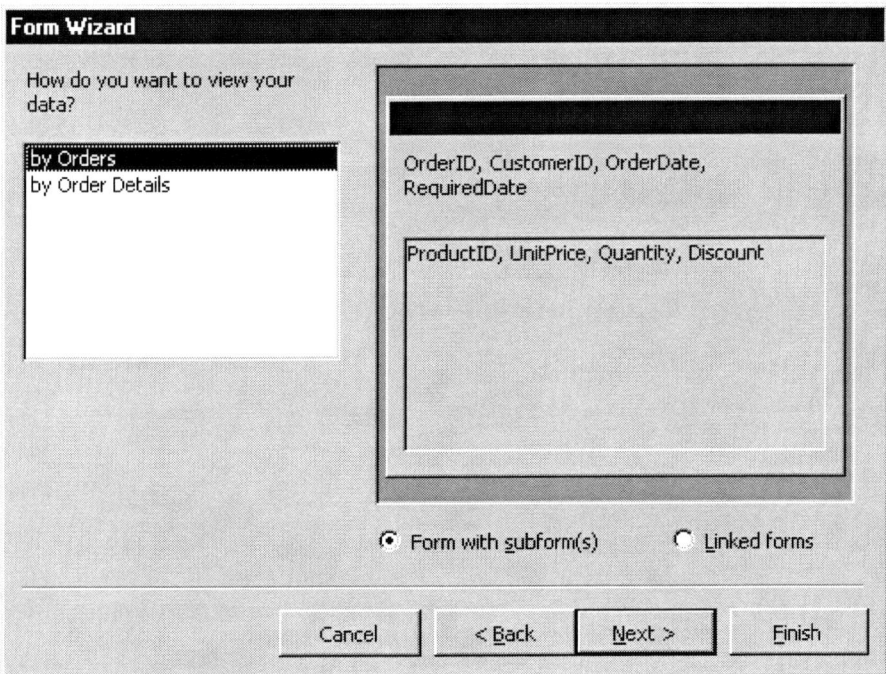

- Keep the options **by Orders** and **Form with subform(s)** selected

- Click **Next >**

- Click the **Tabular** option button for the subform

- Click **Next >**

The **Form Wizard** moves on to the next step, prompting you for a layout for the subform.

A preview of the form appears on the left of the dialogue box.

The Form Wizard moves to the next step, prompting you for a style for your form.

Lesson 6

- Select **Standard** as the style
- Click **Next >**

The **Form Wizard** moves to the last step, prompting you for names for the forms.

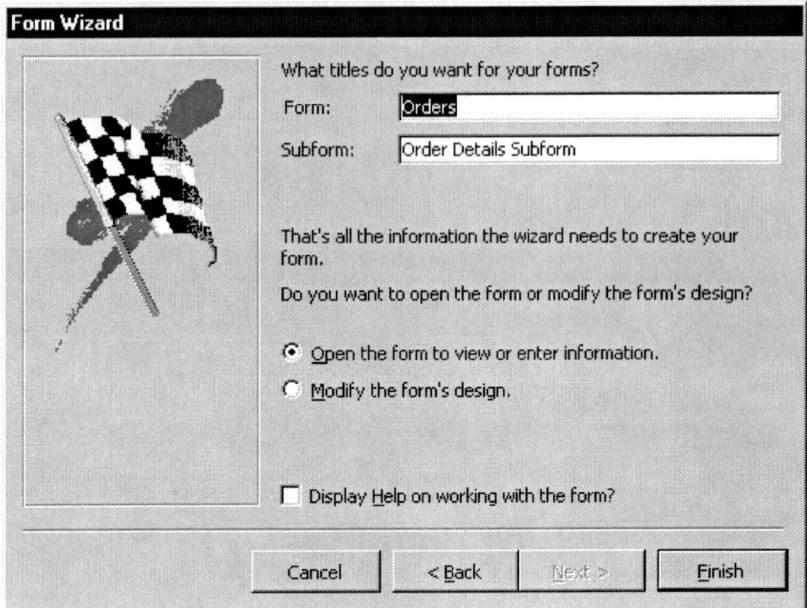

Form Wizard

- Rename the title of the form to
  `Orders Main Form`
- Leave the subform name as it is
- Click **Finish**

A multiple table form is created based on the fields you have chosen from the different tables.

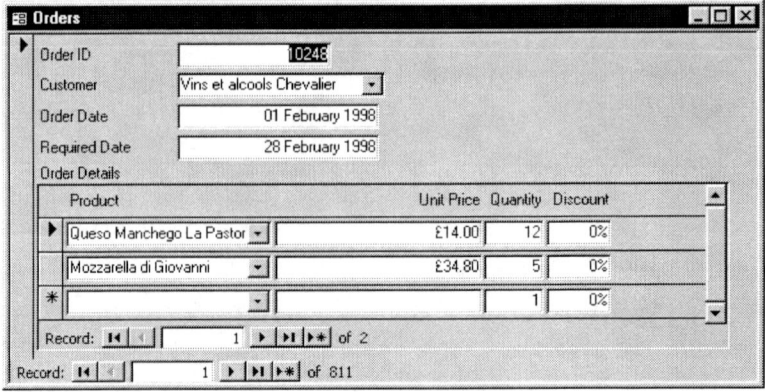

Working with Main and Subform Forms

You can see that the **main form** and the **subform** have their own separate record selector buttons.

When you click the navigation buttons in the main form, the subform refreshes to display only the records related to the linked field in the main form.

Use the navigation buttons in the subform to view additional records or to display related records in linked subforms.

To move between the main/subform using the mouse

TryIT	Action	Result
	• To switch from the main form to the subform, click anywhere in the subform	The cursor moves to the subform.
	• To switch from the subform back to the main form, click a **control** on the main form (not the background)	The cursor moves to the main form.

To move between the main/subform using the keyboard

TryIT	Action	Result
	• Press `Tab` in the last field of the main form	The cursor moves to the first field in the subform.
	• Press `Ctrl`+`Shift`+`Tab` in the last field in the subform	The cursor moves back to the last field in the main form.
	• Press `Ctrl`+`Tab` in the last field of the **subform**	The cursor moves to the next field on the main form or the first field of the next record of the main form.

Lesson 6

To add a record in the main form

TryIT

Action	Result
• Click a **control** in the main form	The cursor moves to the main form.
• On the main form **Navigation Buttons**, click the **New Record** button	You are taken to a new blank main form.
• Enter the data for the record	

To add a record in a subform

TryIT

Action	Result
• Click in the subform	The cursor moves to the subform.
• Click in the last row of the subform datasheet (OR on the subform **Navigation Buttons**, click **New Record**)	The cursor moves to the new record.
• Enter the data for the record	
• Close the form	

Records are automatically saved when you move to another record or create a new record.

Using the SubForm Control

It is possible to add a subform to an existing main form, using the **SubForm/SubReport** control. If you have the **Control Wizards** button selected, Access will provide you with a series of screens that make the addition of a subform a relatively simple operation.

Using the SubForm control allows more control over the design of the subform. You can create and format this subform before adding it to the main form, whereas when you use the wizard, the layout choices are either columnar or tabular.

To add a SubForm control

In this next exercise, we will generate a Customers form using AutoForm and add the Orders form to it as a subform.

TryIT	Action	Result
	• Create a new form based on the **Customers** table using AutoForm	
	• Save the form as **Customers** and open it in design view	The **Customers** form is displayed in **Design** view.
	• Maximise the form design window	
	• Drag the bottom edge of the **Detail** section to make the form about double its existing height	
	• On the **Toolbox** toolbar, click **SubForm/SubReport**	The cursor changes to a cross-hair.
	• In the **Detail** section, click on the form under the existing fields to position the subform	The **SubForm Wizard** starts.

Lesson 6

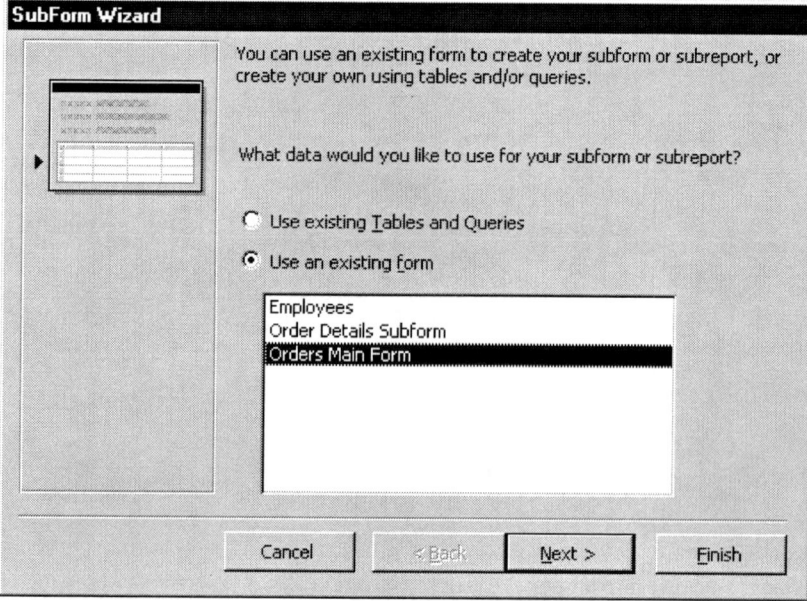

SubForm Wizard

- Click the option button **Use an existing form**
- Select **Orders Main Form**
- Click **Next >**

The **SubForm Wizard** moves to the next step, defining which fields link the main form to the subform.

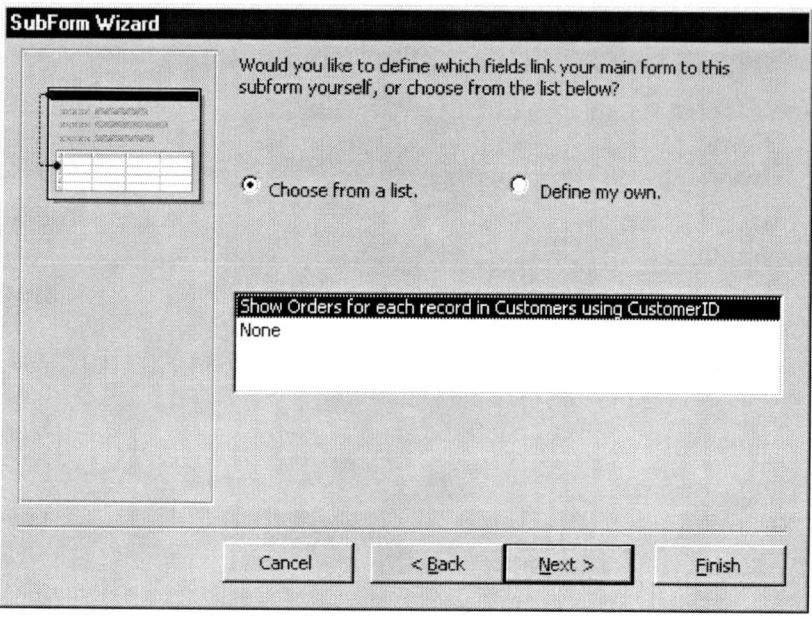

Building and Modifying Forms

- Leave **Show Orders for each record in Customers using CustomerID** selected

- Click **Next >**

- Leave the title as it is

- Click **Finish**

The **SubForm Wizard** moves to the last step, prompting for a title.

The **Orders** form is added to the **Customers** form and displayed below.

- Preview the form in form view
- Save the form then close it
- Close the database

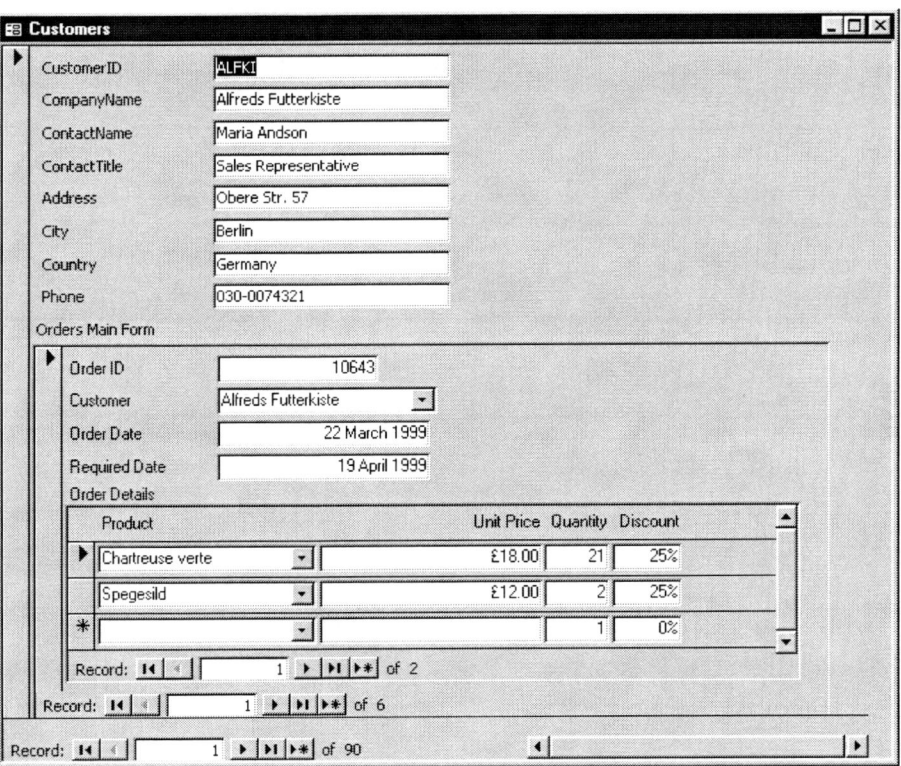

Multiple table form

Notes

Review Questions

(1) What sections make up a form?

(2) What is a control?

(3) What is an unbound control?

(4) How do you add a graphic to a form?

(5) Why would you use a multi-table form?

(6) When would you use a SubForm control?

Answers on the next page.

Lesson 6

Review
Answers

(1) i) Detail
ii) Form header and footer
iii) Page header and footer

(2) An item on a form such as a field name, a field label, a heading, a calculated control

(3) An unbound control is not attached to an underlying table and can be used to create calculations

(4) i) In Design view, select the Image control button on the toolbox
ii) From the Insert Picture dialogue box, select the folder which contains the graphic, then select the graphic and click OK

(5) When you need to see information from more than one table

(6) When you need more control over the design of a subform than the Form Wizard allows

Skills Summary — Review

Congratulations on successfully completing LESSON 6. You can now create and customise user forms.

Review objectives...

- ☐ Modify a form in **Design** view using form **sections** and **controls**
- ☐ View a form's **properties**
- ☐ Add a **graphic** to a form
- ☐ Create a **calculated** control
- ☐ Create **multi-table** forms

Lesson 6

Notes

Going Further

Going Further

Switchboard Forms

When a database becomes quite complex, it is a good idea to provide an alternative means by which forms and reports are launched.

The method of selecting these objects from the Database window allows ordinary users to access other development facilities, which could lead to them damaging the database.

Access provides a utility called the **Switchboard Manager**, which can add a **switchboard** form to an existing database.

The switchboard is a form designed to let the user open a limited range of database objects. You can set the switchboard to startup when the database is opened, preventing users from easily accessing the database window.

 A switchboard does not make the database secure, as users with knowledge of Access will be able to bypass it. Security is discussed in the lesson DATABASE MANAGEMENT starting on page 275.

To create a switchboard

- From the **Tools** menu, select **Database Utilities** then **Switchboard Manager**

If no switchboard has been created previously, a message box is displayed.

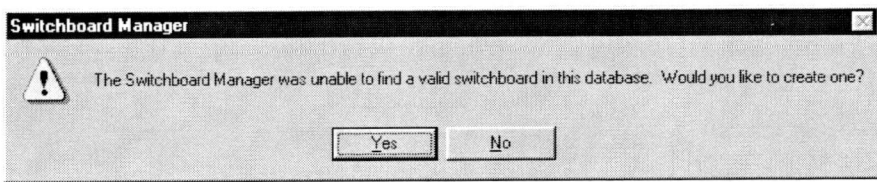

- Click **Yes** if asked to create a switchboard

Lesson 6

The **Switchboard Manager** dialogue box is displayed.

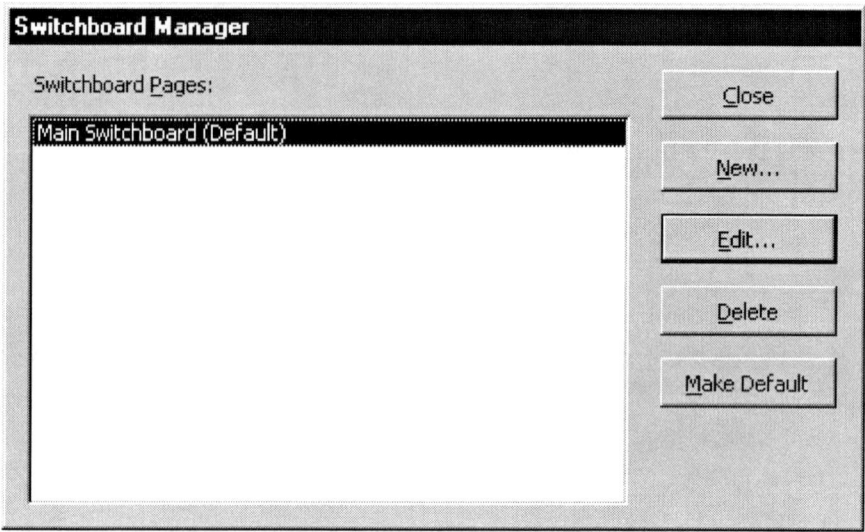

Switchboard Manager dialogue box

- In the **Switchboard Manager** dialogue box, click **Edit...**

The **Edit Switchboard Page** dialogue box is displayed.

- In the **Edit Switchboard Page** dialogue box, click **New...**

The **Edit Switchboard Item** dialogue box is displayed.

Edit Switchboard Page dialogue box

- In the **Text:** box, type the text to display to the user
- In the **Command:** box, select the action to perform (for example, **Open Form...**)
- In the third box, select the object on which to perform the action
- Click **OK**

The **Edit Switchboard Page** dialogue box is displayed again.

Going Further

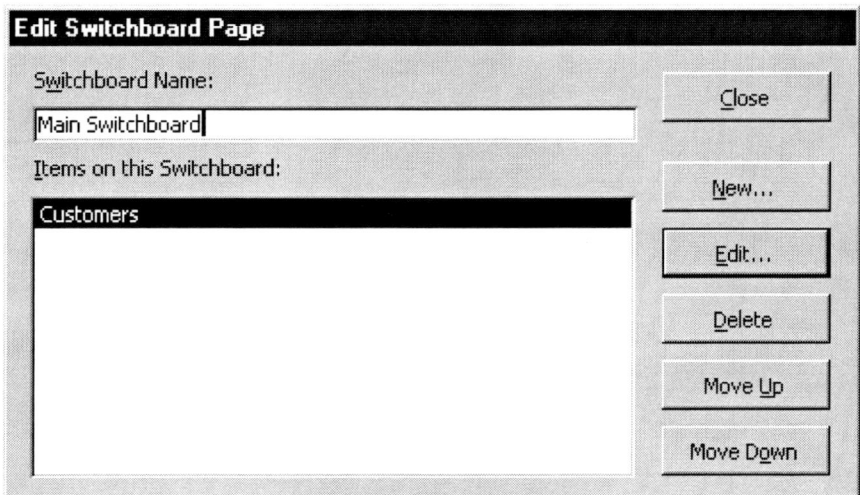

Edit Switchboard Page dialogue box

- Repeat this process until you have added all the switchboard items to the form

You can also use the **Switchboard Manager** to create switchboards that branch to other switchboards if your database is complex.

 If you expect to customise your switchboard form extensively, it is often easier to recreate the switchboard whenever you make extensive modifications to the database.

Lesson 6

To open a switchboard automatically at startup

- From the **Tools** menu, select **Startup...**

The **Startup** dialogue box is displayed.

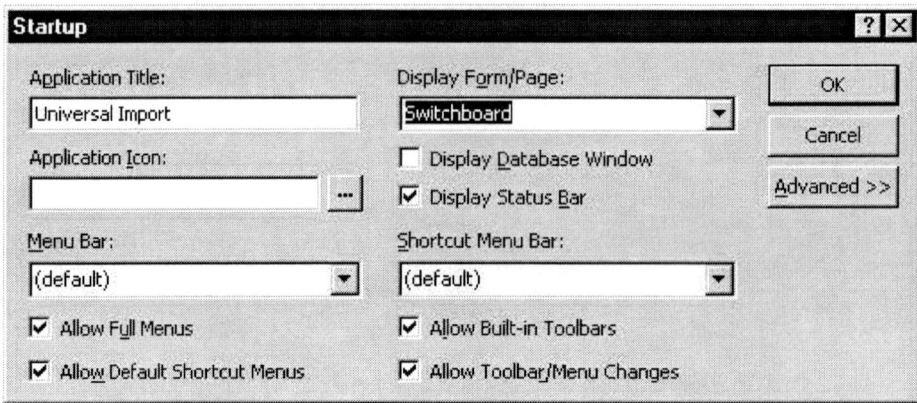

Startup dialogue box

- From the **Display Form/Page:** drop-down arrow, select **Switchboard**
- Uncheck **Display Database Window**
- Click **OK**

The **Switchboard** form will now open automatically when you load the database. The **Database** window will no longer display.

At any stage that you need to display the **Database** window, select **Unhide...** from the **Window** menu or press F11.

Lesson 7 — Reports and Charts

In this lesson you will learn how to use some of the advanced reporting features in Access and how to create charts.

Lesson objectives...

- ☐ Understand report **sections** and **controls**
- ☐ Apply **grouping** and **sorting** in reports
- ☐ Create a **multi-column** report
- ☐ Produce a **summary** report
- ☐ Add **calculated fields** to a report
- ☐ Create a **chart**
- ☐ Create a **subreport**

Jump lesson...

If you can already customise reports you can learn how to create data access pages in PUBLISHING DATA ON THE INTERNET on page 209.

Customising Reports

Reports are an effective way to present data in a printed format. With reports you can group and summarise the data producing detailed listings or brief summaries, you can display running and grand totals, and you can include data from several tables with the use of a query.

The tools used in report design are quite similar to those for form design. It is generally best to use the wizard to create a basic report and then customise it. Reports are also divided into sections and controls work in much the same way as on forms.

Report Sections

The information in a report is divided into sections.

- A **report header** appears at the top of the first page of a report, and displays the title of the report.

- The **page header** displays the heading for each column of data at the top of every page of a report.

- The **detail** section displays the fields of the records from the table or query you have chosen.

- A **page footer** displays at the bottom of every page of the report.

- The **report footer** appears on the last page of the report.

- The **GroupHeader** and **GroupFooter** properties allow you to create a group header or a group footer for a selected field or expression in a report. They can be used to summarise or label data in a specific group of records. (For example, when the **GroupHeader** property is set to **Yes** for the country, each country will begin with the country name followed by the associated records.)

Applying Sorting and Grouping to Reports

You can choose grouping levels while designing a report using the Report Wizard. You can also add and edit grouping in design view.

To create a report with the Report Wizard

In this exercise we will first create a basic Customers report using the **Report Wizard**, and then add grouping levels in design view.

TryIT	Action	Result
	• Open the **UNIVER_7** database	The **Database** window is displayed.
	• Start the **Report Wizard**	The **Report Wizard** is launched.
	• From the **Tables/Queries** drop-down arrow, select **Table:Customers**	
	• Add these fields in the following order to the report: **Country** **City** **CompanyName** **ContactName** **ContactTitle** **Address** **Phone**	The **Country, City, CompanyName, ContactName, ContactTitle, Address, and Phone** fields are moved to the **Selected Fields**.
	• Click **Next >** three times	The wizard moves through the next two steps without making any alterations.
	• Select **Tabular** and **Landscape** for the layout and orientation	
	• Click **Next >**	
	• Select the **Corporate** style	
	• Click **Finish**	The **Customers** report is created.

Lesson 7

To setup grouping levels in design view

*Try*IT	Action	Result
	• Click the **View** button on the toolbar to switch to **Design** view	
	• On the **Standard** toolbar, click **Sorting and Grouping** (**OR** from the **View** menu, select **S**orting and Grouping)	The **Sorting and Grouping** dialogue box is displayed.

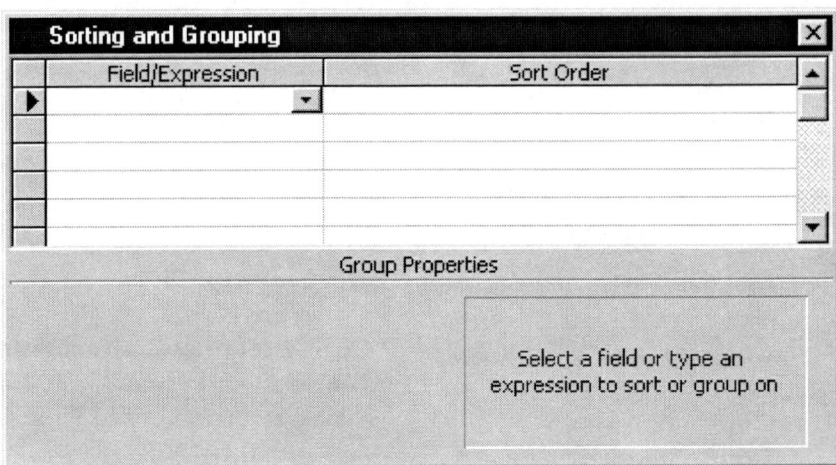

Sorting and Grouping dialogue box

Grouping records creates an additional section on the report form. A group header and a group footer can be displayed and both can be used for calculating and displaying group totals.

Fields used for grouping should be selected **before** fields used only for sorting. Fields used for grouping are identified by the **Grouping** icon in the left margin.

Below is a description of the **Properties** panel in the **Grouping** options:

Property	Action
Group Header	**Yes** or **No** **Yes** displays a separate band on the report as the start of a new section when the field data changes.
Group Footer	**Yes** or No **Yes** displays a separate band on the report as the end of the current section when the field data changes.
Group On	**Each Value** At every change in data a new group section is started. **Prefix characters** Use a prefix for grouping instead of the whole field. A new group is created only at a change of prefix.
Group Interval	Usually one for grouping on Each value. Set the number of characters to check when grouping on prefix characters. For example, to group ABCYY and ABCZZ together, set the group interval to three for the first three characters.
Keep together	**No** Allows heading and detail lines to be split on separate pages. **With first detail** Starts a new page if header and at least one detail line cannot fit on the same page. **Whole group** Starts a new page if group cannot fit on current page.

Lesson 7

TryIT	Action	Result
	• Click the drop-down arrow in the **Field/Expression** column	
	• Select **Country**	
	• In the **Properties** panel set the **Grouping** options	
	• Click the drop-down arrow in **Group Header**	
	• Select **Yes**	
	• Click the drop-down arrow in **Keep Together**	
	• Select **With First Detail**	
	• In the **Sort Order** column, select **Ascending**	The **Country** field is grouped in **Ascending** order.
	• Repeat the steps above to select **City**	The **City** field is grouped in **Ascending** order.

The fields are grouped in the sequence they are selected. You can move grouping levels up and down by clicking-and-dragging on the row selector.

To sort records

As well as grouping by fields, you can sort by fields without grouping them. Sorting changes the sequence in which records will appear on the report in the detail section. Fields used for **Grouping** should be selected **before** fields used only for **Sorting**.

TryIT	Action	Result
	• Click the drop-down arrow in the **Field/Expression** column	
	• Select **CompanyName**	
	• In the **Sort Order** column, select **Ascending**	The **CompanyName** field is sorted in **Ascending** order.

Reports and Charts

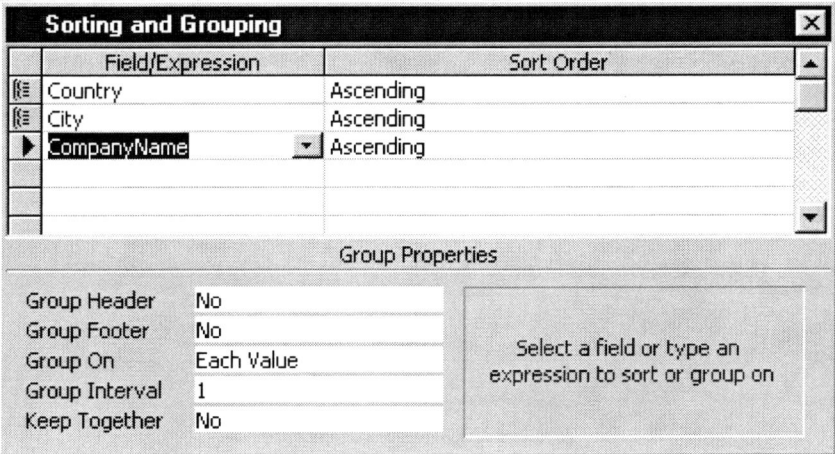

Sorting and Grouping dialogue box

- Close the **Sorting and Grouping** dialogue box
- In **Page Header**, delete the **Country** and **City** *labels*
- Select the **Country** field
- Move the **Country** field into the group header created for it
  The **Country** field is moved to the group header.
- Format the **Country** field to be **16pt** and **bold**
- Resize the text box if necessary
- Resize the **Country Header** to leave a small area of blank space below the field
  Blank space in the section will appear in the report.

- Move the **City** field into the group header created for it
  The **City** field is moved to the group header.
- Make the field **12pt** and **italic**
- Indent the field from the **Country** field by about **1cm** (**½ inch**)
- Resize the text box if necessary
- Resize the **City Header**

Lesson 7

- From the **File** menu, select **Save**
- Click the **Print Preview** button on the toolbar

The report is displayed in **Print Preview**.

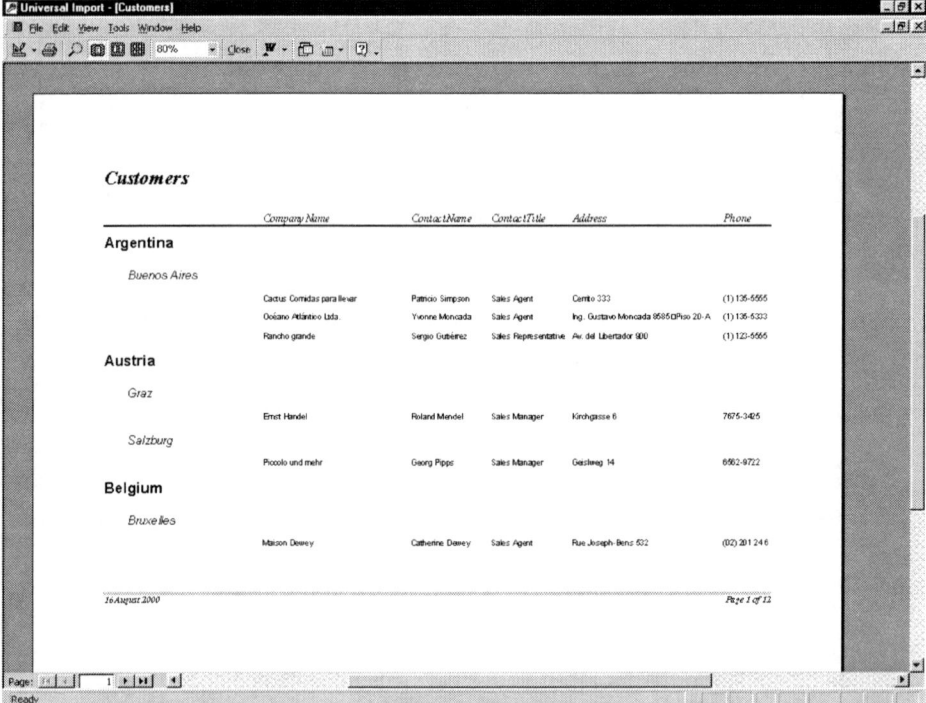

Customers report

Modifying Field and Section Properties

When printing reports, the fields can be set to shrink or grow vertically to fit the data being printed. This is useful where company names and addresses may vary considerably in size. This means the printed fields do not have to be sized for the largest entry in the database, but each record will only take up as much vertical space as required.

The position of page breaks in reports can be controlled by setting the **Keep Together** property in the **Grouping and Sorting** dialogue box, or the **Force New Page** property of the report detail sections. If no Grouping function is in place the page ends when it is full.

The report needs a few more refinements. The CompanyName and Address details are not displaying in full.

> Fields can be set to shrink and grow vertically only. The field width always remains the same, and text word wraps within the field where needed.

TryIT	Action	Result
	• Click the **View** button on the toolbar to switch to **Design** view 	
	• Click the **CompanyName** field in the **Detail** section	
	• Display the Property Sheet if necessary and click the **Format** tab	
	• In the **Can Grow** field, select **Yes**	The **CompanyName** is now able to adjust vertically as and when required.
	• Repeat the steps above for the **Address** field	

Lesson 7

- Click the **Detail** bar
- Check that the **Can Grow** field is set to **Yes**

Properties for the detail section are displayed.

> If the fields are set to **Can Grow** but the report section is not, the data is truncated if it is too long for the section.

- From the **File** menu, select **Save**
- Click the **Print Preview** button on the toolbar

The report is displayed in **Print Preview**.

Creating a Multi-Column Report

If you do not have many fields to show, you may want to use more than one column in your report.

Columns are setup in the **Page Setup** dialog box, where you can also change the page orientation, paper size and margins. These settings are saved with the report.

To create a multi-column report

In this exercise, we will create a multi-column report showing company names only.

TryIT	Action	Result
	• Switch to **Design** view	
	• From the **File** menu, select **Save As...**	The **Save As** dialog box is displayed.
	• Save the report as `Customers with Columns`	A copy of the report is created.
	• Delete the **ContactName**, **ContactTitle**, **Address** and **Phone** fields	

Reports and Charts

- Drag the **CompanyName** field left (to just to the right of the **City** field)

- Delete the controls in the **Page Header** and drag the bar up so that it takes up no space

The revised report should look like the one below.

- From the **File** menu, select **Page Setup...**

- Click the **Columns** tab

The **Page Setup** dialogue box is displayed.

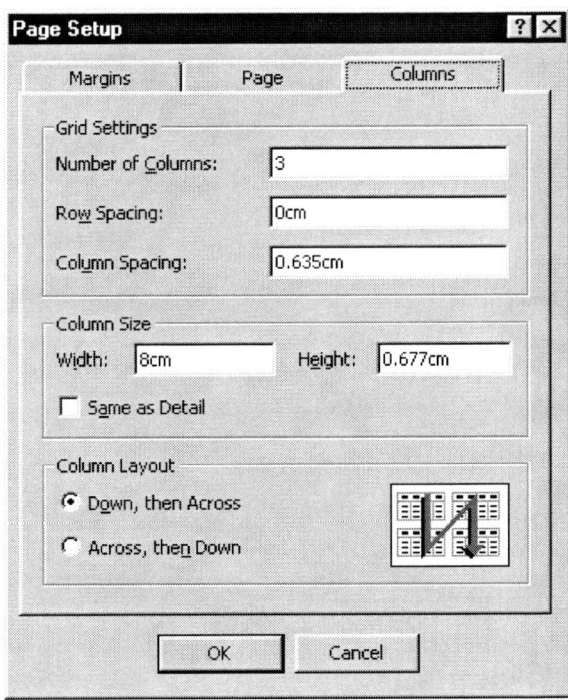

Page Setup - Columns dialogue box

Lesson 7

- In the **Number of Columns** box, type 3
- In the **Width** box, type 8 cm (or 3.15 inches)
- In the **Column Layout** panel, select **Down, then Across**
- Click **OK** then save the report
- Click the **Print Preview** button on the toolbar

    The multi-column report is displayed.

- Close the report

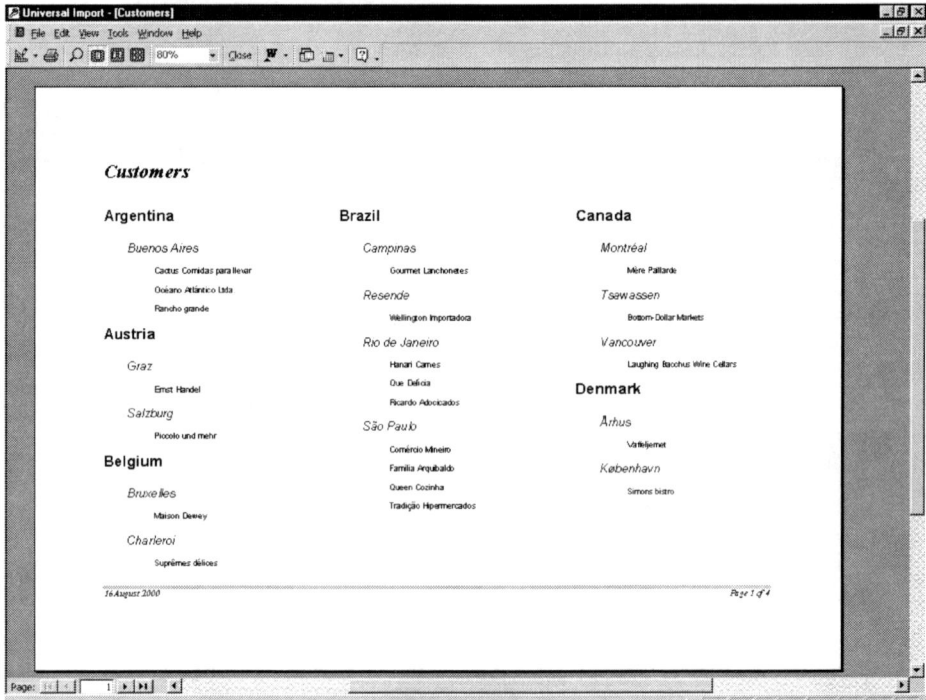

Multi-column report

Adding Calculations to a Report

As with forms, controls on reports can be **bound, unbound** or **calculated**.

Controls are added using the **Toolbox** toolbar.

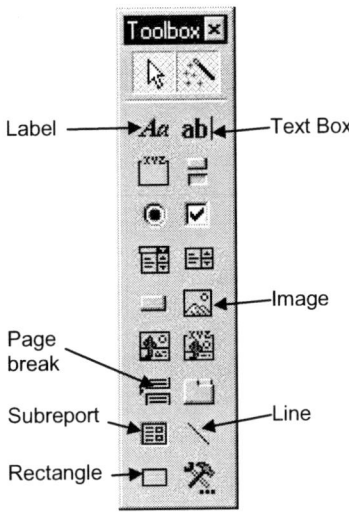

A **bound** control is tied to a field in an underlying table or query. You use bound controls to display values from fields in your database.

An **unbound** control is not attached to a table. As well as having unbound graphics controls, you can use a text box control to perform calculations on a report.

Calculated controls

A **calculated** control uses an expression as its data source. An expression can use data from a field in an underlying table or query of a form or report, or from another control on the form or report.

You can create an expression by typing it in manually or by using the Expression Builder.

To create a calculated control

The **Stock List** report has already been created for this exercise. However, we need to add a few refinements.

TryIT	Action	Result
	• From the **Database** window, select the **Reports** tab • From the **Reports** tab, select the **StockList** report • Click **Design**	The **StockList** report is opened in **Design** view.
	• From the **Toolbox**, select the **Text Box** tool • Click on the **Detail** section of the report, in the space below the **Stock Value** heading • Delete the text box *label* • Display the Property Sheet for the new text box control	A **Text Box** control is created. The **Properties** of the control are displayed.
	• On the **Other** tab, in the **Name** property, type Stock Value • On the **Data** tab, in the **Control Source** property, type `=[UnitPrice]*[UnitsInStock]` • Set the **Format** property to **Currency** • Size and position the text box to fit in with the other controls • Save and preview the report	This calculation takes the Unit Price and multiplies it by the Units in Stock. The figures will display with a currency symbol.

To create a summary calculation

Calculated controls placed in header and footer sections can display summary calculations.

TryIT	Action	Result
	• Create a text box as above for a calculated control in the **Report Footer** section (below the Stock Value column)	A text box is created.
	• In the **Name** property, type `Total Order Value`	This calculation totals the unit price multiplied by the units on order and displays the results in the Report footer on the last page.
	• In the **Control Source** property type `=Sum([UnitPrice]*[UnitsInStock])`	
	• Set the **Format** property to **Currency**	
	• From the **File** menu, select **Save**	The report is saved.
	• Click the **Print Preview** 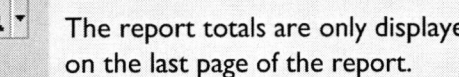 button on the toolbar	The report totals are only displayed on the last page of the report.
	• Close the report	

Creating Charts

A **Chart** form or report displays data in a graphical way to provide comparisons between data values or relative data types. For example, the value of orders placed (a numeric field) by country, or a count of customers (a text field) by country.

Charts can be created in forms and reports. In most cases it is best to use the **Chart Wizard** to create a chart.

Charts are edited using the **Microsoft Graph** application. Graph is used by all the Office products to create and edit charts, so you may well have used it before.

Microsoft Graph must be installed to run the Chart Wizard. Access does not install it by default in a **Typical** setup.

To create a chart using the Chart Wizard

At least one of the fields to be used in the chart must have a Number, Currency or AutoNumber field.

The query **Order Values by Country** to be used for this exercise is already setup.

TryIT	Action	Result
	• From the **Database** window, select the **Reports** object • Click **New** [New]	The **New Report** dialogue box is displayed.
	• From the **Report** list, select **Chart Wizard** • From the **Choose the table or query** list, select **Order Values by Country**	
	• Click **OK**	The **Chart Wizard** starts.

Reports and Charts

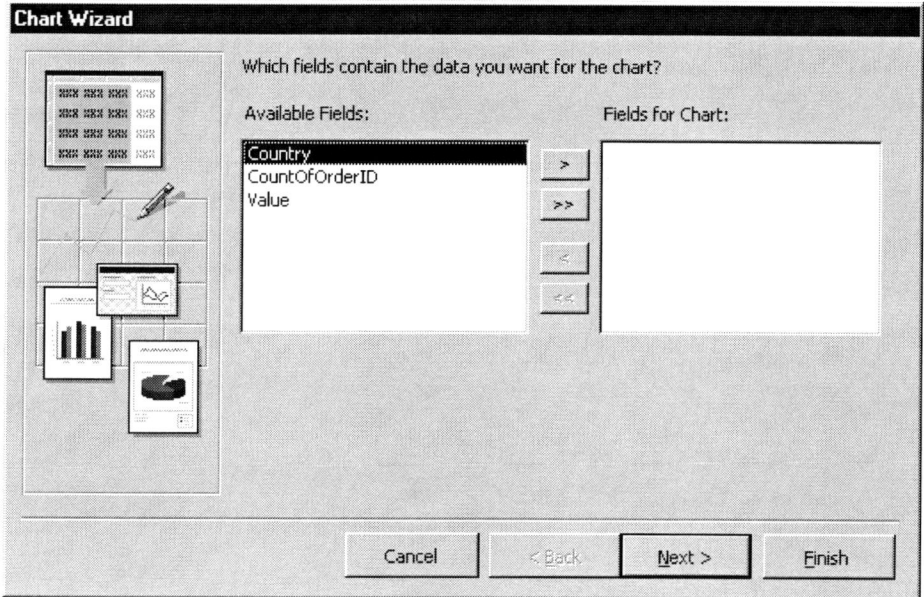
Chart Wizard

- Add the **Country** and **Value** fields to the chart
- Click **Next >**

The **Country** and **Value** fields move to the **Fields for Chart** list.

The next page of the wizard lets you pick a chart type.

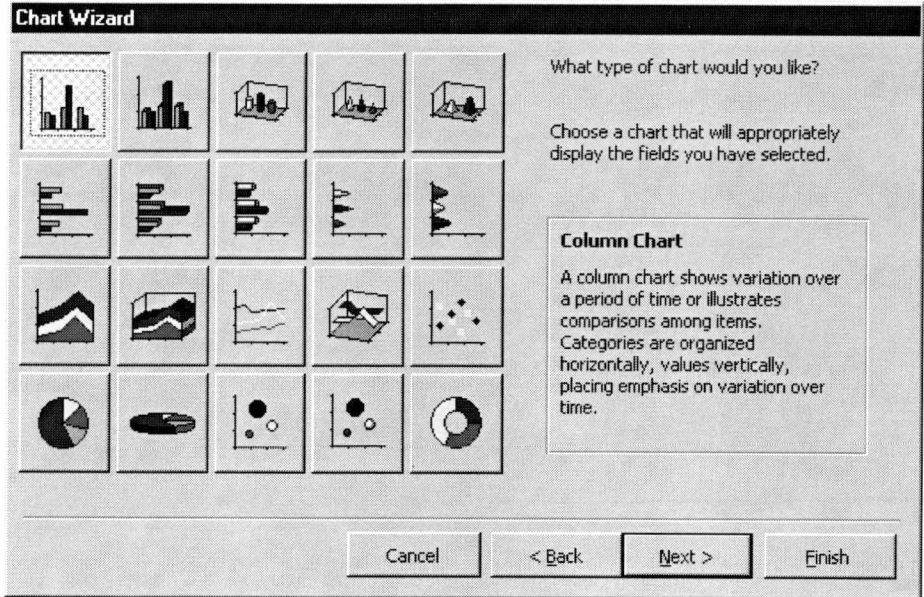
Chart Wizard - Choosing a chart type

Lesson 7

As you click each chart icon, a description is displayed in the panel on the right. Many of the chart types are variations on a theme. The most common types are:

- **Bar** - to compare values
- **Column** or **line** - to compare values (often over a period of time)
- **Area** - to compare values over time and show how the total value breaks down
- **Pie** - to show how a total breaks down

- From the **Chart types** select the **3-D Cone Bar Chart**

- Click **Next >**   The next page of the wizard is displayed.

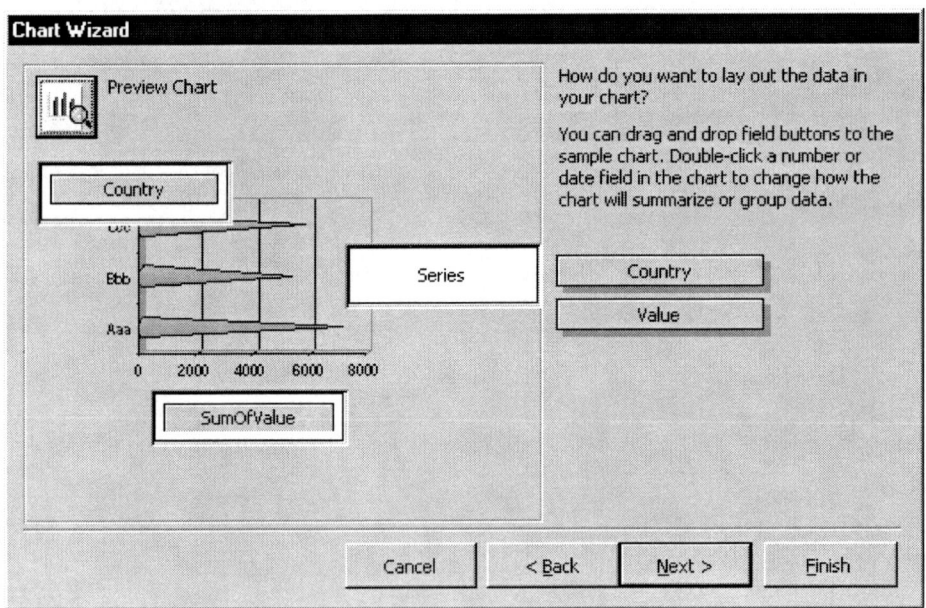

Chart Wizard - setting up the layout

An example chart layout is displayed using the fields you selected. Modify the chart by moving the fields between the **Data**, **Axis** and **Series** boxes. The **Data** box always produces a numeric result from the selected fields (for example, counting text fields, and summing numeric fields).

Access has not set the chart up correctly (the **Country** field should provide the **Series** labels). Also, we will change the data calculation to show an average of values instead of the sum.

- Click-and-drag the Country field from the Axis box (in the top-left) to the empty **Series** box

  The Country field is used to provide data series labels.

- Double-click the **SumOfValue** field

- Select the **Avg** function

  The **Summarize** dialogue box is displayed, allowing you to select a different aggregate function.

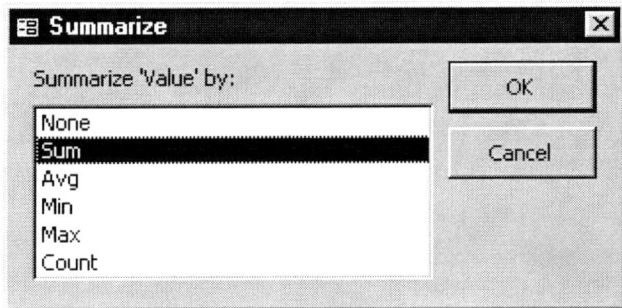

Summarize dialogue box

- Click **OK**
- Click the **Preview Chart** button

  The chart is redrawn to show the average of values.

  In **Print Preview** you can see the sample layout of the chart.

- Click **Close**
- Click **Next >**

  To return to the Chart Wizard.

  The wizard moves to the final dialogue box.

Lesson 7

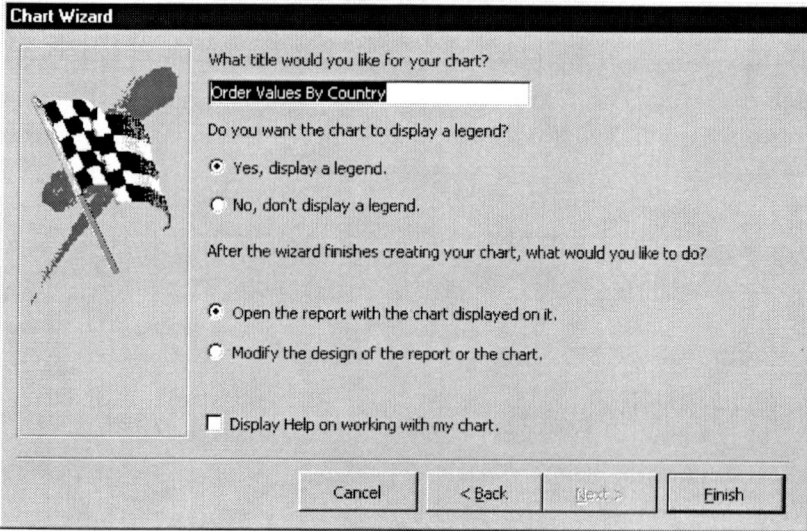

Chart Wizard

- Click the **Yes, display a legend** option button

- Change the title to read **Order Values by Country Chart**

- Click **Finish**

- Save the chart as Order Values by Country Chart

The chart is created and displayed in **Print Preview** mode of the report.

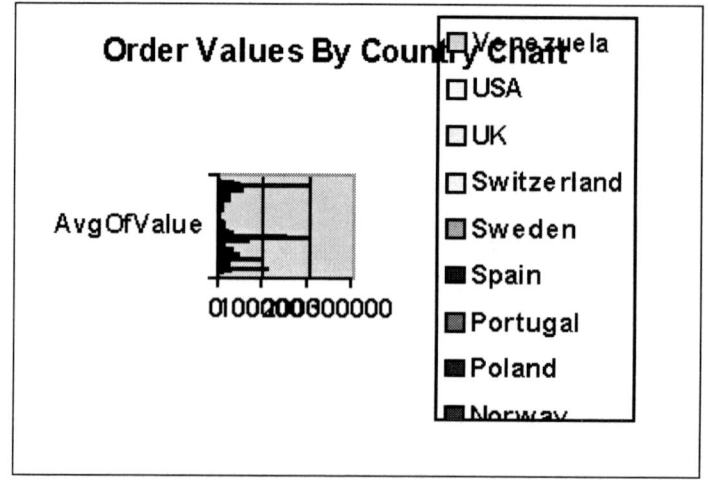

Modifying the Chart

The chart is displayed on the report as an **Unbound Object Frame**. You can change attributes such as the control's size and position or, its border properties in report design view.

Modifications to the chart itself are made in **Microsoft Graph**. You can use Graph to change the colours and text used in the chart, alter the chart type, add elements such as a legend or title, and so on.

The chart's data comes from the underlying table or query and is updated automatically like any other report.

To change the size of the chart control

When you change the size of a chart control in the report, the size of the chart itself is not affected. It is a good idea to resize the control first to give yourself plenty of space to work in while editing the chart with Graph.

TryIT	Action	Result
	• Switch to design view	
	• From the **View** menu, select **Page Header/Footer**	The page header and footer are hidden.
	• Make sure the Property Sheet is displayed then click the chart object once to select it	The **Property Sheet** displays properties for the 'Unbound Object Frame'.
	• On the **Format** tab, change the **Height** and **Width** of the control to 10cm (3.94 inches)	The chart itself does not appear any different.

Now that we have space to work in, we will start MS Graph to edit the chart.

Lesson 7

To use MS Graph to edit the chart

*Try*IT	Action	Result
	• In design view, double-click anywhere on the chart to load **Microsoft Graph**	Microsoft Graph is started.

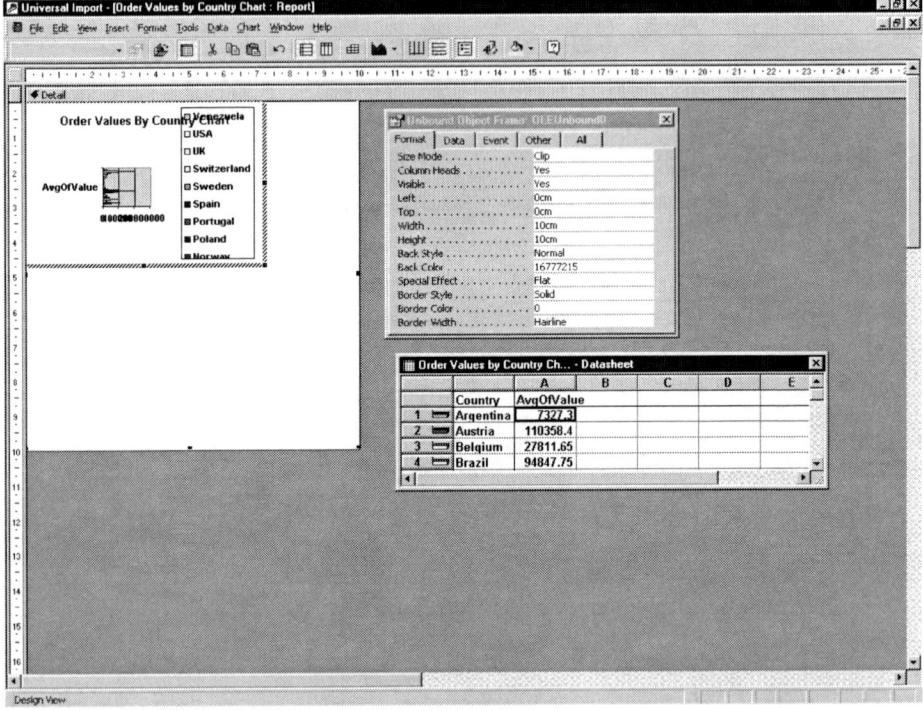

MS Graph

MS Graph is an example of **Object Linking and Embedding (OLE)**. The chart object is edited "in-place", so Graph's toolbars and menus replace those of Access.

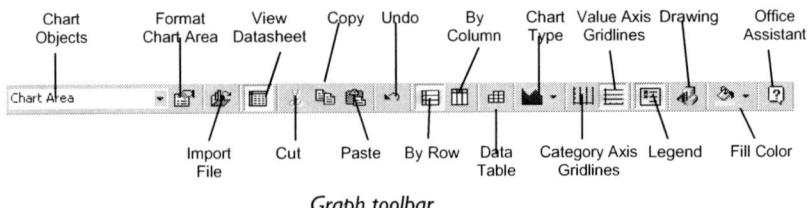

Graph toolbar

Reports and Charts

The following table describes the functions of some of the buttons on the **Graph** toolbar.

Click	To
Chart Area ▼ **Chart Objects**	Select the chart object that you want to change.
Format Chart Area	Set borders, fill colours and fonts for your chart in the **Format Chart Area** dialogue box.
View Datasheet	Display the datasheet window, allowing you to add or edit data.
By Row	Associate chart data series with horizontal rows on the datasheet.
By Column	Associate chart data series with vertical columns on the datasheet.
Data Table	Display a table beneath the chart that contains its data.
Chart Type	Display a palette of 14 chart types. Clicking any one applies that chart type to the active chart.
Category Axis Gridlines	Control whether major vertical gridlines, indicating large groupings of values or categories, are visible on the chart.
Value Axis Gridlines	Control whether major horizontal gridlines, indicating large groupings of values, are visible on the chart.
Legend	Add a legend to the right of the plot area and resize the plot area to accommodate the legend. If the chart already has a legend, clicking the Legend button removes it.
Drawing	Display the **Drawing** toolbar for you to add shapes, arrows and so on to your graph.
Fill Color	Change the fill colour of a selected object.

Before using any of the buttons make sure that you have selected the appropriate chart element to make changes to.

Lesson 7

- Click-and-drag on the bottom corner of the *hashed* border to make the chart fill the whole area of the control (the *solid* border)

    Resize the chart the way you want to see it.

- Double-click the **Legend**

    The **Format Legend** dialogue box is displayed.

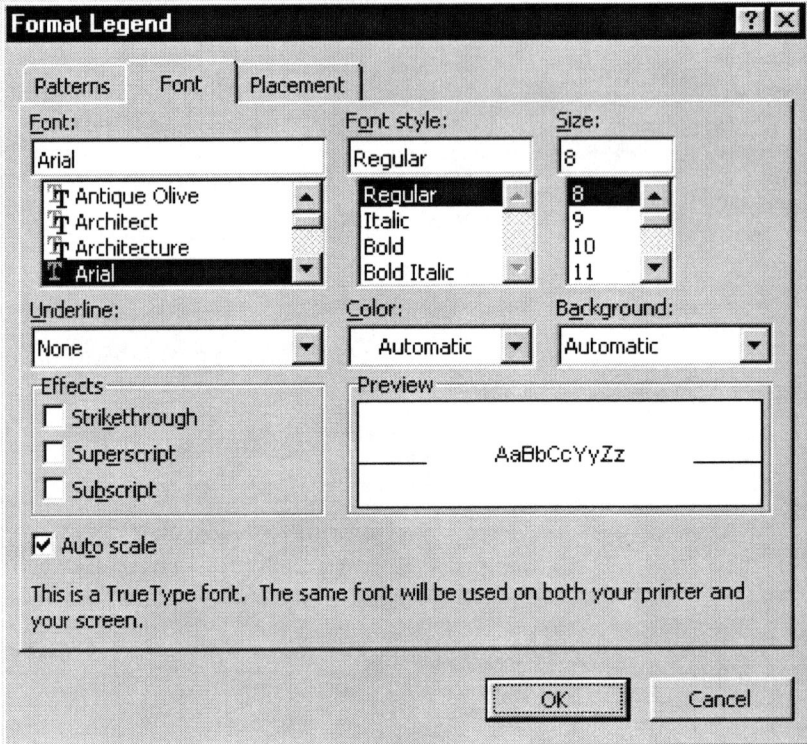

Format Legend dialogue box

- Change the font attributes to Arial, Regular, 8pt

- Click the **Placement** tab

- Select the **Bottom** option and click **OK**

    The legend is moved below the chart.

- From the **Chart** menu, select **Chart Options...**

    The **Chart Options** dialogue box is displayed.

- Click the **Axes** tab

Reports and Charts

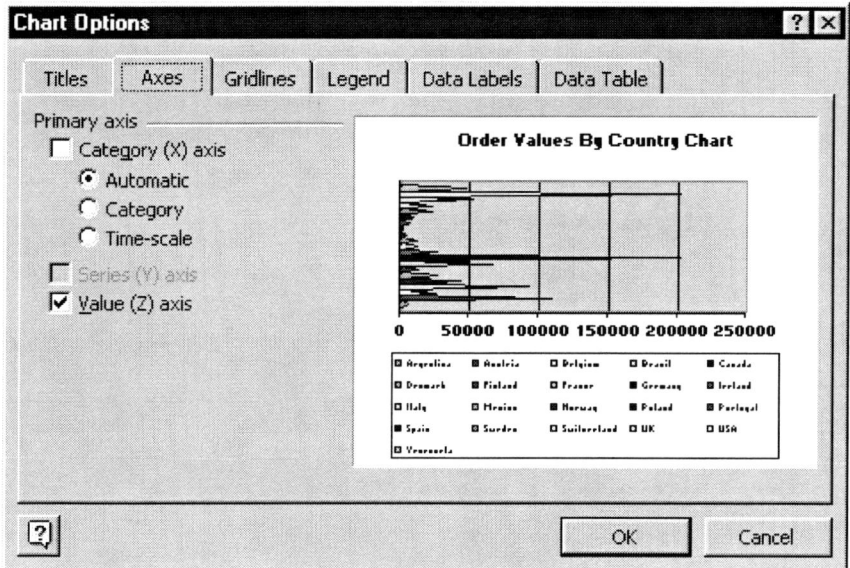
Chart Options dialogue box

- Uncheck the **Category (X) axis** box   This suppresses the display of the axis label.
- Click **OK**
- On the **Chart** toolbar, click the drop-down arrow on the **Chart Objects** list box   The plot area part of the chart is selected.
- Select **Plot Area**
- Click-and-drag the chart area border to make it fill the width of the chart control
- Click in the **Title** box and edit the title to read Average Order Values By Country

- Continue to format different elements of the chart to improve it (for example, adjust font sizes and patterns)
- When you have finished, click away from the chart   Access' menus and toolbars are re-displayed.
- Save and close the report

Lesson 7

Using the SubReport Control

It is possible to add a subreport to an existing report, using the **SubForm/SubReport** toolbox control. If you have the Control Wizards button selected, Access will provide you with a series of screens that make the addition of a subreport a relatively simple operation.

To create a report with subreports

In this exercise, we will create a new report that combines the chart report we just created with another Order Value report.

*Try*IT	Action	Result
	• Create a new report in design view	A report is opened in **Design** view.
	• On the **Toolbox** toolbar, select **Text Label** tool	
	• Create a label in the **Page Header** `Order Values by Country`	The heading for the report is created.
	• Make the label **bold** and change the font size to **12**	
	• Resize the label and section as necessary to fit the text	
	• Ensure that the **Toolbox** toolbar is displayed, with the **Control Wizards** tool selected	
	• On the **Toolbox** toolbar, click **SubForm/SubReport**	The cursor changes to a cross-hair.
	• Click the form at the top left of the **Detail** section	The **SubReport Wizard** starts.

Reports and Charts

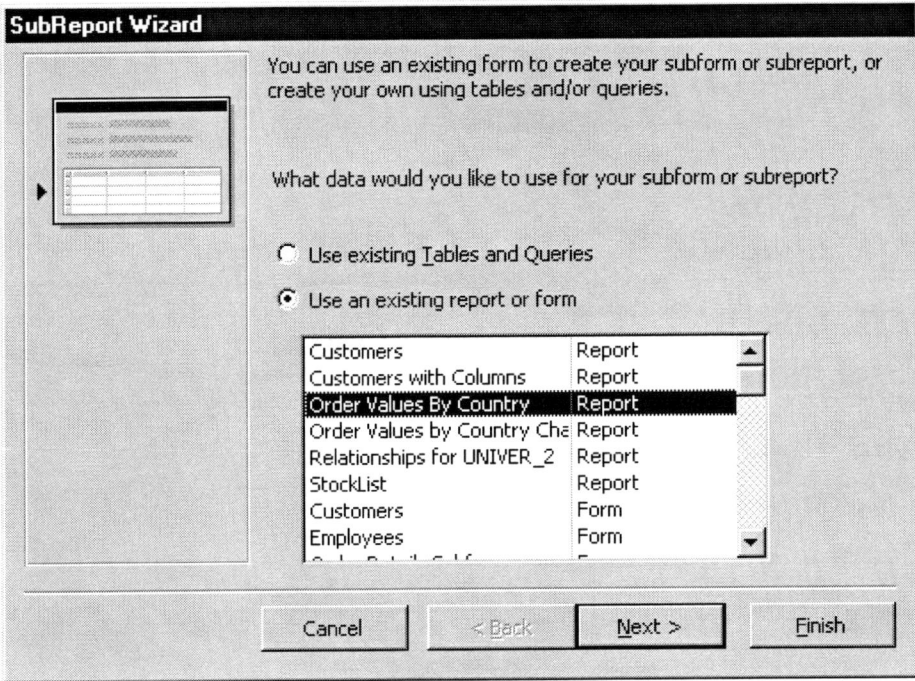

SubReport Wizard

- Select the **Order Values by Country** report

- Click **Finish**
  The subreport is added to the main report.

- Delete the label created with the subreport

The next step is to add the chart as another subreport.

- On the **Toolbox** toolbar, click **SubForm/SubReport**
  The cursor changes to a cross-hair.

- Click below the **Order Values by Country** report
  The **SubReport Wizard** starts.

- Use the SubReport Wizard to add the **Order Values by Country Chart** to the report
  The chart is added to the report.

- Delete the label

Lesson 7

- Save the report as `Order Values` and preview it

- Change the page margins and arrange the subreport controls in design view to get the report on one page

The report may not fit on one page.

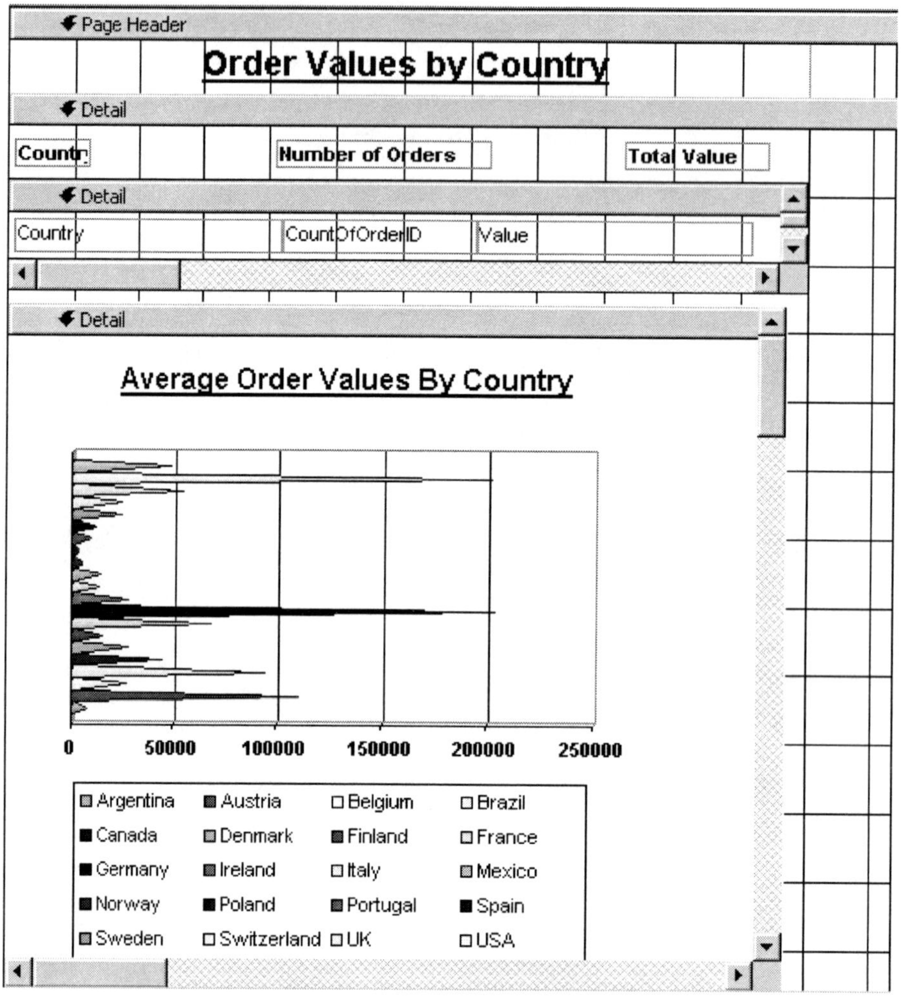

- Save and close the report when you have finished

- Close the database

Review Questions

(1) Is it easier to use the Report Wizard than to try to design your own report from scratch?

(2) How do you modify a report so that a group of records all stay on one page?

(3) Describe the sections in a report.

(4) How do you create a multi-column report?

(5) What is the difference between a bound control and unbound control?

(6) What changes to a chart can be made using Microsoft Graph?

(7) If data changes are required in a chart where do you make the modifications?

(8) What does the SubReport control do?

Answers on the next page.

Review Answers

(1) Yes, it is easier to use the Report Wizard initially to create a report. Once the report is created, you can then make modifications in Design view

(2) Set the Keep Together group property in the Sorting and Grouping dialogue box to Whole Group

(3) i) A report header appears at the top of the first page of a report, and displays the title of the report
ii) The page header displays the heading for each column of data at the top of every page of a report
iii) The detail section displays the fields of the records from the table or query you have chosen
iv) A page footer displays at the bottom of every page of the report
v) The report footer appears on the last page of the report

(4) i) From the File menu, select Page Setup then click the Columns tab
ii) Set the Number of Columns you want and the width

(5) i) A bound control is tied to a field in an underlying table
ii) An unbound control is not attached to an underlying table and can perform calculations

(6) Microsoft Graph is used to edit the chart's appearance (chart type, formatting, legend, title and so on)

(7) Data changes require modifying the underlying table or query

(8) The SubReport control adds another report to the current report (for example, displaying a chart report as part of another report)

Skills Summary — Review

Congratulations on successfully completing LESSON 7. You now know how to customise reports.

Review objectives...

- ☐ Understand report **sections** and **controls**
- ☐ Apply **grouping** and **sorting** in reports
- ☐ Create a **multi-column** report
- ☐ Produce a **summary** report
- ☐ Add **calculated fields** to a report
- ☐ Create a **chart**
- ☐ Create a **subreport**

Lesson 7

Notes

Lesson 8
Publishing Data on the Internet

This lesson shows you how to use hyperlinks and publish to the web.

Lesson objectives...

☐ Create a **hyperlink**

☐ Create an **HTML** file from an Access datasheet

☐ Use an HTML **template**

☐ Create a **data access page**

☐ Create a **grouped** data access page

Jump lesson...

If you can use these web features, learn how to automate database operations using MACROS on page 237.

Putting a Database on the Web

One of the most important changes in computing is the growth of the **internet**, and specifically, the **world wide web**. Most customers expect a company to have a website and to be able to find out about products online.

The web is a collection of HTML documents available on the internet connected by **hyperlinks**, which open the linked document when clicked. Many companies also use an internal web page system (called an **intranet**) to distribute information to their employees.

Access provides the following technology for web-based applications.

- Hyperlinks
- HTML for intra/internet publishing
- Data Access Pages

Hyperlinks

Hyperlinks are shortcuts that you can use in Access to jump to objects (tables, queries and so on) in the current database, another database, or to documents created with Microsoft Word, Microsoft Excel, and Microsoft PowerPoint, and to documents on the global internet or a local intranet.

You can store hyperlinks in fields, tables, forms or reports. You can also create hyperlinks as a label or picture on a form or report, or create a command button on a form that you can click to follow a hyperlink path.

HTML

Datasheets from tables or queries can be published as HTML for inclusion on a web page, however data is not updated automatically.

Data Access Pages

A Data Access Page is a similar to a form or report on a web page. The page is linked to the database and consequently it displays up-to-date information.

Using Hyperlinks in Forms

Hyperlinks can be used on forms, reports and data access pages to link together different parts of a database. You can also use hyperlinks to link to related files or web pages and to provide a link to an email address.

The next exercise looks at creating a hyperlink to an email address from the Orders form to a Customers helpline.

To create a hyperlink

TryIT 	Action	Result
	• Open the database **UNIVER_8**	
	• From the **Database** window, select the **Forms** object	
	• Select **Orders Main Form**	
	• Click **Design**	The form opens in **Design** view.
	• From the **Insert** menu, select **Hyperlink** (**OR** on the toolbar, click **Insert Hyperlink**)	The **Insert Hyperlink** dialogue box is displayed.

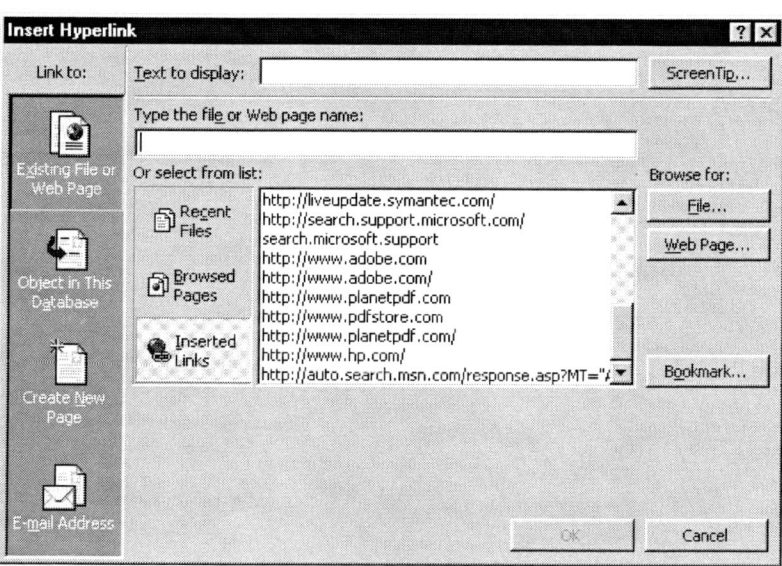

Insert Hyperlink dialogue box

The **Insert Hyperlink** dialogue box is used to create hyperlinks both within or external to your database. The objects on the **Link to:** bar are set out below:

- The **E̲xisting File or Web page** lets you create hyperlinks to other documents or to the Web. You can type in the address or select from the list below.

- The **Objects in This D̲atabase** lets you specify the location within the current database, such as the Products form.

- The **Create N̲ew Page** allows you to link to a document that you have not yet created.

- The **E-m̲ail Address** creates a link that lets users create an email with the correct address in the **To** line.

• On the **Link to:** bar, click **E-m̲ail Address**	As you begin typing, **mailto:** is inserted in front of the address in the **E-mail Address** box, and the same text appears in the **Text To Display** box at the top.
• In the **E-mail Address** box, type `helpline@UniversalImport.com`	
• In the **S̲ubject:** box, type `Orders Help Request`	
• In the **T̲ext to display:** box, select the existing text and type `Email Helpline`	The text displayed is easier to understand.
• Click **OK**	

The **E-mail Helpline** hyperlink appears in the top-left corner of the Orders Main form.

Publishing Data on the Internet

Action	Result
• Point to the hyperlink	The mouse pointer changes to a hand.
• Drag the hyperlink to the right	
• Position the hyperlink in the centre of the available grey area	The hyperlink is now in a more sensible position.
• From the **File** menu, select **Save**	The form is now saved with the hyperlink.
• Click the **View** button on the toolbar to switch to **Form** view	

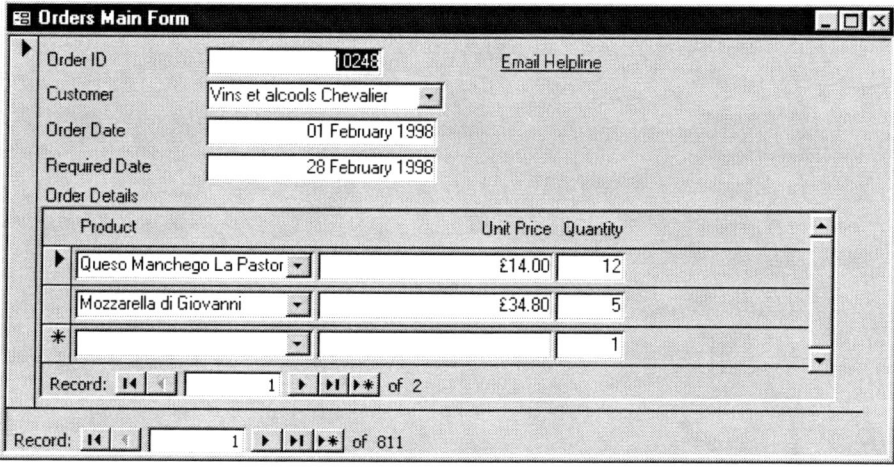

Form with hyperlink

To test the hyperlink

TryIT

Action	Result
• Click the **Email Helpline** hyperlink to test it	**Microsoft Outlook** (or the email application you use) opens, displaying a new message with the subject and address that you have just created.
• Click the **Close** button ⊠ to close **Outlook**	**Outlook** closes.
• Click the **Close** button ⊠ to close the form window	The **Orders Main Form** closes.

Exporting Datasheet Views to HTML

Information that you display in datasheet views, either from select queries or directly from database tables, can be exported for display on an internet or intranet website. Forms and reports can also be exported to HTML format (Hypertext Markup Language) for display on the world wide web.

There are two ways to publish datasheets on a web page.

- **Static** web pages are reports, forms or tables exported to HTML format. If the data changes, the displayed page will not reflect the changes.

- **Active Server Pages** (ASP) are dynamic pages. The web page changes whenever the source data changes. Unfortunately, creating Access Server Pages is beyond the scope of this book.

The topics in this lesson describe how to create material for the web, but not how to publish it. You will need to get the advice of your web server administrator about where to place your HTML files so that they can be accessed on the internet or intranet.

To export a datasheet to HTML

In this exercise, we will create an HTML page from the Products table. Note that you can use the same procedure to create HTML pages from tables, queries forms and reports.

If the table you choose does not exactly meet your requirements, you can apply filters and sorts. However you cannot apply filters to an existing query to limit the records further - it is necessary to change the query definition.

TryIT	Action	Result
	• From **Database** window, select the **Tables** object • Select the **Products** table	

Publishing Data on the Internet

- From the **File** menu, select **Export...**
- From the **Save as type** drop-down list, select **HTML Documents (*.html;*.htm)**

The **Export** dialogue box is displayed.

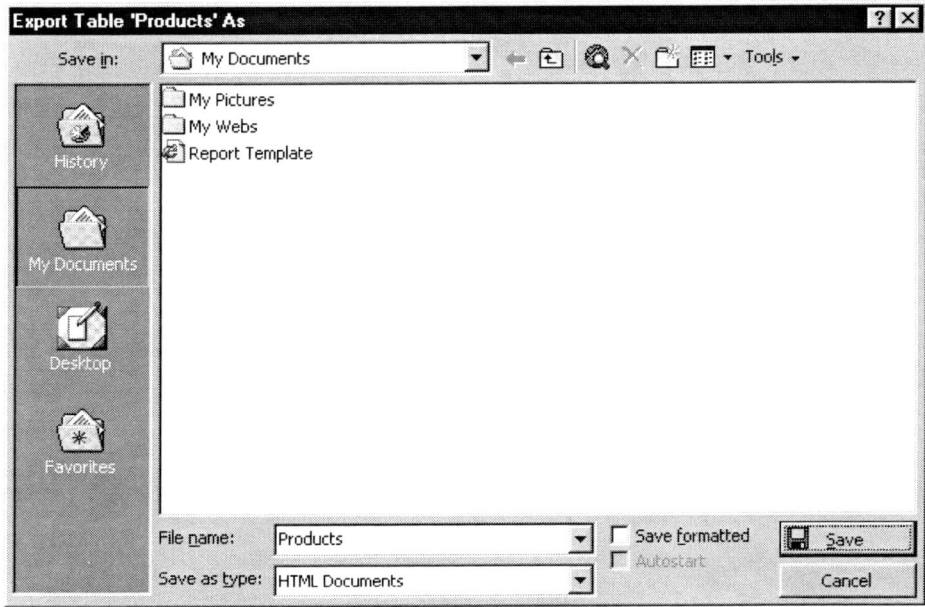

Export dialogue box

- Leave **Products** as the file name
- Click **Save**
- Open the file in your web browser

The document is saved to HTML format.

The data has been exported into a simple table. It is not particularly good to look at, but serves its basic purpose.

To present data more effectively, rather than exporting the table to its own HTML document, you can include it as part of another web page.

Every time your source data changes, it will be necessary to export the data again.

LearnIT MS Access 2000 Expert   Page 215

HTML Templates

An HTML template is basically a web page containing the extra data you want to appear with the table. You can include extra text and graphics or a navigation bar and so on.

You can use any text editor or a web page editor, such as Microsoft FrontPage, to create the template.

Note that this course does not aim to teach you how to create HTML pages, but web pages are quite easy to create and edit. Briefly, an HTML page is made up of **tags**, which instruct the web browser what to display. To create an HTML template for Access, you need to include the **tag**:

```
<!--AccessTemplate_Body-->
```

...where you want the Access table to appear. There are a number of other tags you can use to display a title and add basic navigation. To find out more about these tags, lookup "About HTML Template Files" in the online help.

Here is an example of a simple HTML page that can be used as a template:

```
<HTML>
  <HEAD>
    <TITLE><!--AccessTemplate_Title--></TITLE>
  </HEAD>
  <BODY BACKGROUND="SKY.JPG">
    <H1 ALIGN="CENTER">HTML Sample Report</H1>
    <P ALIGN="CENTER"><!--AccessTemplate_Body--></P>
  </BODY>
</HTML>
```

Your Access template tag should appear between the <Body> and </Body> tags. The <H1> tag indicates a heading. The <P> tag indicates a paragraph. Tags should be in pairs (for example, each <P> tag should have a </P> tag following it.

To add a template to an HTML document

*Try*IT

Action	Result
• Repeat the steps above to create an HTML document	
• In the **Export As** dialogue box, tick the **Save formatted** checkbox	Checking this box prompts Access to use an HTML template.
• Tick the **Autostart** check box	...to display the results in your web browser automatically.
• Click **Save**	Access warns you that an existing file will be replaced
• Click **Yes** to replace the file	The **HTML template** dialogue box is displayed.

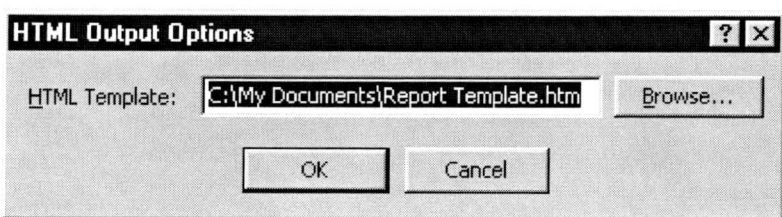

HTML Output Options dialogue box

Access should automatically select the sample template provided (because it is the only HTML file in My Documents).

• If necessary, browse to find **Report Template.htm**	
• Click **OK**	Access outputs your data to an HTML file and automatically launches it in your web browser.

Lesson 8

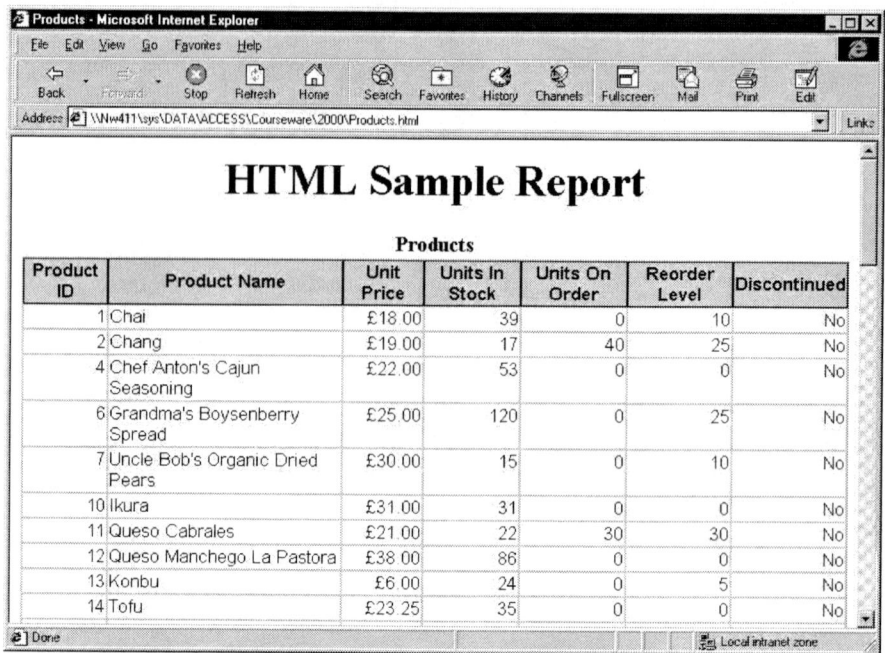

Web page produced with an HTML template

HTML output is suitable for providing a "snapshot" of data. The pages are easy to create and can be viewed in most popular web browsers.

However, if you want to let people **access** or **analyse** data over the web, you should use a **Data Access Page**.

Data Access Pages

Data Access Pages are web pages bound directly to the data in the database. They can be viewed in the web browser **Microsoft Internet Explorer 5**.

Users must also have a licence to use Microsoft Office 2000 in order to use data access pages.

Using **Data Access Pages**, you can:

- Create HTML forms in Access and publish them to the internet (or on an intranet). Any data entered or edited using these pages goes directly into the database.

- Create an interactive data report for users to view and analyse data through IE5. You can create pages with sorting and grouping levels (similar to reports) and add calculated fields. You can also include charts and PivotTable lists. Users can filter or sort data as well.

Unlike other database objects, a data access page is not stored in the database .MDB file. It is a separate HTML page, stored on the HTTP web server. The Access .MDB file does contain a **shortcut** to the page.

As with forms and reports, the easiest way to create a basic page is to use the **Page Wizard**.

To create a data access page using the wizard

TryIT	Action	Result
	• From the **Database** window, select the **Pages** object [Pages]	
	• Select **Create data access page by using wizard**	
	• Click **Open** [Open]	The **Page Wizard** is launched.

Lesson 8

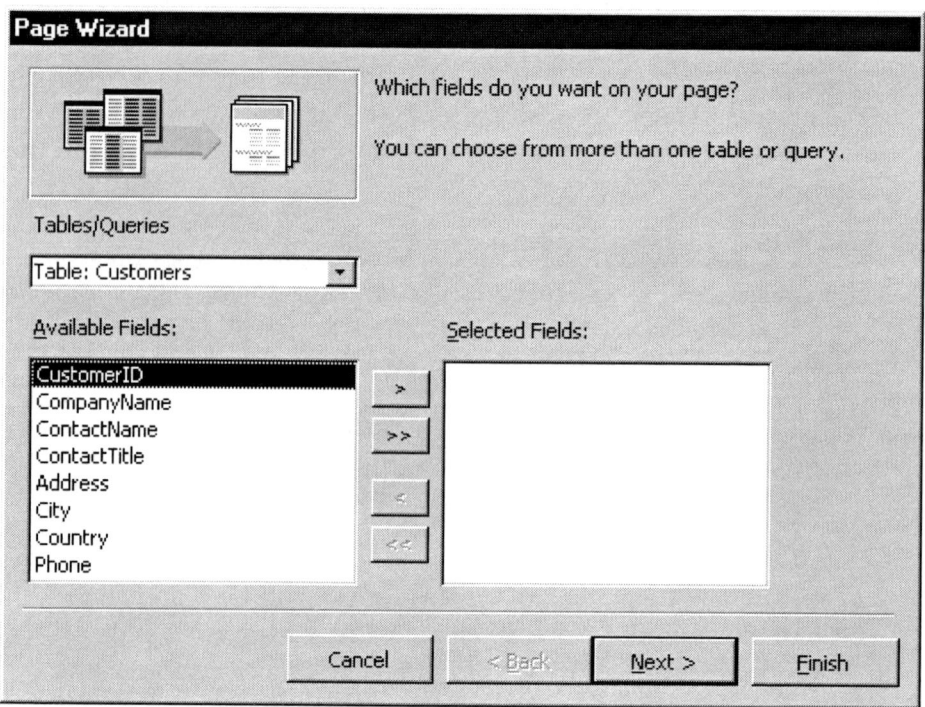

Page Wizard

- From the **Tables/Queries** drop-down arrow, select **Table:Customers**

- From the **Available Fields:**, move all the fields to the **Selected Fields**

- Click **Next >**

The wizard moves to the next step: **grouping levels**.

If you select any grouping levels, the pages will not be editable through the web interface.

If you are creating a page for the purpose of adding and editing records, do not select any grouping levels.

Publishing Data on the Internet

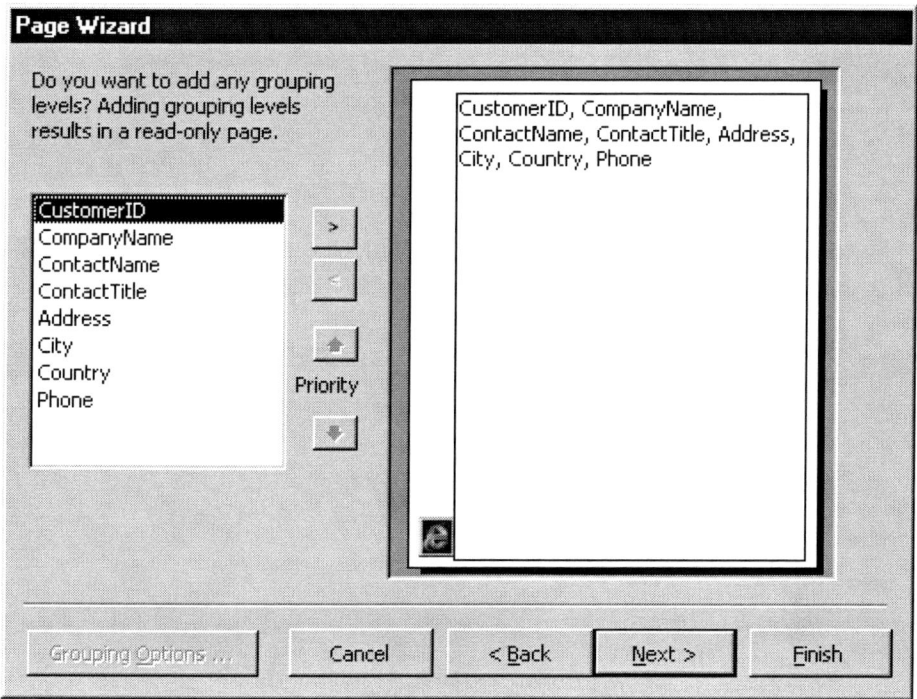

Page Wizard

For this example, we will create a data entry page.

• Click **Next >**	The wizard moves to the next step: choosing the **sort order** for the records.

You can provide up to four levels of sorting for the detail records of the page. Grouping levels imply their own level of sort order, since Access will need to sort the records by the grouping fields.

• Click the drop-down arrow on the first sort box	
• Select **Country**	A sort order is selected.
• Leave the order button set to **Descending**	
• Click **Next >**	The wizard moves to the last stage: choosing a title.

Lesson 8

As well as entering a title, you can provide additional web themes to your pages from those that you installed with Office 2000.

- Keep the default title **Customers**
- Keep **Modify the page's design** selected
- Tick the **Do you want to apply a theme to your page?** check box
- Click **Finish**

The wizard opens the page and also opens the **Theme** dialogue box.

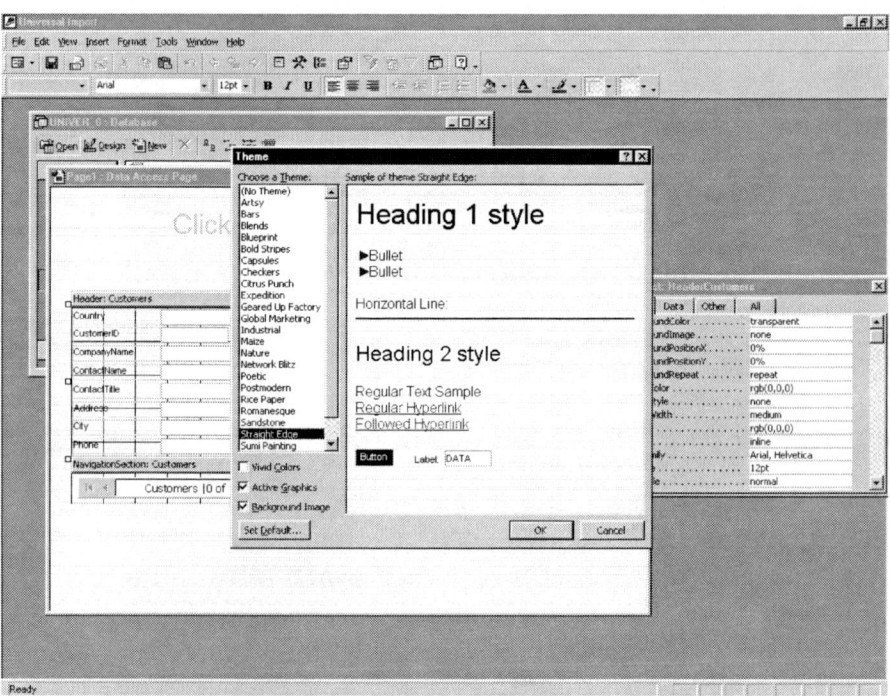

Web Theme selection dialogue box

A theme is like a template design that you can apply to your web page.

Some themes need to be installed on demand. You will need the Office 2000 installation files/CD in order to use these themes.

Publishing Data on the Internet

You can also decide whether to include the following theme elements on your data access page:

- **Vivid Colors** - apply brighter colours
- **Active Graphics** - animate graphics (in a browser only)
- **Background Image** - apply a background to the data access page

• Select the **Romanesque** theme	
• Deselect the **Vivid Colors** and **Active Graphics** options	The data access page is displayed in design view with the new theme applied.
• Click **OK**	

• From the **File** menu, select **Save**	
• In the **File name** box, type `Customers`	
• Click **Save**	Access creates an HTML page

The Data Access Page files are created in the default directory, with a subdirectory **<name>_files**, which contains any images and style sheets required and a small XML file that acts as an index for the rest of the files.

When you move your data access page to your web server, you must keep the HTML file together with the folder of supporting files.

• Click in the **Title** section which says **Click here and type title text** and type `Customer Details`	A title is added to the page.
• Click the **View** button on the toolbar to switch to **Form** view	The data access page is displayed in form view.

Lesson 8

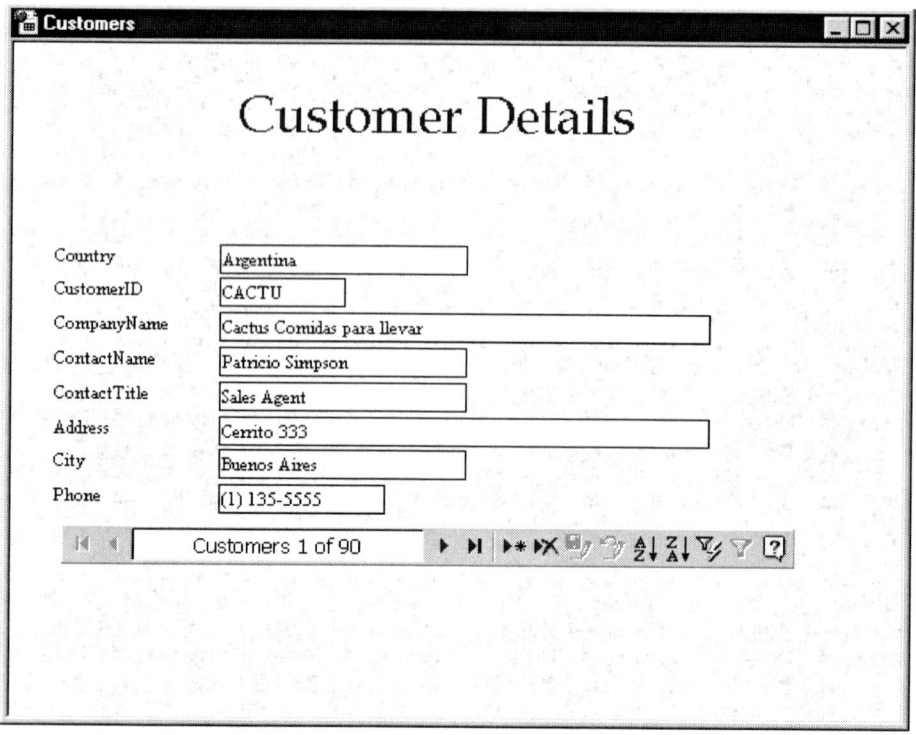

Users can navigate between records using the toolbar on the page. They can also sort and filter data.

As with normal Access forms, data is saved when you move to another record. However, you can force a record to save by clicking ![save]. You can undo changes by clicking ![undo].

- Practise working with the data access page if you wish
- Save and close the page

Do not publish a data access page on the internet without understanding the implications for the security of the database (and potentially your company's computer network).

The basics of Access security are discussed from page 276 on, but this does not cover internet security. Seek further training or advice before publishing a link to a database containing confidential or sensitive information.

Creating a Grouped Data Access Page

A data access page where grouping has been applied can only be used to analyse records, not to add or edit them.

To create a grouped data access page

TryIT	Action	Result
	• Start the **Page Wizard** • From the **Customers** table, add the **CompanyName** field • From the **Products** table, add the **ProductName** field • Click **Next >**	The grouping page of the **Page Wizard** is displayed.

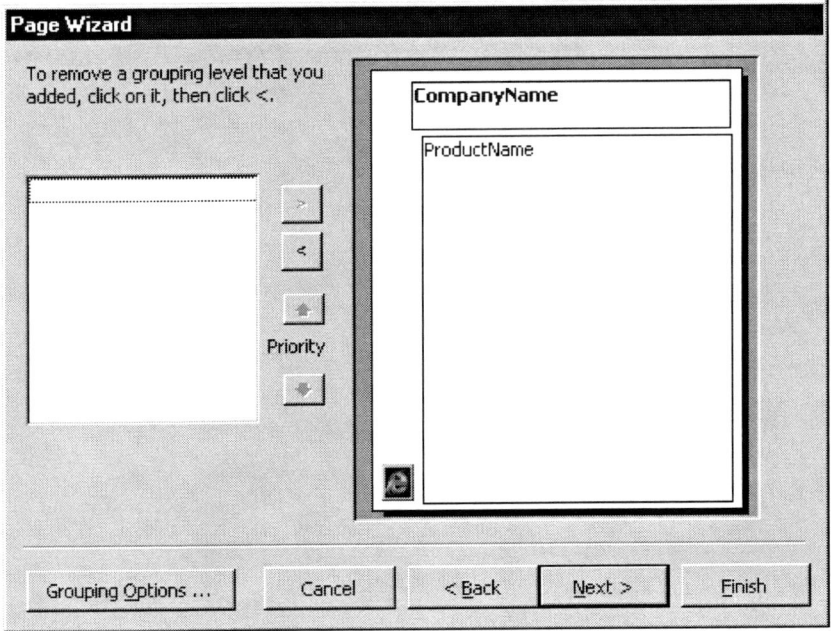

Page Wizard - Grouping options

	• Select **CompanyName** as the next grouping level • Click **Next >**	The group is previewed in the right-hand panel. The next screen prompts you for a sort order for detail records.

Lesson 8

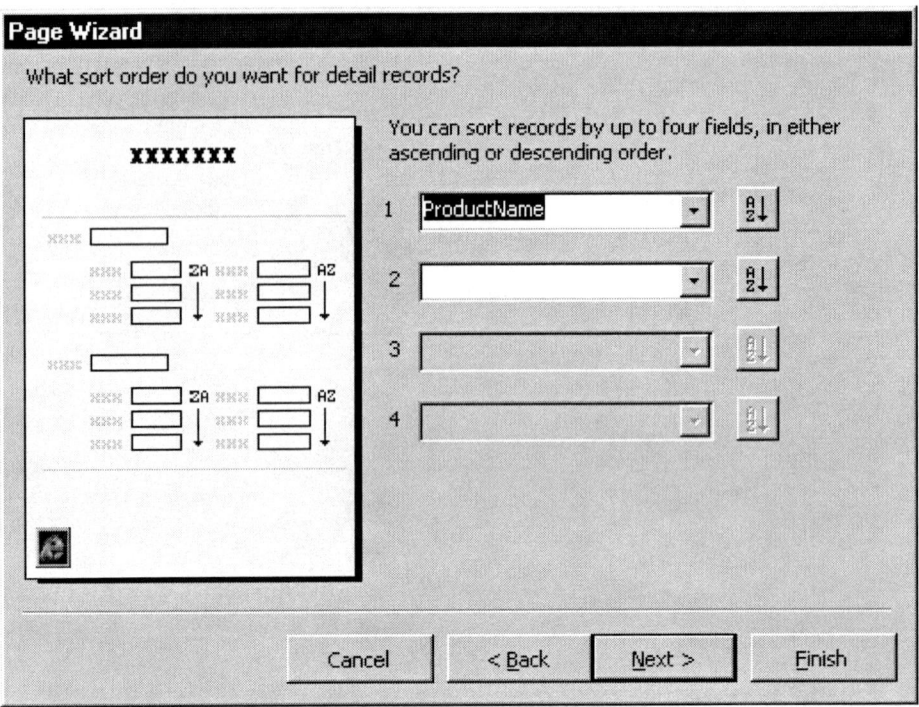

Page Wizard - Detail records sort options

- Select **ProductName** as the field to sort on

- Click **Finish**

- Save the page as **Products By Customer**

The page is opened in design view.

The HTML page is created.

As you can see, the page is not very well formatted. The label and group button do not fit in the header section and the text in the navigation bars does not indicate their purpose very well.

Modifying the Design of a Data Access Page

A full discussion of how to edit data access pages is beyond the scope of this course, but this topic describes the basic layout of a page and identifies some of the tools you can use.

A data access page is similar to a report, in that it is divided into sections and controls. There is also a Toolbox and Property Sheet.

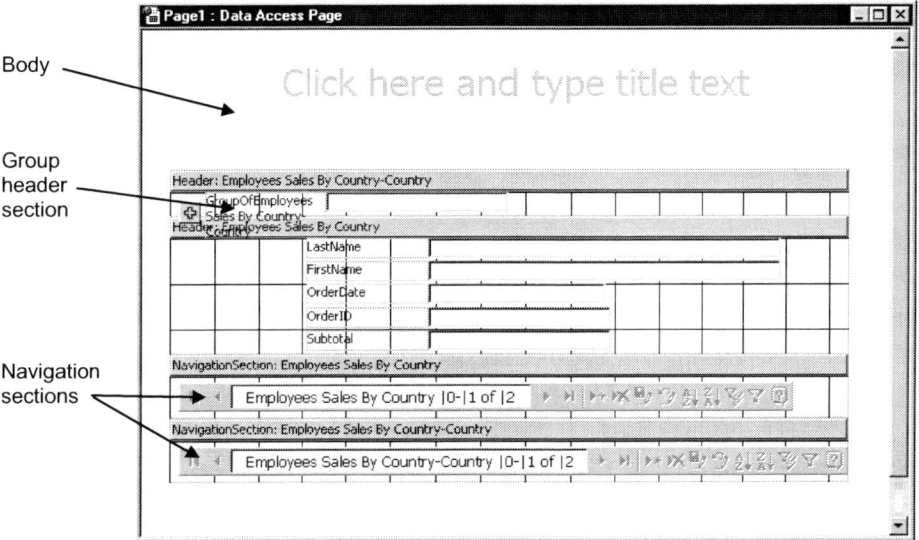

Data access page in design view

The **body** contains the sections (which hold the actual data) and can display a title, text and graphics.

The **sections** available depend on the type of page. **Group headers** are used to display data and totals. The **navigation section** stores a navigation bar for each group header.

You can also display a **group footer**, for calculating totals, and a **caption section** for displaying field labels.

Lesson 8

To modify the group properties of a data access page

The group properties of data access pages are modified using the **Sorting and Grouping** dialogue box.

Each group is identified by the name of the record source.

*Try*IT	Action	Result
	• On the **Standard** toolbar, click **Sorting and Grouping**	The **Sorting and Grouping** dialogue box is displayed.

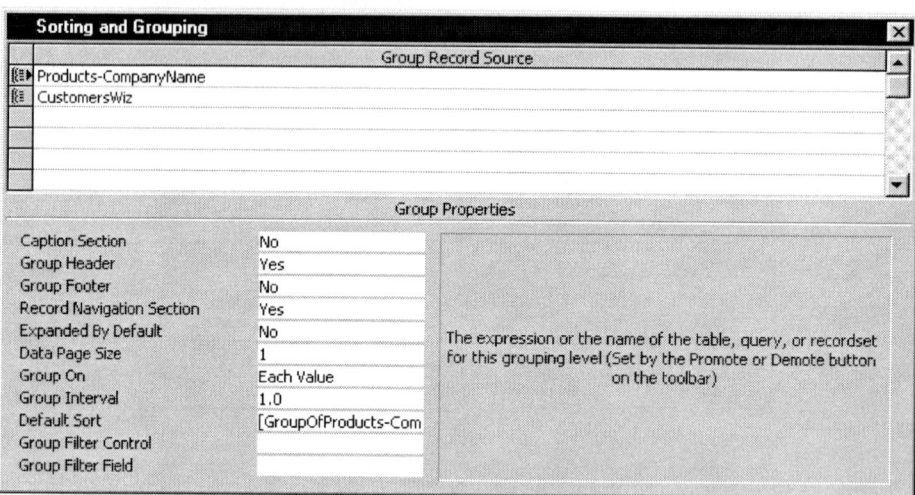

Sorting and Grouping dialogue box

	• Select **Products-CompanyName** • In the **Group Footer** box, select **Yes**	Group Properties for the group header are displayed in the lower panel.
	• For the **Expanded By Default** property, click **Yes**	Detail records will be on view by default

 Expanding detail records in a group section makes the page slower to load, so you may want to keep this option set to **No** if users will be viewing the page over the internet.

Publishing Data on the Internet

- Select **CustomersWiz**
- In the **Data Page Size** box, select **All**
- For **Record Navigation Section**, select **No**
- Click the **Close** button ⊠ to exit the dialogue box

Group Properties for the detail section are displayed in the lower panel.

The navigation bar is removed.

Data Page Size sets the number of records to display on-screen at any one time. Again, setting a lower number here will make the page load quicker.

Data Page Size must always be set to 1 if you want to add and edit records on a data access page.

To modify the data access page

TryIT	Action	Result
	• Click in the title and type `Customer Ordering`	The title is changed.
	• Click the group header	White selection handles are displayed around the object.
	• Drag the bottom handle to make more room in the header	
	• Double-click the label	The label text is selected.
	• Type `Customer`	The label text is changed.
	• Select the data control, remove the border and format it as bold and underline	
	• Complete the page design as shown below	

```
Header: Products-CompanyName
    Customer

Header: CustomersWiz


Footer: Products-CompanyName
```

LearnIT MS Access 2000 Expert   Page 229

To modify the navigation bars

If the page is not used for adding and editing records, many of the buttons on the default navigation bars are unnecessary.

TryIT

Action	Result
• Select the navigation bar	
• Display the **Property Sheet** and select the **Other** tab	
• Click the **ShowDelButton** property and select **False**	The button is removed from the toolbar.
• Remove the following buttons (Double-click a property to set it to false): **Label**, **New**, **Save**, **Undo**	
• Resize the toolbar to fit the remaining buttons	
• Save the page and click **View** to preview it	

To add a control to a data access page

The DAP Toolbox offers many of the same controls that are available for forms and reports: labels, text boxes, combo boxes, command buttons and so on.

In addition there are the following buttons:

- **Bound HTML** to display data, for example the results of a calculation. Text boxes use more resources and should only be used when you want to enter and change data in a field.

- **Scrolling Text** controls the text you enter horizontally or vertically.

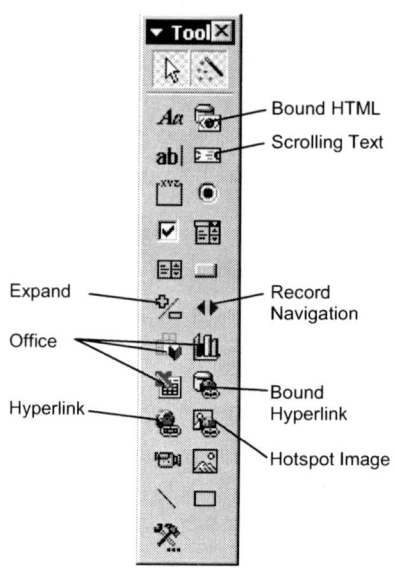

Publishing Data on the Internet

- **Record Navigation** provides various options that deal with record navigation.

- **Bound Hyperlink** this enables the hyperlink to change from record to record.

- **Hotspot Image** is like a hyperlink control, only you place an image in place of the alias text. You click on the image and it takes you to the indicated URL.

- **Office** buttons allow you to add chart, spreadsheet and PivotTable controls

TryIT 	Action	Result
	• Switch back to design view • On the **Toolbox**, select the **Bound HTML** tool • Draw out a small box in the footer • Display the **Property Sheet** for the new control and select the **Data** tab	 The control is added to the page.

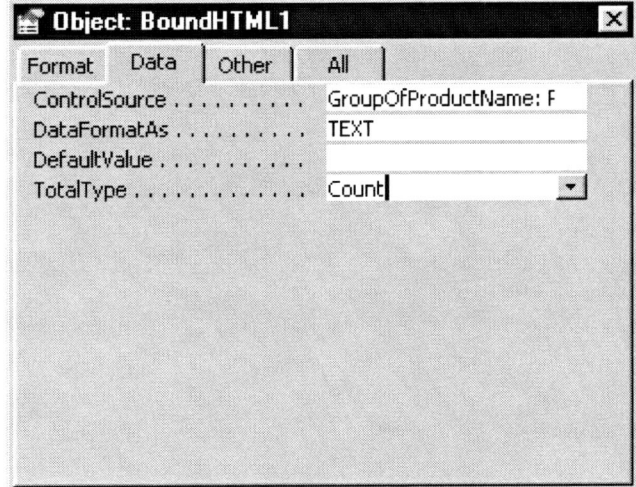

Property Sheet

LearnIT MS Access 2000 Expert — Page 231

Lesson 8

- In the **ControlSource** property, select **ProductName**

- In the **TotalType** box, select **Count**

    The control will show the number of product orders that have been made.

- Add an explanatory label next to the HTML control (`Total Product Orders Placed`)

- Re-format and position the controls as appropriate

- Save the changes you have made

- Preview the page then close it

Review Questions

(1) What is a hyperlink?

(2) Where can you store hyperlinks?

(3) What is HTML?

(4) How do you save a file to HTML?

(5) What is an HTML template?

(6) What is a data access page?

(7) What can't you do if you set Group By fields in a data access page?

(8) What does the Data Page Size property do?

Answers on the next page.

Lesson 8

Review Answers

(1) A hyperlink is a shortcut that you can use in tables or forms to jump to objects in the same database or another database, to documents created with Microsoft Word, Excel and PowerPoint, and to documents on the internet or intranet

(2) i) In fields in tables, forms or reports
ii) As a label or picture on a form or report
iii) As a command button on a form to follow a hyperlink path

(3) HTML (HyperText Markup Language) is the language used to create basic web pages for display on the world wide web

(4) i) From the File menu, select Export...
ii) In the File name: text box, give the file a name
iii) From the Save as type: drop-down list, select HTML documents (*.html;*.htm)
iv) Click Save

(5) An HTML Template is an existing web page used to contain and format an exported datasheet

(6) A data access page works like a form or report. It is an HTML page stored separately from the database (usually on a web server) but can still be used to view or edit records

(7) A data access page with grouped fields cannot be used to add or edit records

(8) The Data Page Size property determines how many records can be seen in a Group Header on a data access page at any one time. This must be set to 1 in order to update records

Skills Summary

Review

Congratulations on successfully completing LESSON 8. You can now prepare database material for publishing on the web.

Review objectives...

- ☐ Create a **hyperlink**

- ☐ Create an **HTML** file from an Access datasheet

- ☐ Use an HTML **template**

- ☐ Create a **data access page**

- ☐ Create a **grouped** data access page

Lesson 8

Notes

Macros

Lesson 9

This lesson shows you how to create and run macros that automate database functions.

Lesson objectives...

- [ ] Know how **macros** work

- [ ] **Create** a macro

- [ ] **Run** a macro

- [ ] Add a macro to a **command** button

- [ ] Use the **Expression Builder** to create a macro

Jump lesson...

If you can create macros, learn about database administration by jumping to DATABASE MANAGEMENT on page 275 or to DATABASE UTILITIES on page 309.

What is a Macro?

A **macro** is a series of actions that run in sequence to perform a task, such as opening a form or report.

Macros can be used to perform repetitive tasks, complex operations, or just to speed up normal operations. In whatever way you need macros, they can dramatically increase productivity when working in a database.

Macros can be attached to **event properties** on forms and reports or to **command buttons**.

An **event** is an action in the Windows environment. Typical events include user actions (such as clicking the mouse button or pressing a key) and the results of user actions (a form opening or closing or entering or exiting a field).

A **command button** is a control placed on a **form** or **report**. The macro will only run if the user clicks the button.

Some of the actions a macro can perform are listed below:

- Open and close database objects
- Show and hide toolbars
- Run a report
- Transfer objects to another database

Where appropriate, **arguments** can be applied to a macro action. For example, the MsgBox command displays a message box:

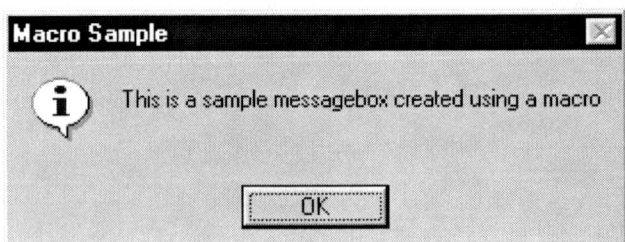

Sample message box produced using a macro

The macro **arguments** determine the type of message box (**Information**), the text in the title bar and body and whether the box plays a beep when it is displayed.

Access Applications

Another important use of macros is to design an Access **application**. Most database users do not need to be able to use all the database design tools offered by Access. In fact, it is usually a good idea to prevent users from being able to use these tools, in order to stop them from damaging the database.

In the next few lessons, you will see some examples of ways to design a **user interface** for your database. An important part of database design is providing the user with the tools they need to operate the database efficiently **and no more!** Macros play a large part in this design process.

Creating a Macro

Macros are stored as a separate set of objects in the database, just like tables, queries, forms and reports.

53 macro actions are available, although some are more frequently used than others.

Before you begin creating a macro, you should plan the actions required for you to complete the task you want to automate. Writing out the steps on paper will make creating a complex macro easier.

To create a simple macro

- From the **Database** window, select the **Macros** object
- Click **N**ew

The **Macro Design** window is displayed.

Lesson 9

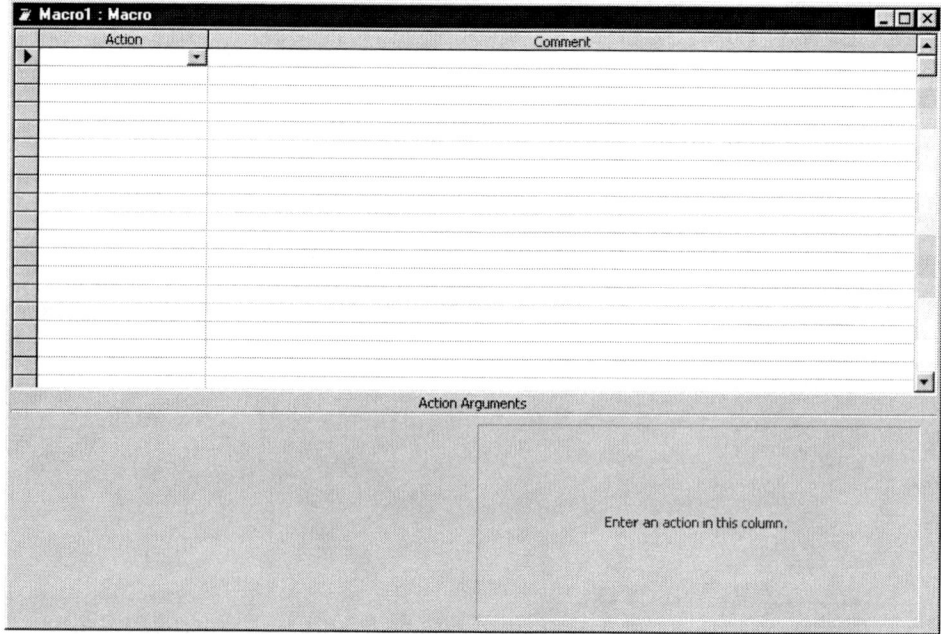

Macro design interface

A macro consists of a series of actions, each of which can be accompanied by an appropriate comment in the top pane of the dialogue box. At the bottom of the dialogue box, the **Action Arguments** section will display additional arguments that are appropriate to the selected action.

- Click in the **Action** drop-down list

The **Action** list is displayed.

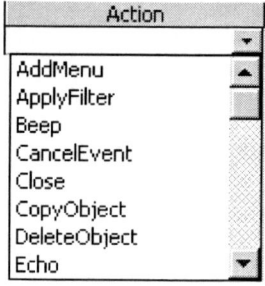

Macro actions

- Select an action
- Add a **comment** if necessary and set the appropriate **arguments**
- Add further actions if required then save the macro

The following table groups actions by the type of operation that they perform.

Category	To	Use
Import/ Export	Send Access objects to other applications	OutputTo, SendObject
	Transfer data between Access and other data formats	TransferDatabase, TransferSpreadsheet, TransferText
Execution	Carry out a command	RunCommand
	Exit Access	Quit
	Run a macro, procedure, or query	OpenQuery, RunCode, RunMacro, RunSQL
	Run another application	RunApp
	Stop execution	CancelEvent, Quit, StopAllMacros, StopMacro
Data in Forms and Reports	Restrict data	ApplyFilter
	Move through data	FindNext, FindRecord, GoToControl, GoToPage, GoToRecord
Miscellaneous	Create a custom menu bar, a custom shortcut menu, global menu bar, or global shortcut menu	AddMenu
	Set the state of menu items on a custom menu bar or global menu bar	SetMenuItem
	Display information on the screen	Echo, Hourglass, MsgBox, SetWarnings
	Generate keystrokes	SendKeys
	Display or hide the built-in or custom command bar	ShowToolbar
	Sound a beep	Beep

Lesson 9

Category	To	Use
Object Manipulation	Copy, rename, or save an object	CopyObject, Rename, Save
	Delete an object	DeleteObject
	Move or resize a window	Maximize, Minimize, MoveSize, Restore
	Open or close an object	Close, OpenForm, OpenModule, OpenQuery, OpenReport, OpenTable, OpenDataAccessPage, OpenDiagram, OpenStoredProcedure, OpenView
	Print an object	OpenForm, OpenQuery, OpenReport, OpenStoredProcedure, OpenView, PrintOut
	Select an object	SelectObject
	Set the value of a field, control, or property	SetValue
	Update data or the screen	RepaintObject, Requery, ShowAllRecords

Running a Macro

Many macros will be used in forms and reports to automate database functions for the user, in which case they are attached to command buttons or event properties (see below). However, you may also want to run macros independently.

To run a macro

- From the **Database** window, select the **Macros** object
- Select the macro then click **Run**

Macro Examples

The following macros demonstrate some of the techniques for effective macro use. The **Comments** column is not shown in these examples. The column named **Arguments** contains the required arguments for each action listed. Some arguments are optional and can be left blank, others are required and Access will prompt for their entry if they are left blank.

Macros can be used to open and close forms, preview and print reports, and change the contents of fields.

The **Add Customer** macro opens a form named Customers in **Add** mode, displays a blank record, maximises the window, and beeps.

To prevent the screen from flickering the **Echo** action is switched off, and the **Hourglass** icon is displayed while the macro is running.

Condition	Action	Arguments	
		Add Customer	
	Echo	Echo On	No
		Status Bar Text	Opening Form
	Hourglass	Hourglass On	Yes
	OpenForm	Form Name	Customers
		View	Form
		Filter	
		Where Condition	
		Data Mode	Add
		Window Mode	Normal
	Maximise		
	Beep		

When opening a form in normal or edit mode the record selection can be restricted by applying a **Filter** or a **Where Condition**.

A previously saved filter or query containing all of the fields in the form can be used to select specific records and sort them into the required sequence.

A **Where Condition** statement can be used to restrict the selected records to a constant selection such as all customers from Germany:

```
[Country]="Germany"
```

...or a floating selection such as all records created within the last seven days:

```
[CreateDate]>=Today-7
```

...or a selection based on data displayed in another form:

```
[Name] = Forms![Contacts]![ContactName]
```

When using this search method **[Name]** is the name of a field in the form you want to open. **Forms![Contacts]![ContactName]** means look for the search data in another form named Contacts in a field named ContactName.

In the Customers form, **View** and **Print** macros may be assigned to separate command buttons. The **View Customer** macro previews a report and the Print Customer macro prints it. To preview or print the report based on data in the form the **Where Condition** can be set:

```
[Country] = Forms![Customers]![Country]
```

When using this search method **[Country]** is the name of a field in the report you want to print. **Forms![Customers]![Country]** means look for the print selection criteria in the form named Customers in a field named Country.

Condition	Action	Arguments	
	View Customer		
	OpenReport	Report Name	Customers
		View	Print Preview
		Filter Name	
		Where Condition	
	Print Customer		
	OpenReport	Report Name	Customers
		View	Print
		Filter Name	
		Where Condition	

In the Customers form the **Close Customer** macro can be assigned to a command button to close the form. If data has been changed but not saved a prompt is displayed to save the data before closing the form. Alternative save options are **Yes** to automatically save changes without prompting, or **No** to close the form and discard any unsaved changes.

Condition	Action	Arguments	
		Close Customer	
	Close	Object Type	Form
		Object Name	Customers
		Save	Prompt

In the **Search Date** macro the cursor is moved to the Date field and the **Find Record** command is run to search for a specific date. The search settings are set as they would be if the Find command was being run manually.

Condition	Action	Arguments	
		Search Date	
	GoToControl	Control Name	Date
	FindRecord	Find What	28-Sep
		Match	Whole field
		Match Case	No
		Search	All
		Search as Formatted	Yes
		Only Current Field	Yes
		Find First	Yes

Conditional macro actions

Macros can be set to run only when a specific condition is met. To continue the condition enter three dots on successive lines. Action lines with no condition set are always run.

- To set macro conditions, on the **Standard** toolbar, click **Conditions**

OR

- From the **View** menu, select **Conditions**

The **Discount** macro performs calculations in a macro instead of using calculated controls on a form. This can speed up some calculations and allows the results to be entered into a bound control, which stores the result in a table.

This macro uses the **SetValue** action to change the contents of fields. Numbers, text, dates or any other value can be set provided it matches the data type of the field.

If the Discount field contains a value greater than 0 (zero) the macro calculates the value of discount on items ordered and displays it in the DiscountValue field. It then calculates the total cost of the items ordered, subtracts the DiscountValue and displays the result in the TotalCost field. If the Discount field contains a value of 0 (zero) a different set of values is entered in the fields.

Condition	Action	Arguments	
Discount			
[Discount]>0	SetValue	Item	[DiscountValue]
		Expression	[Units]*[UnitPrice]*[Discount]
...	SetValue	Item	[TotalCost]
		Expression	[Units]*[UnitPrice]-[DiscountValue]
[Discount]=0	SetValue	Item	[DiscountValue]
		Expression	0
...	SetValue	Item	[TotalCost]
		Expression	[Units]*[UnitPrice]

In addition to changing the entries in fields, the SetValue action can be used to change field properties such as hiding or displaying fields (the **Visible** property) and enabling or disabling fields (the **Enabled** property) to allow or prevent data entry. Field colours and enhancement properties can also be set this way.

In the **Reorders** macro if a product is Discontinued, the StockOnOrder field is disabled to prevent orders being placed and the ReorderLevel field is hidden. If the Discontinued setting is reversed the field properties are changed back to their original settings.

Condition	Action	Arguments	
		Reorders	
[Discontinued]=Yes	**SetValue**	Item	[ReorderLevel].[Visible]
		Expression	No
...	**SetValue**	Item	[UnitsOnOrder].[Enabled]
		Expression	No
[Discontinued]=No	**SetValue**	Item	[ReorderLevel].[Visible]
		Expression	Yes
...	**SetValue**	Item	[UnitsOnOrder].[Enabled]
		Expression	Yes

Because Discontinued is a Yes/No field and can be changed with the mouse or keyboard the macro is placed in both the **On Click** and **On Key Press** properties of the field.

Because the Discontinued status can change from record to record the macro must also be run when changing records so that the currently displayed record is set correctly. To do this it must be placed in the **On Current** property of the form.

Macro messages

A message box macro can be used to warn, question, or inform the user. It halts the macro until the message is acknowledged by the user. The message can be used as a data entry validation method by setting a macro Condition to check, or the message can be displayed every time the macro is run.

The **Discontinued** macro displays two different messages when a product is discontinued. The first message is only displayed when there is currently stock on order, and prompts for the order to be cancelled. The second message is always displayed when the item is discontinued, prompting for a new discounted price to be entered and moving the cursor to the Unit Price field. Additionally the reorder level is automatically set to 0 (zero).

Condition	Action	Arguments	
		Discontinued	
[Discontinued]=Yes And [UnitsOnOrder]>0	MsgBox	Message	Cancel stock on order !
		Beep	Yes
		Type	Critical
		Title	Stock Cancellation
[Discontinued]=Yes	MsgBox	Message	Enter discounted price
		Beep	Yes
		Type	Warning
		Title	Discounted Item
...	SetValue	Item	[ReorderLevel]
		Expression	0
...	GoToControl	Control Name	UnitPrice

These macro actions could either be incorporated within the Reorder macro, or created separately and applied to the After Update property of the Form.

Design Solving Macros

The next exercise will work through creating a macro that solves a design problem that occurs when entering records in a relational database - that of having to add a new parent record during the entry of a child record.

While it is possible to create multiple-user forms for the purpose of amending existing records, creating a form for data entry poses a different requirement. The form must be a simple as possible in order to make the entry of data as simple and efficient as possible.

Multiple user forms often provide an interface that is cluttered and hard to work with. Taking the **Universal Import** database as an example, an important form will be the **Order Entry** form. Each order that is added to the database is linked to an associated customer, which is fine, as long as no new customers decide to call up and place orders!

Rather than get the sales operative to minimise the order entry form in order to add a new customer, you will add a command button to the form which will use a macro to open a New Customer form in which to add the new customer details.

TryIT 	Action	Result
	• Open the database **UNIVER_9** • From the **Forms** tab, open the **Orders Main Form**	The form should be similar to the one below.

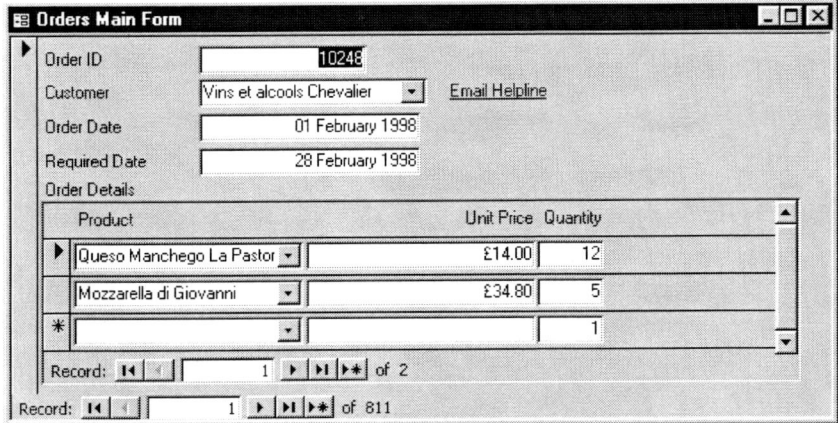

Orders Main Form

Lesson 9

This form is good for quickly adding new orders. All it needs is a form that can be "popped-up" when a new customer calls with an order.

The actions that you will have to take in the macro are as follows:

- Open the Customers form
- Add a new record - you could get the user to add their own record, but as you will see this is possible in a macro

The user will then enter the details for the new Customer record. This new information will need to be transferred back to the calling form once the addition of the new record is complete. Therefore another macro is required to close the form.

The following actions need to be added to the **OpenCust** macro:

Action	Parameter	Value	Explanation
OpenForm	Form Name	Customers	Opens the form
	View	Form (default)	Opens in form view rather than design, print preview...
	Filter Name	[Leave Blank]	
	Where Condition	[Leave Blank]	
	Data Mode	Add	Will open immediately for adding a new record
	Window Mode	Dialog	Will open in a separate window

Macros

TryIT	Action	Result
	• From the **Database** window, select the **Macros** object • Click **New** 📄 New	The macro window opens.

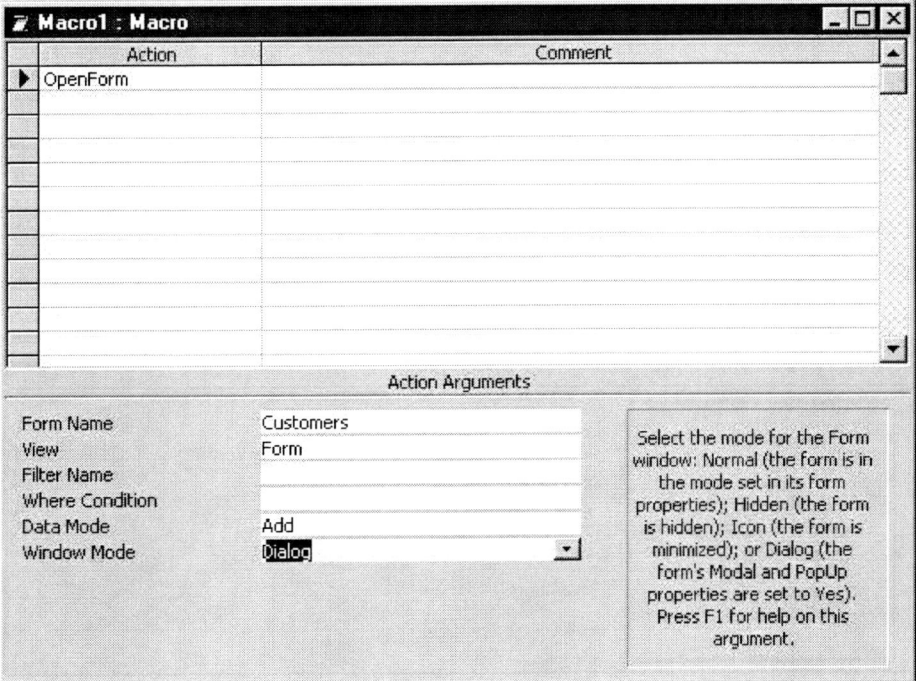

	• From the **Action** drop-down arrow, select **OpenForm**	
	• From the **Form Name** drop-down arrow in the **Action Arguments** pane, select **Customers** • Leave the view as **Form**	The form will open in form view, rather than design, print preview and so on.
	• From the **Data Mode** drop-down arrow, select **Add**	The **data entry** mode for the form will be **Add** to allow adding new records.
	• From the **Window Mode** drop-down arrow, select **Dialog**	The form will open in a separate window.

Lesson 9

- Click the **Close** button ⊠ to close the macro window
- Click **Yes** to save the changes
- In the **Macro Name** box, type `OpenCust`
- Click **OK**   The macro is saved as **OpenCust**.

Opening the form in **Add** data mode makes the form quicker to load (since Access does not need to load existing records into memory). If you want to update existing details, choose **Edit**. To create a form to view records only, choose **Read Only**.

Adding a Macro to a Command Button

The next stage is to add a command button to the Orders form in which to add the macro.

To add the macro to a command button

TryIT	Action	Result
	• Open the **Orders Main Form** in design view	
	• Display the **Toolbox** if necessary and make sure the **Control Wizards** are activated	
	• Select the **Command Button** tool from the **Toolbox**	
	• Add it to the form	The **Command Button Wizard** starts.
	• In the **Command Button Wizard** screen, select the **Miscellaneous** category	
	• Select the **Run Macro** option	

Macros

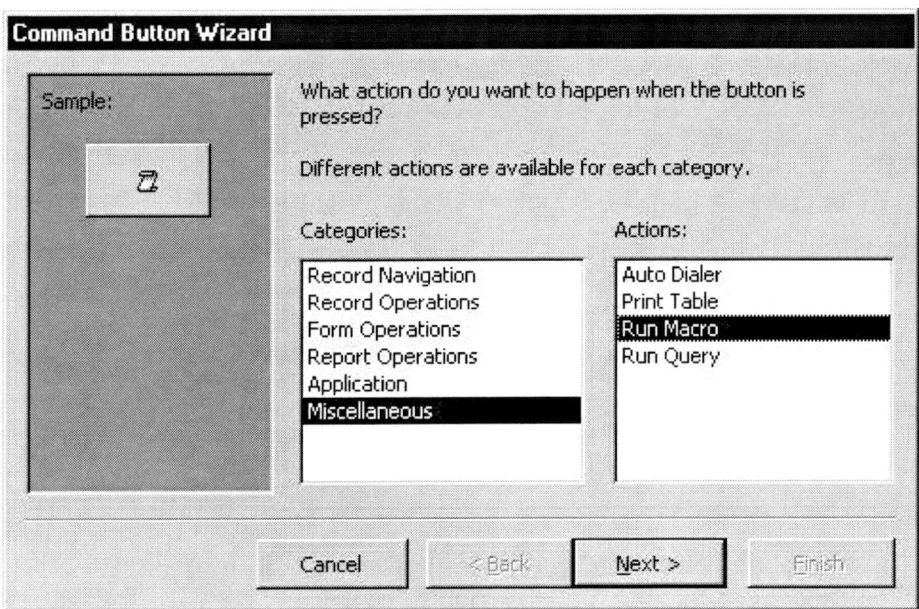
Command Button Wizard

• Click **Next >**	You are prompted to choose a macro.
• Select the **OpenCust** macro you have just created	
• Click **Next >**	This screen lets you label the button.
• Select **Text:** option button	
• Type Add Customer	
• Click **Next >**	This screen lets you name the control.
• For the name of the button, type cmdAddCust	
• Click **Finish**	The form is redisplayed with the new button.

• Save the form then switch to **Form** view	The form is displayed in form view.
• Click the **Add Customer** button to test it	The **Customers** form is displayed.

Using the Expression Builder to Build a Macro

The next stage of the exercise is to create a macro that will close the **Customers** form and update the customer list in the Orders form.

This macro will have to perform the following actions:

- **SetValue** - sets the value of the **CustomerID** combo box to the CustomerID value that you have just entered
- **Close** the Customers form and return to the Orders Main Form
- **Requery** the **CustomerID** combo box control - this will update the **CustomerID** list to include the customer that you have just added to the **Customers** table

To add the values to the parameters of the **SetValue** action, you can either type them from the fields above, or use the **Expression Builder** in the following way:

TryIT	Action	Result
	• Close the **Customers** form • Create a new macro	A new macro window opens.
	• From the **Action** drop-down arrow, select **SetValue**	
	• Select the **Item** parameter field in the **Action Arguments**	
	• Click the ellipses button (...) at the end of the parameter row to launch the **Expression Builder**	The **Expression Builder** is displayed.

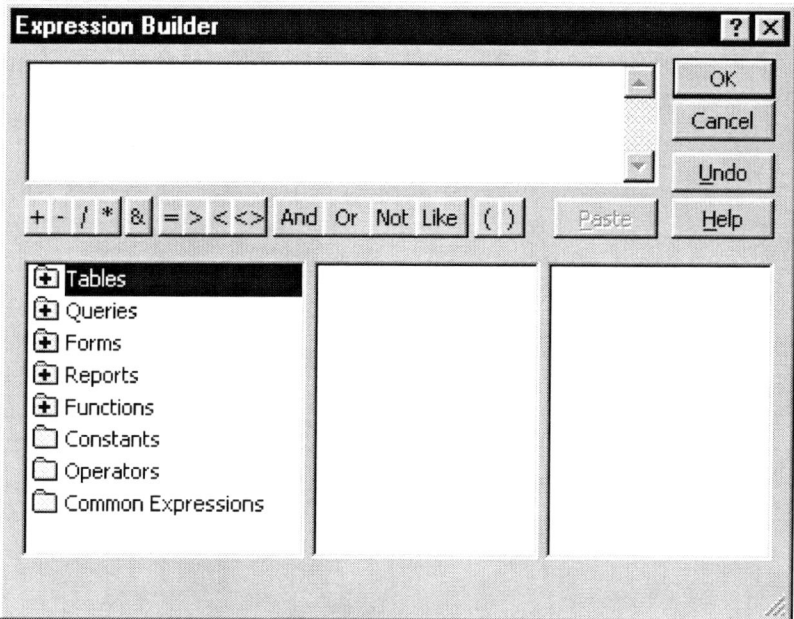

Expression Builder

The **Expression Builder** is a tool that aids the building up long or complex expressions. It contains a blank box at the top where the expression is created, a selection of buttons to help build the expression, and three columns at the bottom.

The right column displays a selection of field properties or functions depending on the items selected in the left and middle columns.

Expression Builder objects

The Expression Builder contains a list of all the objects in the database - tables, queries, forms and reports, and each of the controls within those objects. It also contains a list of functions and commands that can be used in expressions.

The left column lists all the tables, forms, queries and built-in functions that are available. Clicking the **plus (+)** symbol next to an object type such as **Tables** displays an expanded list of available tables. Select the **Functions** object, then **Built-in Functions** to display a list of formula functions.

The middle column lists a selection of controls and field names or function categories depending on the item selected in the left column. Select a control to paste into the Builder panel or select a function category.

The right column may display nothing, a selection of field properties, or a list of functions depending on the items selected in the left and middle columns.

To create an expression

TryIT	Action	Result
	• Double-click the plus sign (⊞) against **Forms**	The **Forms** list is expanded.
	• Double-click the plus sign (⊞) against **All Forms**	The **All Forms** list is expanded.
	• Click **Orders Main Form**	
	• In the middle pane, select **CustomerID**	
	• Click **P**aste	The value is added into the expression pane.
	• Click **OK**	The selected value is added to the arguments field.

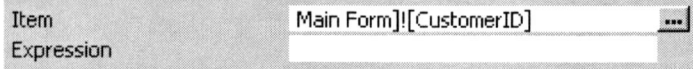

	• Click in the **Expression** argument field	
	• Click the ellipses button (...) at the end of the parameter row to launch the **Expression Builder**	The **Expression Builder** is launched again.

Macros

- Expand the objects list on the left hand pane until the **Customers** form is selected

- In the middle pane, select **CustomerID**

- Click **P**aste   The value is added into the expression pane.

- Click **OK**   The selected value is added to the **expression** field.

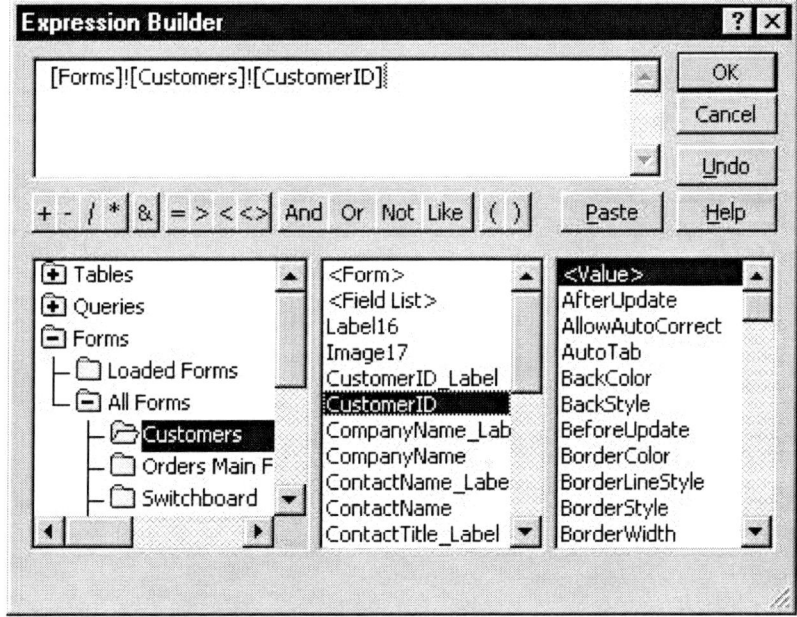

Expression Builder

TryIT

Practice

- Continue to add the macro actions following the table overleaf

If you followed the exercise above, the first action **SetValue** has already been carried out.

Lesson 9

Action	Parameter	Value	Explanation
SetValue	Item	[Forms]![Orders Main Form]![CustomerID]	Copy the value from the Customers table to the Orders table
	Expression	[Forms]![Customers]![CustomerID]	
Close	Object Type	Form	Close the form
	Object Name	Customers	
Requery	Control Name	CustomerID	Update the values for the Customer control on the Orders Main Form
Repaint Object	Object Type	Form	Refresh the form to display the new information
	Object Name	Orders Main Form	

 For more information on macro actions, query the online help with the name of the action or press F1 while adding the action to a macro.

Your completed macro should look like this:

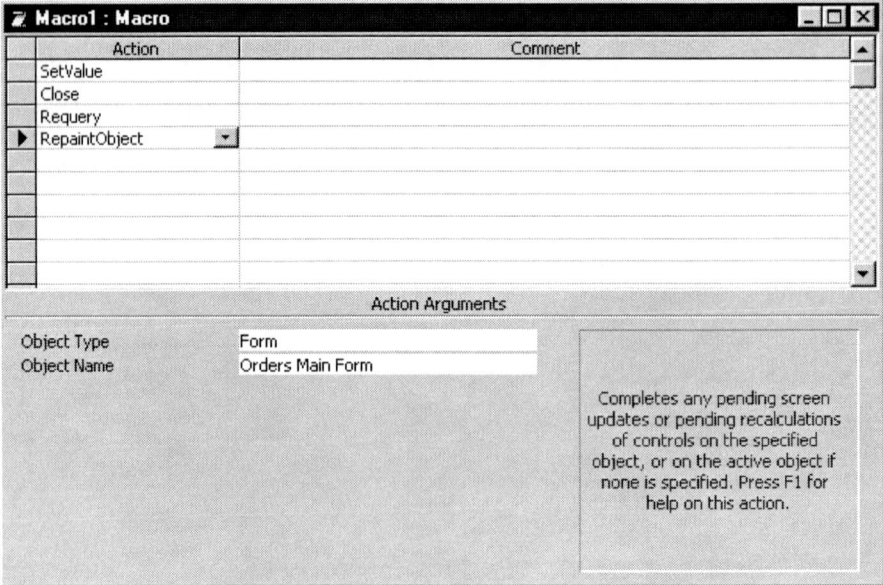

Macros

TryIT	Action	Result
	• Click the **Close** button ☒ to close the macro window • Click **Y**es to save the changes • In the **Macro Name** box, type `CloseCust` • Click **OK**	 The macro is saved.

Now we need to add the macro to a command button on the **Customers** form.

TryIT	Action	Result
	• Open the **Customers** form in design view • Add a **Command Button** ▭ to the form	The **Customers** form opens in design view. The **Command Button Wizard** starts.
	• In the **Command Button Wizard** screen, select the **Miscellaneous** category • Select the **Run Macro** option then click **N**ext > • Select the **CloseCust** macro you have just created • Click **N**ext > • Select **Text:** option button • Type `Return to Orders` • Click **N**ext > • For the name of the button, type `cmdCloseCust` • Click **F**inish	 You are prompted to select a macro. You are prompted to add a label. You are prompted to enter a name for the macro. The form is redisplayed with the new button.

Lesson 9

- Click the **Close** button ☒ to close the form

- Click **Y**es to save the changes

- Open (or switch back to) **Orders Main Form**

You are prompted to save the form.

The form opens.

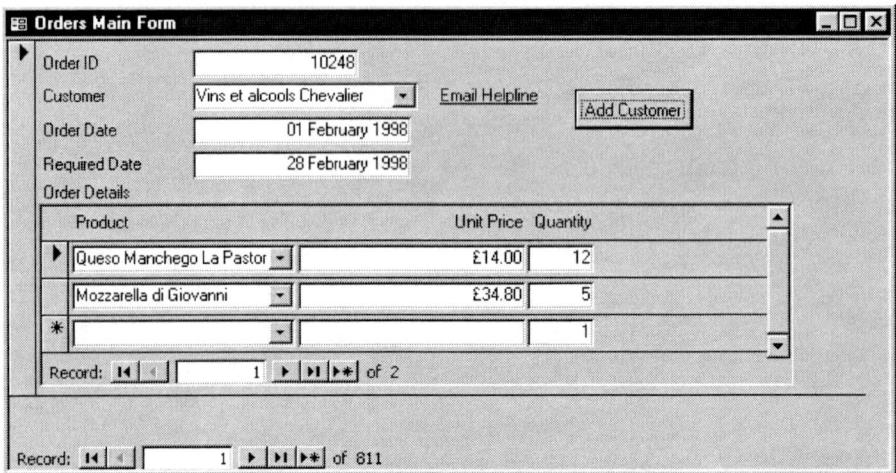

- Add a new record and click the **Add Customer** button to test the macros

- Close the database

It is important to add a new record before pressing the **Add Customer** button, otherwise the process will change the current customer's name. Further database design would be required to solve this usability problem.

You can also run macros in response to events. Select the object to attach to the macro to and click the **Events** tab in the Property Sheet. Select the macro from the drop-down list in the appropriate event.

Any further discussion of this topic is beyond the scope of this course, but if you want to know more about the basics of events, lookup "Events: Making your database objects work together" in the online help.

Review Questions

(1) What is a macro?

(2) Where are macros stored?

(3) When does a macro run?

(4) What should you do before creating a macro?

(5) What is an Action Argument?

(6) What is a Where condition?

(7) What is a Command Button?

(8) What is the Expression Builder?

_____

Answers on the next page.

Lesson 9

Review Answers

(1) A macro is a series of steps (or actions) that run in sequence to perform specific tasks

(2) Macros are stored under the Macros object in the database

(3) i) Select the macro then click run
    ii) Attach the macro to an event property of an object (for example, clicking a Command Button)

(4) Plan the actions required to complete the task you want to automate

(5) Action Arguments are the properties of macro actions, describing how the action is to operate. For example, the arguments of the OpenForm action indicate which form to open and can specify view, data and window mode, filter and where condition

(6) A Where condition can be used to specify criteria in the macro arguments, for example to display a subset of records in a form

(7) A Command Button is a control on a form or report that allows the user to initiate an action (such as running a macro)

(8) The Expression Builder contains a list of all the objects in the database - tables, queries, forms and reports, and each of the controls within those objects. It also contains a list of functions and commands that can be used in expressions

Skills Summary

Review

Congratulations on successfully completing LESSON 9. You can now develop macros for automating database functions.

Review objectives...

- ☐ Know how **macros** work

- ☐ **Create** a macro

- ☐ **Run** a macro

- ☐ Add a macro to a **command** button

- ☐ Use the **Expression Builder** to create a macro

Lesson 9

 Going Further

Designing Menus Bars and Toolbars

In order to complete the design of an Access application, menus and toolbars can be customised to display only appropriate buttons and menu items, and displayed or hidden as and when needed. Shortcut menus can also be created which appear when the right mouse button is clicked.

Custom menus and toolbars can be set to display automatically when a form or report is opened by selecting them in the properties list. To open or close the standard Access menus and toolbars at any time a macro action can be attached to the appropriate property.

To create a custom menu bar or toolbar

- From the **Tools** menu, select **Customize...**

The **Customize** dialogue box is displayed.

- Click the **Toolbars** tab

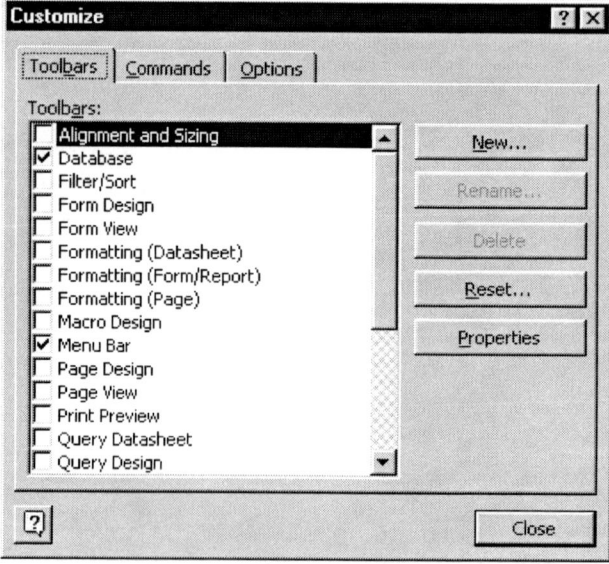

Customize - Toolbars dialogue box

- Click **New...**

The **New Toolbar** dialogue box is displayed.

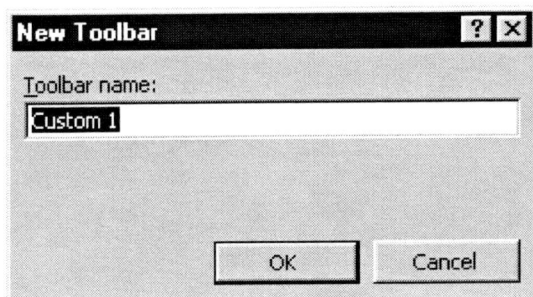

New Toolbar dialogue box

- In the **Toolbar name** box, enter the name of the new menu or toolbar

- Click **OK**

The new bar is displayed.

New toolbar

- Add buttons and menu items as appropriate (see "Customising Menus and Toolbars" below)

To create a menu bar or shortcut menu

- From the **Customize** dialogue box, create a new toolbar
- Add appropriate items to the bar (see "Customising Menus and Toolbars" below)
- Drag the new toolbar away from its default position (over the top of the **Customize** dialogue box)
- Click **Properties**

The **Toolbar Properties** dialogue box is displayed.

Lesson 9

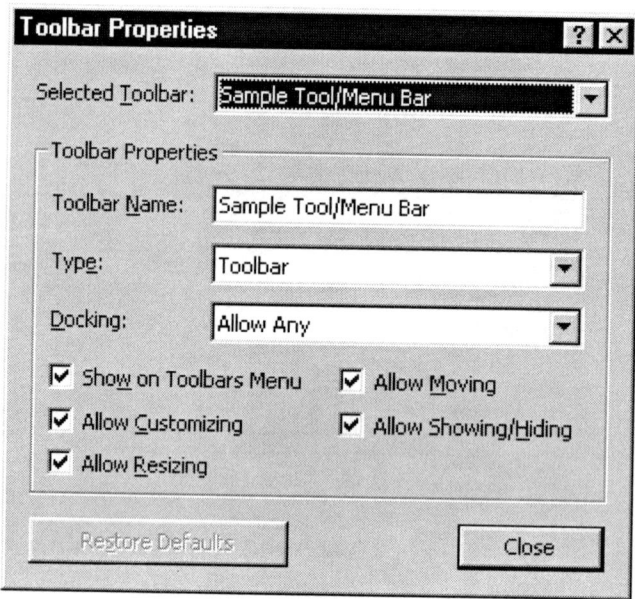

Toolbar Properties dialogue box

- In the **Type:** box, select **Menu Bar** for a new menu bar

The toolbar is changed to a menu bar.

New Menu bar

- Click **Close**

 To create a shortcut menu, select **Popup** in the **Type:** box and follow the on-screen instructions. To assign a shortcut menu to a control, in design view display the **Properties** sheet ( ) and select the relevant control. On the **Properties** sheet, click the **Other** tab and click in the **Shortcut Menu Bar** box. Select a shortcut menu from the drop-down list.

Customising Menus and Toolbars

While the Menu bar traditionally contains menus and toolbars contain toolbar buttons, in fact either type of bar can contain both menus and buttons.

To add a custom menu item to a menu bar or toolbar

- Ensure the menu or toolbar to add the menu item to is visible
- From the **Tools** menu, select **Customize...**

The **Customize** dialogue box is displayed.

- Select the **Commands** tab then from the **Categories** box, select **New Menu**

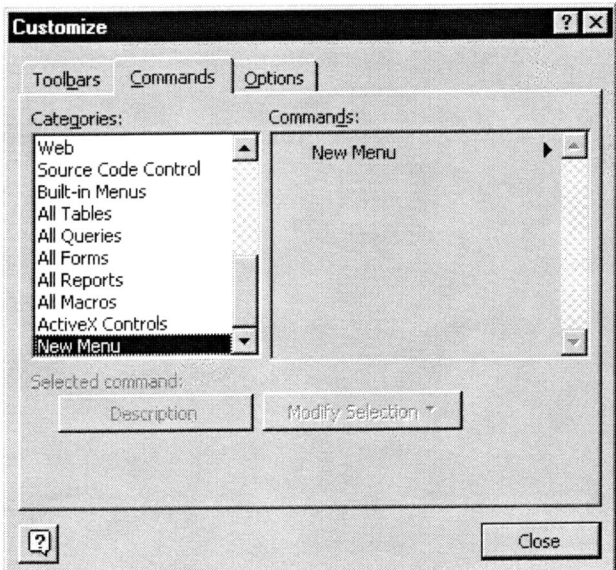

Customize - Commands dialogue box

- From the **Commands** box, click-and-drag **New Menu** to the required Menu bar or toolbar
- Right-click **New Menu** on the Menu bar or toolbar and then type a name in the **Name** box followed by `Enter`

You can now add commands to the new menu.

Lesson 9

- From the **Categories** list, select a menu item category

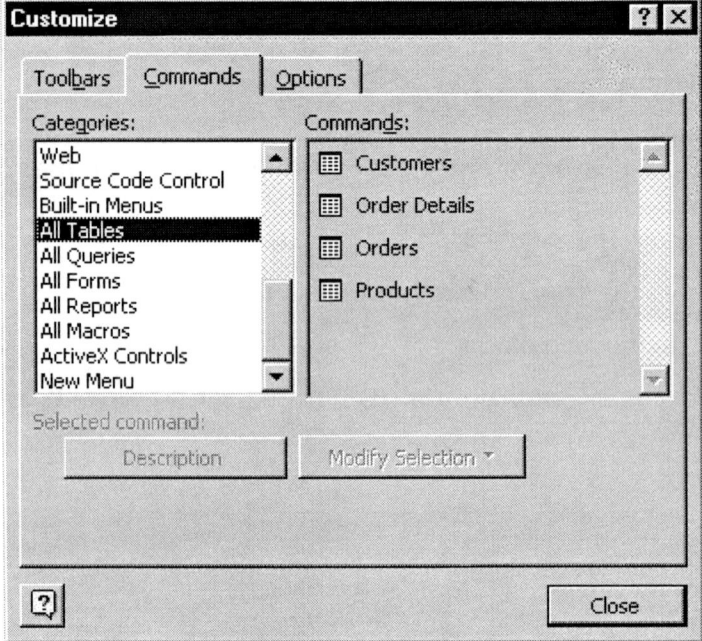

Customize - Commands dialogue box

- From the **Commands** list, click-and-drag a menu item to the menu button
- When the menu pull-down is displayed drop the menu item onto the pull-down button

Drop-down menu box

- Repeat for each menu item to appear in the menu pull-down list
- Click **Close**

Create new toolbars and set them up with all of the required buttons, rather than customising the buttons on the standard Access toolbars. To return a customised Access toolbar to its default setting, click the **Reset...** button in the **Customize** dialogue box.

To add a custom button to a menu bar or toolbar

Custom menu or toolbar buttons can be assigned to run a macro.

- Ensure the menu or toolbar you want to add a custom button to is visible

- Display the **Customize** dialogue box, click the **Commands** tab and select the **File** category

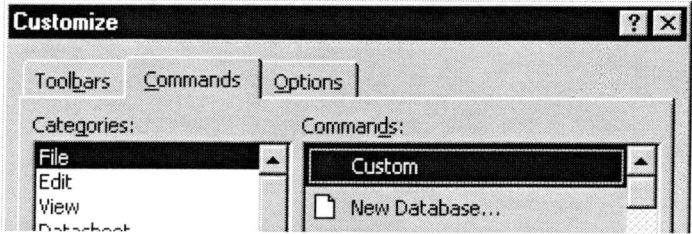

Customize - Commands dialogue box

- From the **Commands:** box, select **Custom** and drag it to the toolbar

- Click the **right** mouse button on the toolbar **Custom** button

The **Custom** toolbar/menu option dialogue box is displayed.

- In the **Name** box enter the name to display on the button

OR

- Click **Change Button Image** and select a button icon

- Select **Properties**

The **Control Properties** dialogue box is displayed for the selected menu/toolbar.

Custom toolbar/menu option dialogue box

Lesson 9

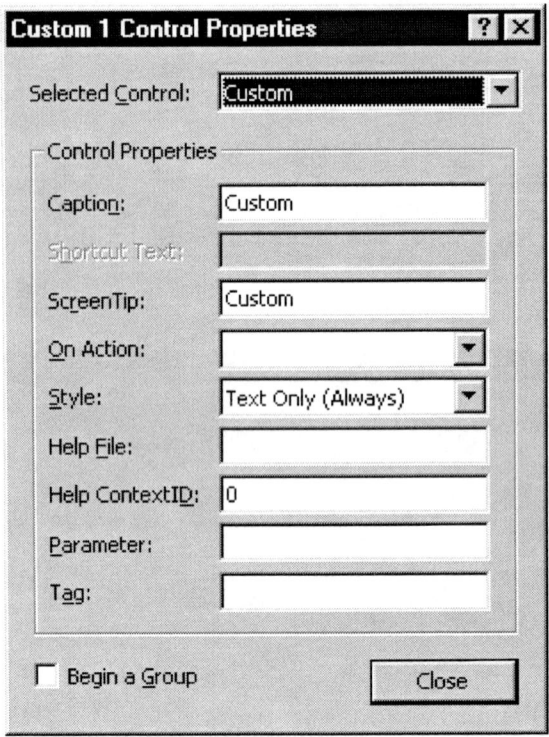

Control Properties dialogue box

- Click the **On Action** pull-down button and select a macro from the list
- Click **Close**

To edit a button image

- Display the toolbar containing the button image
- From the **Tools** menu, select **Customize...**
- Right-click the button image on the toolbar to be edited and from the shortcut menu choose **Edit Button Image...**

The **Button Editor** dialogue box is displayed.

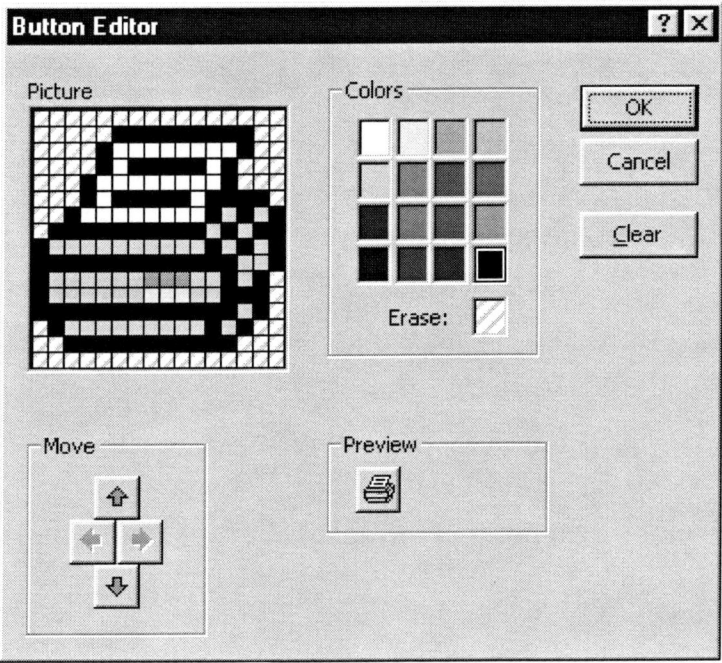

- To edit the existing image, select a colour and fill the pixels of the image

- To draw a new button image, choose the **Clear** button and then follow the step above

 Images can also be copied and pasted from other buttons or graphics applications. With the **Customize** dialogue box displayed, right-click the button image you want and select **Copy Button Image**. Then right-click the new button and select **Paste Button Image**.

To display the button image

Toolbar buttons can display an image, an image and text or just text.

- With the **Customize** dialogue displayed, right-click the macro button
- Select **Default Style** to display just the image

OR

- Select **Text Only** to display just the button name

OR

- Select **Image and Text** to display both name and image

To remove a menu item or toolbar button from a toolbar

- Display the **Customize** dialogue box
- Click-and-drag the button or menu off the bar

To delete a custom menu bar or toolbar

All of the menu bars and toolbars are displayed in the **Customize** dialogue box. Only custom bars created with the **New** button can be deleted.

Custom bars always appear at the bottom of the list.

- Display the **Customize** dialogue box
- From the **Toolbars** box, select the custom bar to be deleted
- Click **Delete**
- Click **Close**

Customising Startup

Database startup defaults can be set in the **Startup** dialogue box, in order to prepare the database for use when it is loaded.

To customise database startup settings

- From the **Tools** menu, choose **Startup**...

The **Startup** dialogue box is displayed.

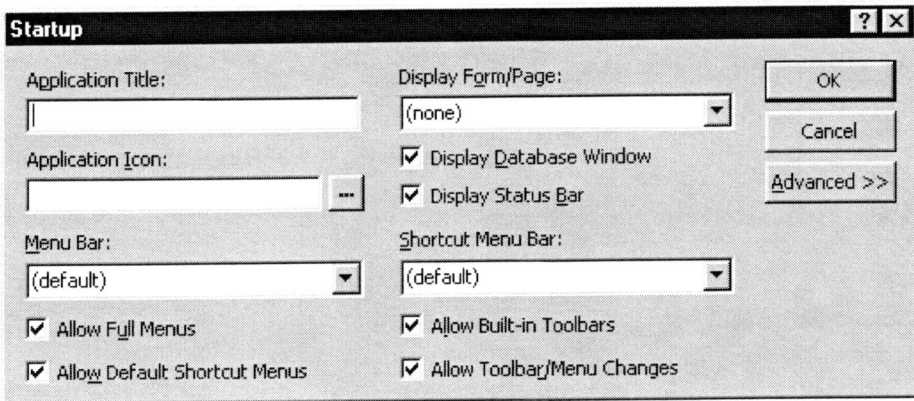

Startup dialogue box

- Set the required startup options (refer to the table overleaf)
- Click **OK**

Startup Option	Action
Application Title	Enter the name to display on the application window title bar. This name is displayed on the window's Taskbar also.
Application Icon	Click the Builder button to select an icon to display on the application window Title bar and the Taskbar.
Menu Bar	Enter the name of a custom menu to display.
Allow Full Menus	Select the check box to enable or restrict the standard menu options available.
Allow Default Shortcut Menus	Select the check box to enable or disable the standard shortcut menus.
Display Form	Select the form to display automatically at startup.
Display Database Window	Select the check box to hide or display the Database window.
Display Status Bar	Select the check box to hide or display the Status bar.
Shortcut Menu Bar	Enter the name of a custom shortcut menu to display.
Allow Built-in Toolbars	Select the check box to allow or restrict toolbar selection to all or only customised toolbars.
Allow Toolbar/Menu Changes	Select the check box to allow or restrict customisation of toolbars and menus.
Advanced >>	Set additional options such as viewing the macro codes if an error occurs, and to use Access Special Keys.

⚠ Menu and toolbar settings in the **Startup** dialogue box are defaults only and are overridden by specific settings contained in Form and Report properties.

Lesson 10 — Database Management

Regular maintenance is essential in order to keep a database working effectively. All databases must be backed up regularly to avoid loss of data. A database may also need to be made secure from unauthorised access. This lesson gives you a basic introduction to database administration.

You will require a blank floppy disk to complete part of this lesson.

Lesson objectives...

- ☐ Apply a **password** to limit access to a database
- ☐ **Backup** and **restore** a database
- ☐ **Compact** and **repair** a database
- ☐ **Encrypt** a database to make it unreadable to any program other than Access 2000
- ☐ Use the **Database Splitter**

Jump lesson...

You can learn about additional management tools in DATABASE UTILITIES on page 309.

Database Administration

Typically, most databases are used by more than one person in an organisation.

Access databases are setup to be used by several people at once and are designed to allow fast, convenient access to a fairly large number of users. Normally a database file will be stored in a shared network folder, where users can access it easily.

In a situation where several people are using the same database, it is important that one person is **responsible** for administering and securing the database.

Databases will usually contain valuable and confidential information. It is important to protect your organisation's data against accidental or deliberate damage or theft.

Security is usually enforced by:

- **Restricting access to the database**

Only users who need to use the database should be able to open it at all. Other users should have no access to the file whatsoever. This can be achieved by setting access permissions on the shared network folder.

Access to the folder and to the database itself can be further controlled by setting **passwords** and by **encrypting** the information in the database file.

- **Restricting permissions of allowed users**

A user who only needs to view data in the database does not need, and should not be allowed, to change its structure - or even to change records!

It is possible to create different **types** (or **groups**) of database user to achieve this. The basics of this topic are discussed in the **GOING FURTHER** section (page 295).

- **Backing up and encrypting data**

The remainder of this lesson discusses basic security and administration tools that you can use to manage your databases.

Setting a Database Password

Password security can be independently applied to each database. Whenever the file is opened, the user is prompted for the password.

A password is only of use if it restricts access to the database to the people who are supposed to know it.

Passwords should be changed regularly, be about 7-10 characters long and should ideally contain a mixture of letters and digits.

Do not use someone's name or date of birth as a password. TRAIN users not to reveal the password to others.

If a password is written down, it should be stored securely, preferably offsite (away from your place of work). Note that it IS very, very important not to forget a database password, as if you do, you will NOT be able to access your data.

To set a password on the database, you must open the database in **Exclusive** mode.

Under normal circumstances, Access opens a database in **Shared** mode, so that other people can open and work in the same database at the same time. Because you are setting a password on the database, it follows that you will have to be the only one using it.

To open a database in exclusive mode

TryIT

Action	Result
• In Access, from the **File** menu, select **Open...**	The contents of the current folder are displayed.
• Select **UNIVER_10.MDB**	
• Click the **drop-down arrow** to the right of the **Open** button	Additional options are displayed.

Lesson 10

Open button drop-down menu

 If you select the Open button rather than the drop-down arrow on the right of the button, you will open the database in Shared mode.

Action	Result
• Select **Open Exclusive**	The database is opened in **Exclusive** mode.

When a database is opened in Exclusive mode, users trying to open the same database will get the following dialogue box.

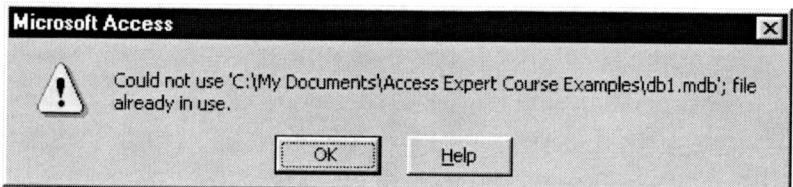

Trying to open a database already open in Exclusive mode

To set a password

TryIT

Action	Result
• From the **Tools** menu, select **Security** then **Set Database Password...**	The **Set Database Password** is displayed.

Set Database Password dialogue box

Page 278   LearnIT MS Access 2000 Expert

Database Management

- In the **Password:** field, enter the password (ver5atility)
- In the **Verify** box, enter the password again (ver5atility)
- Click **OK**   The password is accepted.

 Access passwords are case sensitive - be especially careful of the Caps Lock button when typing your password.

If you have not opened the database exclusively (see earlier in this section), the following dialogue box is displayed:

- Close the database
- Try to open the database exclusively   The **Password Required** dialogue box is displayed.
- Enter the password and click **OK**   The database opens.

Password Required dialogue box

Lesson 10

To remove a password

Again, the database must be opened in **Exclusive** mode to remove a password.

*Try*IT	Action	Result
	• From the **T**ools menu, select **Security** • From the submenu, select **Unset D**atabase Password...	The **Unset Database Password** dialogue box is displayed.

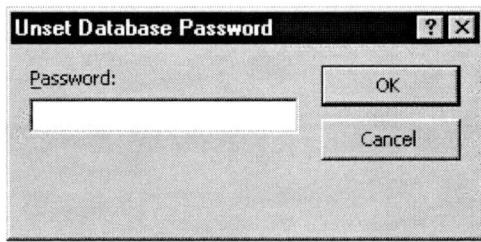
Unset Database Password dialogue box

	• In the **P**assword box enter the password (ver5atility) • Click **OK**	If the password is incorrect, the following dialogue box is displayed.

Error message

Backing Up a Database

It is always good practice to make regular backup copies of a database to prevent loss of data.

You should consider backing up the database:

- When you have entered or amended large amounts of data
- Before and after making alterations to the structure of the database
- Before installing software or otherwise reconfiguring the PC on which the database is stored
- If a database is used regularly, you should devise a plan for making regular backups (daily **and** weekly backups on different media)

Keep several backup disks and rotate them in sequence, as even backup copies can become corrupted or defective.

A simple backup process involves copying the file to another place - this could be:

- Another directory on your hard disk
- A shared area on your network server
- A floppy disk or other removable media

Access databases are held as single files with a .MDB extension, making them easy to locate and manage. You should however ensure that all users have closed the database before backing up.

Lesson 10

To backup the database

The exercise below uses Windows Explorer and will copy the database file from **My Documents** to a floppy disk in the **A:** drive.

TryIT	Action	Result
	• Close the database • On the **Windows Taskbar**, click **Start** • Move the mouse pointer up to the **Programs** menu, then down to **Windows Explorer** • Click the **Windows Explorer** item	The **Start** menu is displayed. The **Programs** menu appears. Windows Explorer starts.
	• Open the **My Documents** folder • Select **UNIVER_10.MDB** • Click the right mouse button • Select **Copy** • Put a blank floppy disk into the PC's **A:** drive.	The contents of the folder are displayed. The shortcut menu is displayed. The database file is copied to the Clipboard.
	• In Windows Explorer, open the **A:** drive • Click the right mouse button • Select **Paste**	The contents of the floppy disk in the A: drive are displayed. The database file is pasted from the Clipboard to the floppy disk.

 It is good practice to store at least one backup copy **offsite** (that is, away from your place of work). This protects your data against theft, fire or other accidents.

Restoring a Database from Backup

Restoring a database is only necessary when there is a problem with the original database.

 It is however, very important to **test** the backup copies you make regularly to check that the backed-up database functions correctly.

For this exercise, the process means copying the database back from the floppy disk and overwriting the database file in **My Documents**.

TryIT	Action	Result
	• In Windows Explorer, open the **A:** drive	The contents of the **A:** drive are displayed.
	• Select **UNIVER_10.MDB**	
	• Click the right mouse button	The shortcut menu is displayed.
	• Select **C**opy	The database file is copied to the Clipboard.
	• Open the **My Documents** folder	The contents **My Documents** are displayed.
	• Click the right mouse button	
	• Select **P**aste	A warning message checks whether you want to overwrite the existing file.
	• Click **Y**es	The database file is pasted from the Clipboard to **My Documents**.

Compacting and Repairing a Database

As you continue to use your database you will find that it starts to take up a frustratingly large amount of disk space.

When you make alterations to objects in an Access database, for example deleting tables and forms, Access does not reclaim the space. You can do this manually by **compacting** the database.

When you compact a database you are essentially **defragmenting** it, tidying up the data and filling in the spaces.

Compact a database regularly. Compacting usually speeds up the queries in your database, because the records are reorganised in a more efficient manner, which reduces the time needed to retrieve those records once the database has been compacted.

When multiple users use a database over a network, it is quite easy for errors to occur in the MDB file - the database becomes **corrupted**. Usually Access will warn you that this is the case, but you may simply notice that a database is behaving erratically and frequently crashes. If this occurs, running **Compact and Repair** can usually fix any problems.

If **Compact and Repair** does not fix a corrupt database you will need to restore the database from a backup, which of course you have been making regularly!

The **Compact and Repair** operation itself is a simple one-step menu command. However you must ensure that no-one else has the database open before attempting to compact it.

To compact and repair a database

TryIT

Action	Result
• Open the **UNIVER_10** database • From the **T**ools menu, select **D**atabase Utilities • Select **C**ompact and Repair Database...	Access automatically compacts and repairs the database at the same time.

Always make sure that all users close the database before starting this exercise.

Running Compact and Repair Automatically

You can set Access to compact and repair your database automatically each time you close the database.

Compacting only takes place if in doing so, the size of the database can be reduced by 256 kilobytes or more.

TryIT

Action	Result
• From the **T**ools menu, select **O**ptions then click the **General** tab • Tick the **C**ompact on Close check box • Click **OK** • Close the database	In future when you close the database, Access will automatically check whether it needs to be compacted.

Compacting does not occur if you close a database that is currently opened by another user.

LearnIT MS Access 2000 Expert — Page 285

Encrypting and Decrypting a Database

An unauthorised user could access your data by bypassing Access entirely. An Access database file can be opened and the contents viewed by a variety of text editing utilities.

You can guard against this by encrypting your database. Encryption uses built-in tools to ensure that the data is unrecognisable when viewed from text editors and word processors.

When a file is encrypted the encryption is transparent to Access, and has no noticeable effect on the performance of a database.

Be aware that encryption by itself does not prevent other users from using Access to open and read an encrypted database. To prevent this, you must also set a password (see page 277).

To encrypt a database

Encryption allows you to use the same name and location of the old database file, or to save the file to a new encrypted file and keep the original file.

You cannot encrypt or decrypt a database when it is open. The encrypt or decrypt process fails if another user has the database open.

*Try*IT	Action	Result
	• From the **Tools** menu, select **Secur**i**ty**	
	• From the submenu, select **Encrypt/Decrypt Database...**	The **Encrypt/Decrypt Database** dialogue box is displayed.

Database Management

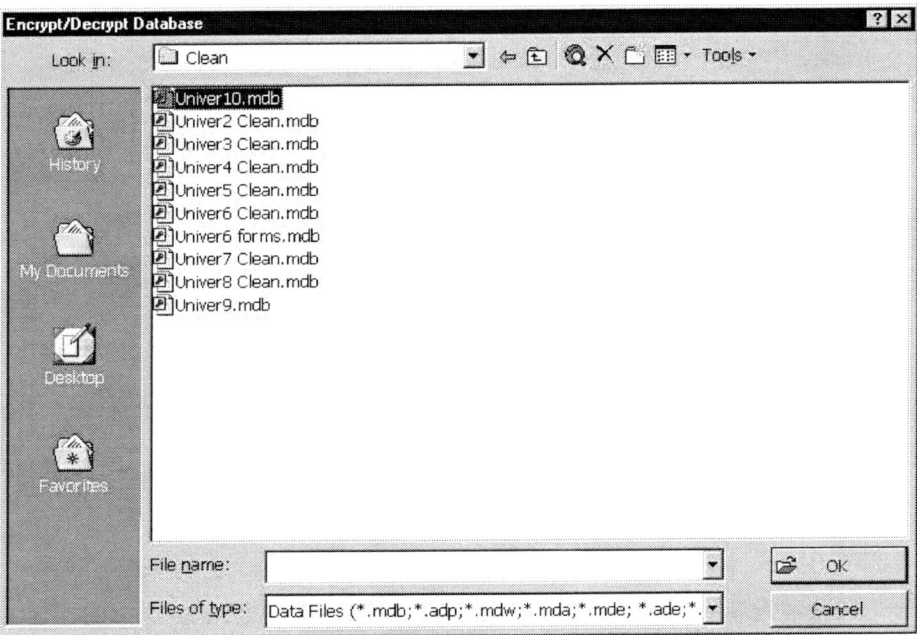

Encrypt/Decrypt Database dialogue box

• Select **UNIVER_10.MDB**	The **Encrypt Database As** dialogue box is displayed.
• Click **OK**	
• Leave the file name as it is	
• Click **Save**	The database is encrypted to a new file.

To decrypt a database

■ From the **Tools** menu, select **Security** then **Encrypt/Decrypt Database...**

The **Encrypt/Decrypt Database** dialogue box is displayed.

■ Select the database to decrypt and click **OK**

The **Decrypt Database As** dialogue box is displayed.

■ Enter a new file name for the encrypted file and click **Save**

The decrypted database is saved to a new file.

Splitting a Database

You can reduce the size of a database by splitting it. This procedure splits the database into two files: one that contains the tables (called the **back-end database**) and the current database file that contains the queries, forms and so on.

This technique stores all the data in one location, but allows each user the ability to create forms and reports in their own database files.

Before splitting the database, make a backup copy and check that you can restore it correctly.

TryIT

Action	Result
• Open **UNIVER_10** • From the **Tools** menu, select **Database Utilities** then **Database Splitter...**	The **Database Splitter Wizard** dialogue box is displayed.

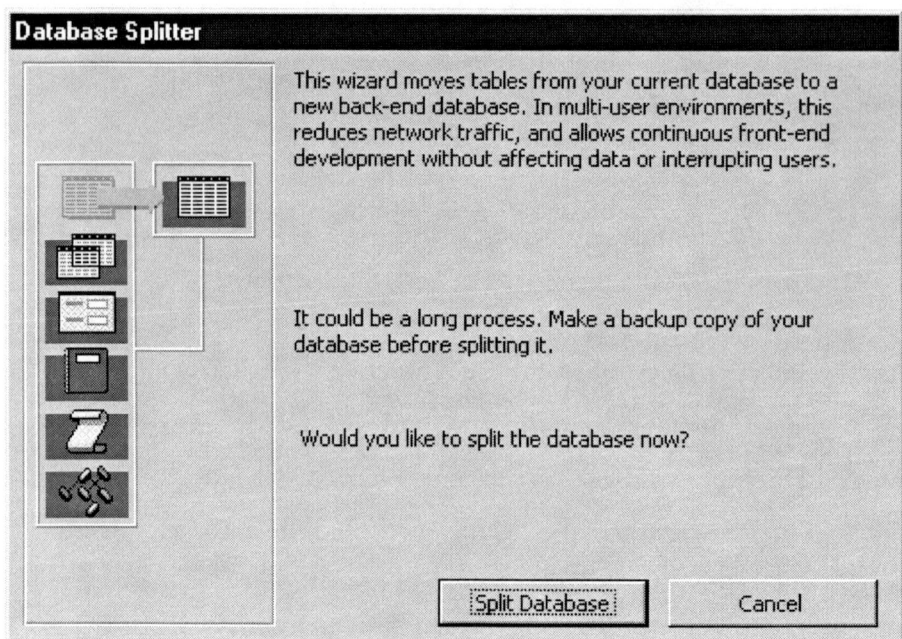

Database Splitter Wizard

Database Management

- Click **Split Database**

The **Create Back-end Database** dialogue box is displayed.

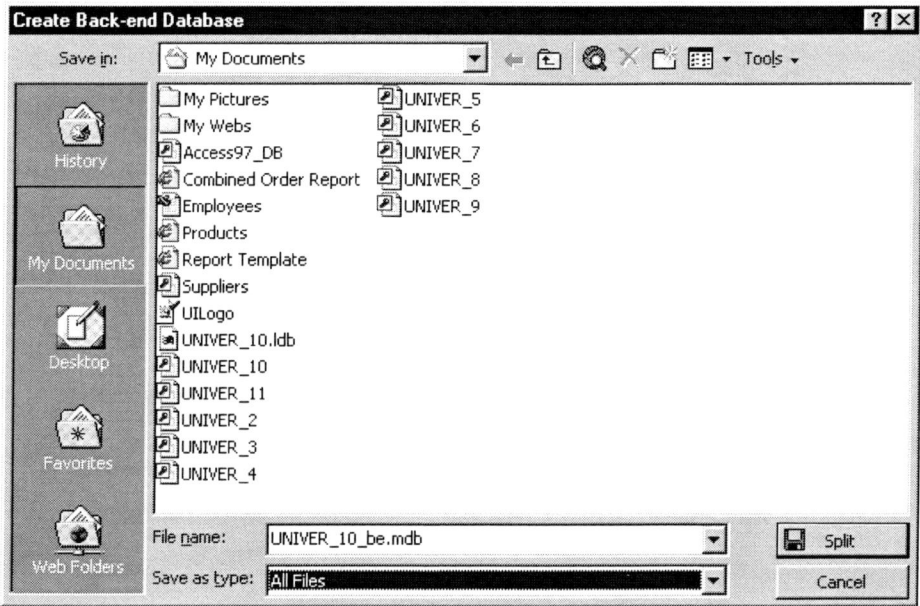

Create Back-end Database dialogue box

The default file name for the Back-end database is:

```
[original file name]_be.mdb
```

Although you can change this name, it is advisable to accept the default as it is an easy-to-recognise file name for the back-end database.

You will probably need to select a new folder though (for example, a shared network folder).

- Leave the file name prompted by Access

- Click the **Split** button

Access splits the database into two files. When Access has completed splitting the database, the message below is displayed.

Lesson 10

Database Splitter message box

- Click **OK**

All the tables are removed from the existing database, and replaced with links to the back-end database.

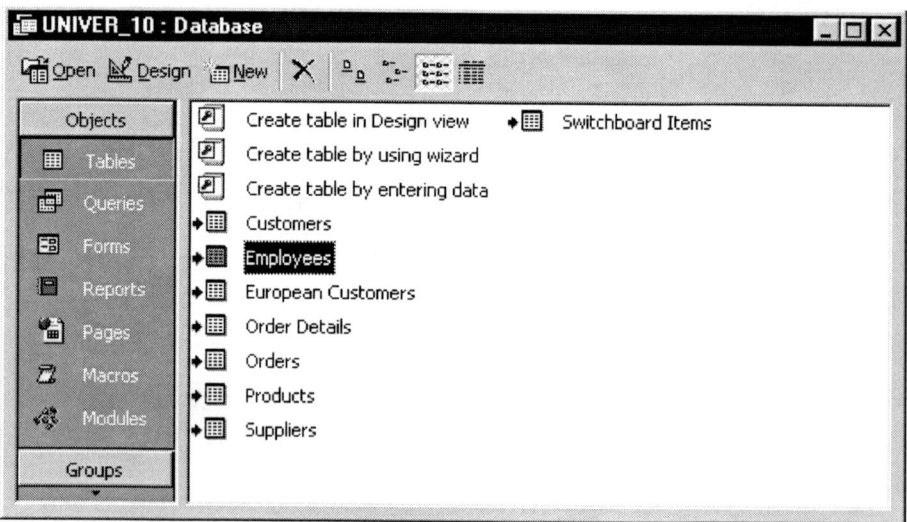

Split database

Use the **Linked Table Manager** (see page 91) to update tables if the location of the back-end file has to be changed.

Review Questions

(1) How do you open a database to set a password?

(2) How do you set a password?

(3) What should you remember about passwords?

(4) When should you backup a database?

(5) What does compacting a database mean?

(6) What is encryption?

(7) What happens when you split a database?

Answers on the next page.

Lesson 10

Review Answers

(1) Open the database in Exclusive mode

(2) i) From the Tools menu, select Security then select Set Database Password...
iii) Type in your password
iv) Retype the password in the Verify box

(3) i) Remember the password! - If a password is written down, it should be stored securely, preferably offsite (away from your place of work)
ii) A password is only of use if it restricts access to the database to the people who are supposed to know it - TRAIN users not to reveal their password to others.
iii) Passwords should be changed regularly
iv) Passwords should be about 7-10 characters long and should ideally contain a mixture of letters and digits
v) Never use someone's name or date of birth as a password

(4) i) It is always good practice to make regular (daily and/or weekly) backup copies of a database to prevent loss of data
ii) When you altered a large number of records
iii) When you have made alterations to the structure of the database

(5) Compacting a database optimises the efficiency of a database, reclaims unused space and tidies up the database

(6) Encrypting a database renders the database unrecognisable when viewed from text editors and word processors

(7) Splitting a database splits the database into two files. The first file contains the tables with the data. The second file contains the queries, forms, reports and so on for users to work with independently of the data

Skills Summary

Review

Congratulations on successfully completing LESSON 10. You now know the basics of database maintenance and administration.

Review objectives...

- ☐ Apply a **password** to limit access to a database

- ☐ **Backup** and **restore** a database

- ☐ **Compact** and **repair** a database

- ☐ **Encrypt** a database to make it unreadable to any program other than Access 2000

- ☐ Use the **Database Splitter**

Lesson 10

Notes

Going Further

Managing Shared Databases

The following notes cover the basics of managing shared databases in Access. Please note that this is an advanced topic, which also requires some knowledge of operating system security in order to put into practice.

If you are going to be responsible for shared databases in your organisation you should definitely seek further training.

When a database is to be shared by several users in a network or workgroup situation, the problem of multiple access arises. Should two people be able to access the same database at the same time? What will happen if they try to change the same record? In a multi-user environment, Access controls data access and editing by means of **locking**.

Locking dictates the amount of access that is available to multiple users who are trying to use the same database at the same time. What you are basically trying to do when applying locking is to balance **concurrency** with **consistency**. That is, to allow the maximum amount of users to access information in the database (**concurrency**), while ensuring that the information that they receive is of a consistent and repeatable nature (**consistency**).

Access has four levels of data locking to prevent data editing conflicts on shared databases.

File locking
Table locking
Record locking
No locking

File locking — Highest Consistency — Lowest Concurrency

↑ ↓

No locking — Lowest Consistency — Highest Concurrency

To set file locking

File locking is simply a case of opening a database in **Exclusive mode**. This locks an open database to prevent other users from opening it and editing it.

To set single record locking

Record locking allows several users to edit the same table at the same time, but prevents them from editing the same record.

- From a **Query** or **Form Design** window, select **Properties** (Ensure that the Form Background is the selected object in a form)

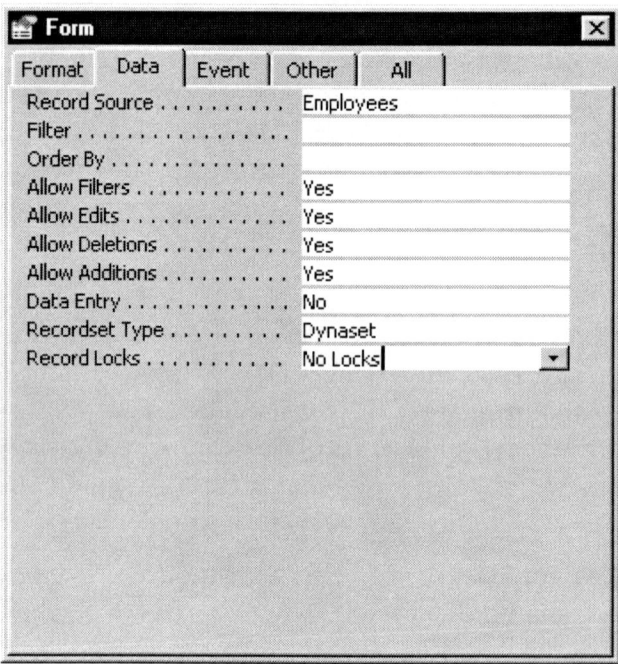

Form Properties

The **Record Locks** property allows you to set the level at which Access will lock accessed records - the default is **No Locks**

Record Locks options

Going Further

- Set the **Record Locks** property to **Edited Record**

When the record being viewed is being edited by another user a ⊘ symbol is displayed in the left margin. The record edit cannot be edited until it is saved by the other user. The screen will be updated with the changes when the records are refreshed.

Locked record symbol

To set table locking

When working on a specific table in a database all records in the table can be locked to prevent other users editing it concurrently. The table can still be viewed, or used in queries and reports by other users.

- Set the form or query's **Record Locks** property to **All Records**

If you attempt to open a locked form or query already opened by another user a record locking message is displayed.

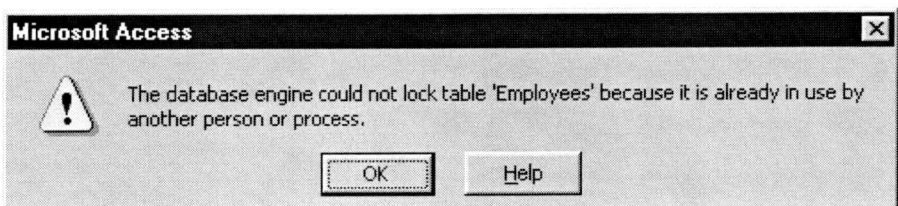

Locked table message

Reports based on locked queries can be used normally.

Setting Default Locking Properties

Access allows defaults to be set for file and record locking. When files are opened, or when queries and forms are created the default setting is automatically applied, but can be changed when required.

To set locking defaults

- From the **Tools** menu, select **Options...**

The **Options** dialogue box is displayed.

- Select the **Advanced** tab

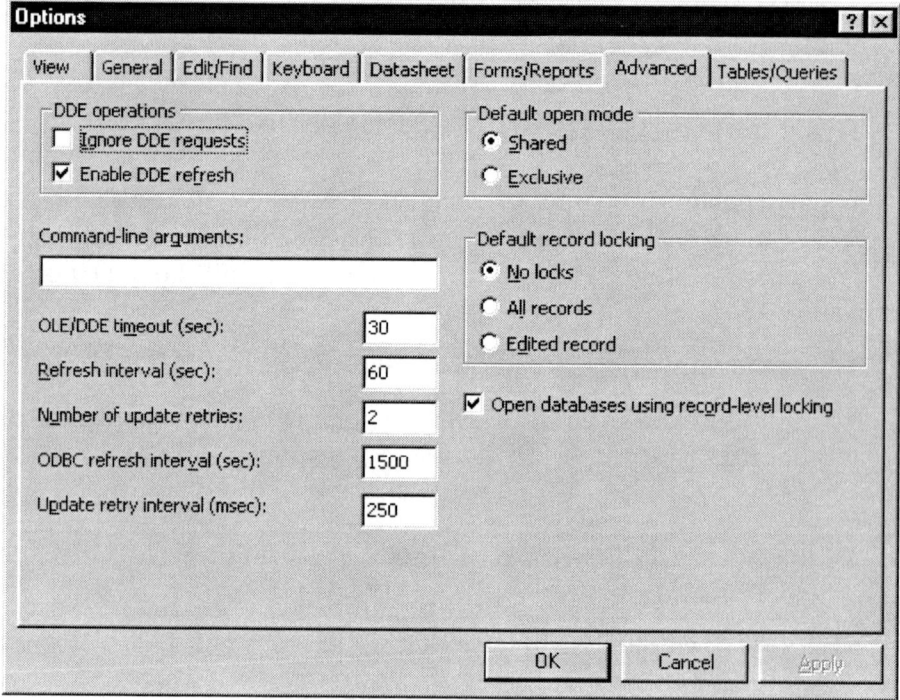

Options - Advanced dialogue box

- From the **Default Record Locking** panel, select a record locking option
- From the **Default Open Mode** panel, select a file locking option
- Click **Apply**
- Click **OK**

Creating Groups and Users

Database password protection is share-level security. A single password applies to the entire database file, and is used by all users. It does not prevent a user from starting Access and opening a different database.

Creating **groups** and **users** applies protection to Access itself, preventing non-authorised users from running Access at all. It also allows each user to be granted specific permissions to use a limited range of database functions such as adding but not deleting records, or viewing but not editing records.

There are three levels of **user** who may use a database.

- **Administrators** have full control of the database and can make any required modifications to it

- **Users** are regular users granted permission to open and work in the database - they can be given selective permission to modify the data and structure of the database

- **Guests** are occasional users who are granted limited access to the database

Groups are a simple method of categorising users for administrative purposes. There are two default groups: **ADMINS** and **USERS**.

By default, **both** of these groups have permissions at **Administrator** level. Anyone who is added to either of these groups can add, delete, and edit, in any Access function.

There is one default user, named **Admin**, who belongs to both the ADMINS and USERS groups. Because both groups are set to Administrator level, the user named Admin can perform any and all actions in the database. The default setting for Access is to recognise every user who starts Access as the **Admin** user with full access and functional privileges.

Security is always switched on and cannot be switched off, although it is not apparent to most users. Only when levels of user access are set up does the security appear to take effect and ask for logon identification.

The group and user settings are stored in the **SYSTEM.MDW** workgroup information file in the **Windows\System** directory .

Before modifying any of the security options make a **backup copy** of this file, **and** any databases created while this file was in use. If you forget the password or login names you will not be able to start Access. You must restore **SYSTEM.MDW and** the database files from the backups.

When granting permissions, it is best to create group names first and set permissions for the groups, then add users to the appropriate groups. The users are automatically granted the highest level of permissions of whichever groups they belong to.

The default users and groups are shown in the table below.

Group	User	Password	Permissions
ADMINS	Admin	None	Administrator
USERS	Admin	None	Administrator
GUEST	Guest	None	

To create a new group

- Make a backup of your Access databases and the **SYSTEM.MDW** file and check that you can restore them correctly

- From the **Tools** menu, select **Security** then select **User and Group Accounts**

The **User and Group Accounts** dialogue box is displayed.

- Select the **Groups** tab

Going Further

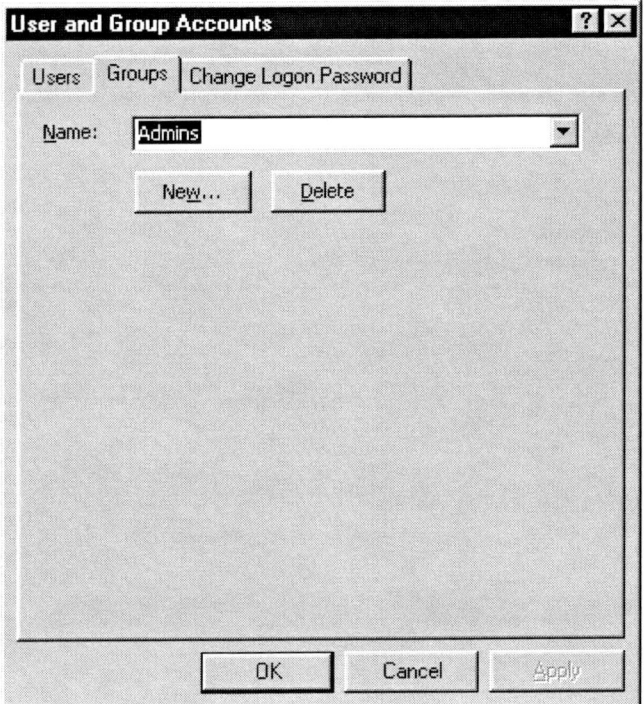

User and Group Accounts - Groups dialogue box

- Click **New**...

The **New User/Group** dialogue box is displayed.

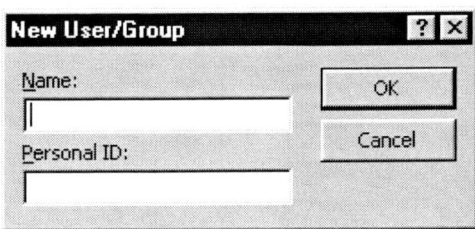

New User/Group dialogue box

- In the **Name:** box, enter the name for the new group

- In the **Personal ID:** box, enter a personal identification code for the group

Access uses the Personal ID in order to identify groups to which a user belongs. The Personal ID can be 4 to 20 characters long and is case-sensitive.

- Click **OK** to exit both dialogue boxes

Lesson 10

To create a new user

- From the **Tools** menu, select **Security** then select **User and Group Accounts**
- Click the **Users** tab

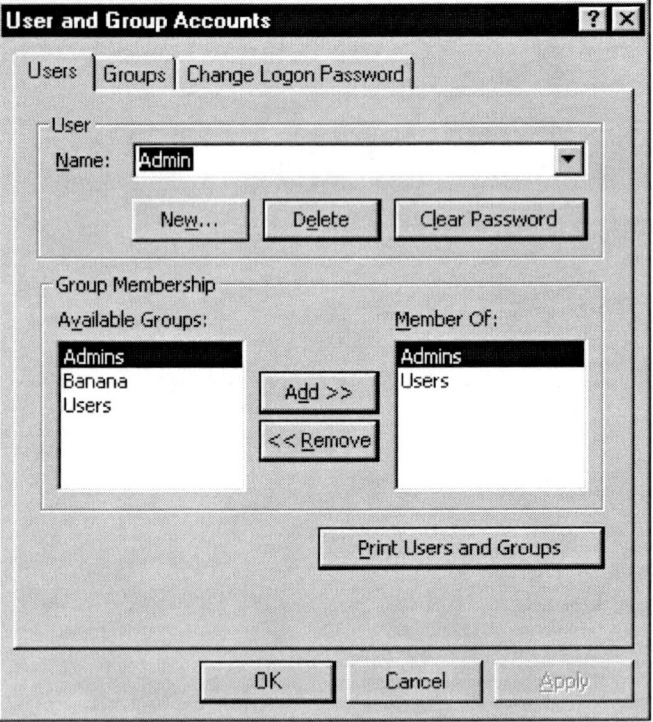

User and Group Accounts - Users dialogue box

- Click **New...**

The **New User/Group** dialogue box is displayed.

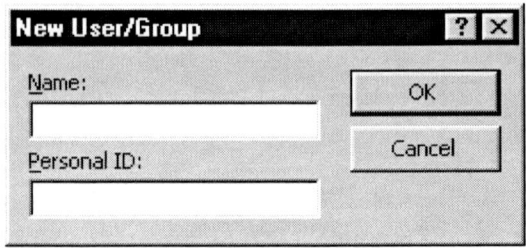

New User/Group dialogue box

Going Further

- In the **Name** box, enter the name for the new user
- In the **Personal ID** box, enter a personal identification code for the user
- Click **OK**

The **User** dialogue box is redisplayed.

- In the **Available Groups** box, select an assignment group for the new user
- Click the **Add>>** button to display the group name in the **Members of** box
- Repeat for each groups to which the user will belong
- Click **OK**

The actual permissions granted are the highest permissions of any group in the **Members of** box.

All users automatically belong to the USERS group, which cannot be removed from the **Members of** box and has a default permission of Administrator.

You must reset USERS to have **NO** permissions before any other changes can take effect (see page 306).

To set or change a user password

When a new user is created the password is left blank. A user password can only be set by closing Access and then logging on as that user.

- From the **Tools** menu, select **Security**
- From the **Security** submenu, select **User and Group Accounts**

The **User and Group Accounts** dialogue box is displayed.

- Select the **Change Logon Password** tab

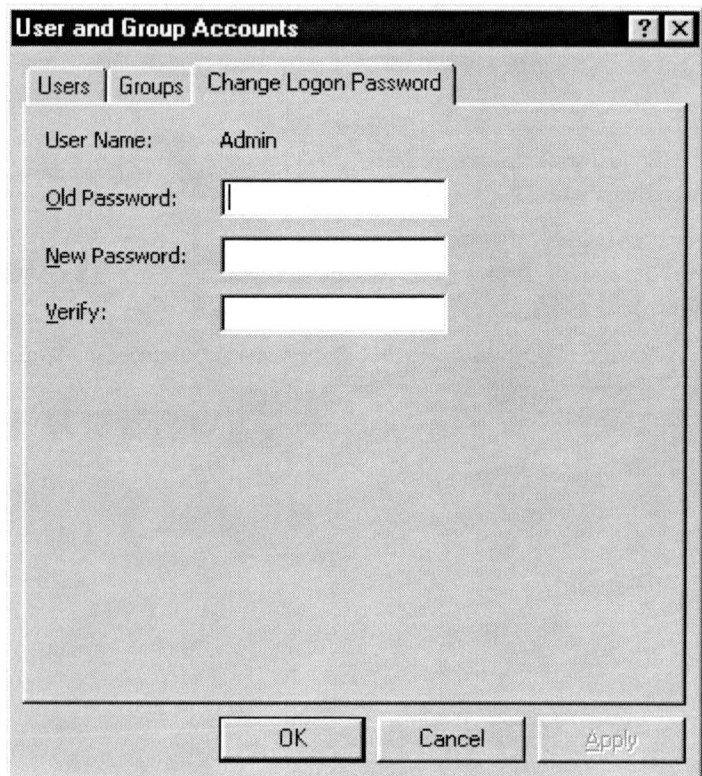

User and Group Accounts - Change Logon Password dialogue box

- In the **Old Password:** box enter the existing password if there is one
- In the **New Password:** box enter the new password
- In the **Verify:** box enter the new password again
- Click **Apply** then **OK**

A user password can only be changed by logging on with that user name.

To remove a password

If a user forgets their password they will not be able to start Access. However, any user with Administrator rights can clear the password of another user to give them access.

If you are a user:

- From the **Tools** menu, select **Security**
- From the submenu, select **User and Group Accounts**

The **User and Group Accounts** dialogue box is displayed.

- Select the **Change Logon Password** tab
- Enter the current password in the **Old Password** box
- Leave the **New Password** box, **Verify** box empty
- Click **Apply**
- Click **OK**

If you are an Administrator:

- From the **Tools** menu, select **Security**
- From the submenu, select **User and Group Accounts**

The **User and Group Accounts** dialogue box is displayed.

- In the **User** panel, in the **Name** box select the user name from the pull-down list
- Click **Clear Password**
- Click **OK**

Setting User Permissions

The Access security system allows each group or individual user permission to perform specific actions when using a database. For example, adding records but not deleting them, creating new reports, but not creating new queries. A user automatically obtains the highest level of permissions of those granted to himself or any groups he belongs to.

Separate permission levels are set for each type of Access object - tables, forms, reports and so on.

To set permissions

- Open the database you are setting permissions for
- From the **Tools** menu, select **Security** then from the submenu, select **User and Group Permissions**

The **User and Group Permissions** dialogue box is displayed.

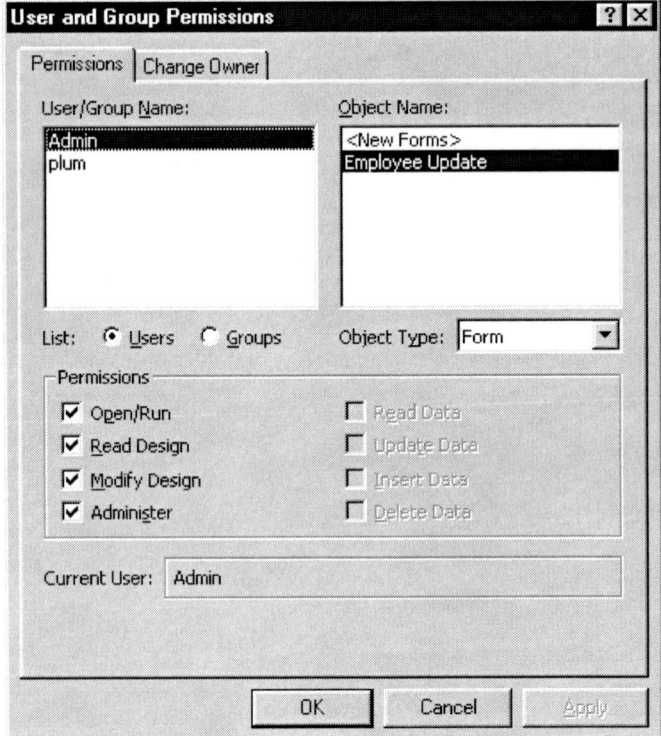

User and Group Permissions dialogue box

- Select the **Users** or **Groups** selection button to see the appropriate list of names
- From the **User/Group Name:** box, select a name
- From the **Object Type:** pull-down list, select an object
- From the **Object Name:** box, select the object(s) to grant permissions for
- From the **Permissions** panel, select the check boxes of the permissions to set
- Repeat for the process for each type of object, and each user or group
- Click **Apply** then click **OK**

Assigning Ownership

Every object created in Access is **owned** by the user who created it, the default owner being the user named **Admin**. The owner has full permissions at Administrator level for the object(s) owned.

Ownership can be transferred to a single user or to a group of users giving them full permissions for the owned object(s).

The owner of an object can grant or remove permissions for that object to other users. The owner of the database can grant or remove permissions for all objects contained in the database.

To change ownership

- From the **Tools** menu, select **Security** then **User and Group Permissions**

The **User and Group Permissions** dialogue box is displayed.

- Select the **Change Owner** tab

Lesson 10

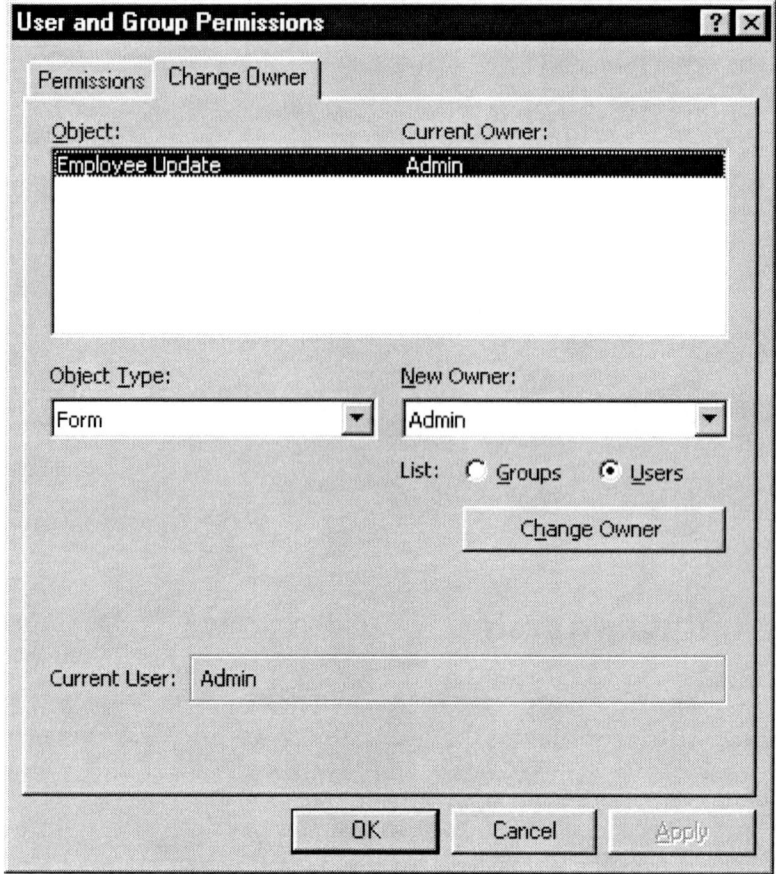

User and Group Permissions - Change Owner dialogue box

- From the **Object Type:** pull-down list, select an object
- From the **Object:** box, select the object(s) to change ownership for
- Select the **Groups** or **Users** selection button to see the appropriate list of names
- From the **New Owner:** pull-down list, select a name
- Repeat the process for each type of object, and each user or group
- Click **Apply** then click **OK**

Database Utilities

Lesson 11

Several extra database utilities are available to help you design and run a database.

Lesson objectives...

- ☐ Analyse a database with the **Table Analyzer**

- ☐ **Replicate** a database

- ☐ **Convert** a database to another file format

The Table Analyzer

Even if you followed the tips on **normalisation** in LESSON 1 carefully, you still may not have arrived at the best design for your database. If your database has a table that contains duplicate information in one or more fields, you can use the **Table Analyzer Wizard** to split the data into related tables so that you can store data more efficiently.

Either you can specify the tables that you want the wizard to create or you can have the wizard normalise the table for you.

After you have defined the proposed new tables, the wizard helps you to reconcile data that the original table repeated inconsistently.

In the last step, you can create a query to view all the information from the split tables in a single datasheet that is similar to your original table.

To use the Table Analyzer Wizard

TryIT	Action	Result
	• Open **UNIVER_11** • On the **Tools** menu, point to **Analyze** and then click **Table** • Click the **Show Me** buttons	 The **Table Analyzer Wizard** starts and displays the first of two introductory windows that explain what the wizard can do. ...to get a better idea of the kinds of problems the wizard can solve and to see how the wizard works.

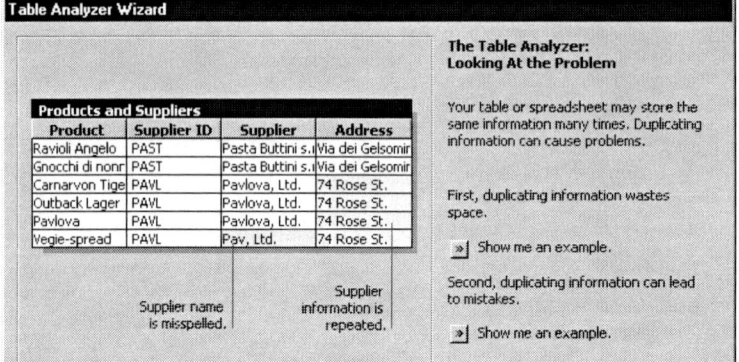

Table Analyzer Wizard

Database Utilities

- After seeing the examples, click **N**ext >

- Select the **Customers** table
- Click **N**ext >

The Table Analyzer Wizard moves through the introductory pages.

The wizard moves to the next step, where you pick the table to analyse.

The next page lets you choose whether to let the wizard normalise the table.

- Leave the option button **Y**es, **let the wizard decide** selected

- Click **N**ext >

The Table Analyzer Wizard examines the Customer table and creates two extra tables.

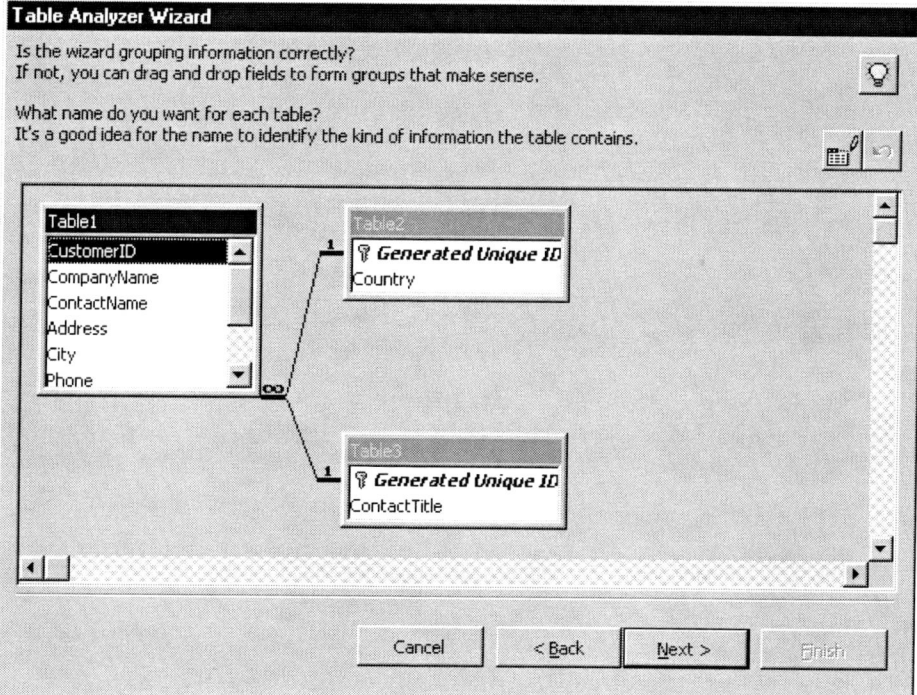

The Table Analyzer Wizard suggests splitting the Country and ContactTitle fields from the Customers table.

Lesson 11

Sometimes these tables may need some adjustment if the wizard does not get it absolutely right, but you can drag-and-drop fields to make better sense of the groups.

However, there is nothing to change in our exercise.

To rename the tables

TryIT	Action	Result
	• To rename a table, click on the table name • Click the **Rename Table** button (OR double-click the table's **Title** bar) • Ignore **Table1** as there is already a table called **Customers** • Rename **Table2** to **Country** • Click **OK** • Rename **Table3** to **ContactTitle** • Click **OK** • Click **Next >**	 The tables are renamed. The wizard moves to the next step.

The next step is to identify the primary key fields in the proposed tables. If no field has unique values, the wizard adds a **Generated Unique ID** field.

	• Click **Next >**	The primary keys will be generated by the wizard. The next page highlights some "errors" identified by the wizard.

Database Utilities

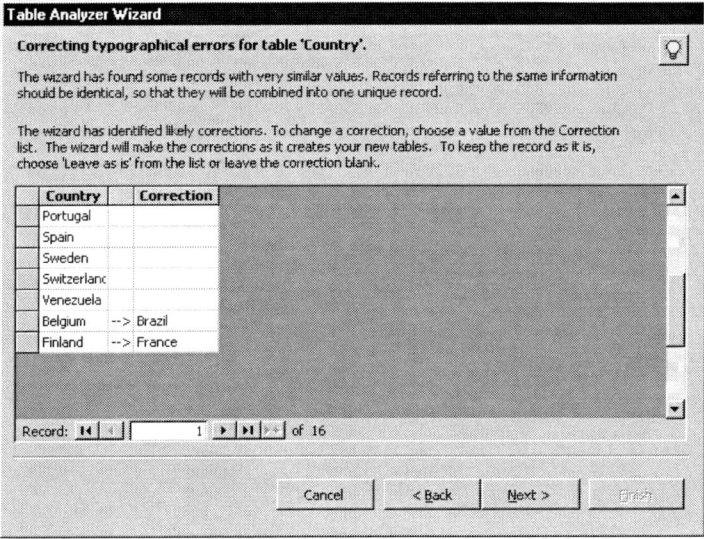

The countries identified are not duplicates (!) and therefore should be left as they are.

- In the **Correction** field, click the drop-down list against **Belgium** and **Finland** and select **Leave as is**

- Click **Next >**

- In the next step for the **ContactTitle** table, correct the **Owner/Marketing Assistant** to **Owner**

- Click **Next >**

Leave as is inserted in the **Correction** field.

In the final step, the wizard prompts to create a new query that has the same name as the original table. Old queries, forms and reports based on the original table will now use the new query and will continue to work seamlessly.

- Leave the option button **Yes, create the query** selected

- Click **Finish**

The wizard also creates relationships amongst the new tables.

Replicating a Database

Replication allows you to create multiple copies of a database. You would create a replica database for someone working off-site (for example, employees working from home, field sales staff or travelling representatives).

In replication, the original database becomes the **Design Master**. You can create as many **replica** copies of the database as are required. You can add and edit records in either replicas or the Design Master, but you can only make **structural** changes to the database in the Design Master.

To keep the different versions of the database up-to-date, replicas need to be **synchronised** with the **Design Master**. If a conflict arises between entries in the databases, you can choose which values are correct.

When you convert a database to be used with replication, Access adds a number of system tables to track both the design and data changes.

> Replication is also an alternative to **sharing** a database file over a local network. Replication helps to reduce network traffic, as users are working on different copies. It is also possible to make backups of the Design Master while users continue to work on the replicas.

As with most other administration functions, the database must be opened exclusively in order to setup replication. It is also a good idea to backup the database before setting up replication.

To create a replica

TryIT

Action	Result
• From the **Tools** menu, select **Replication** then select **C**reate Replica... • Click **Y**es to close the database	The message box below is displayed.

Database Utilities

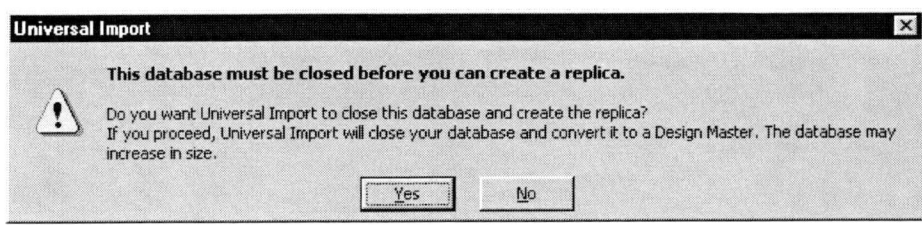

Replication warning message

Access starts to convert the current copy of the database into the **Design Master**. After some time, the warning message below is displayed.

Only one Design Master exists per replica set.

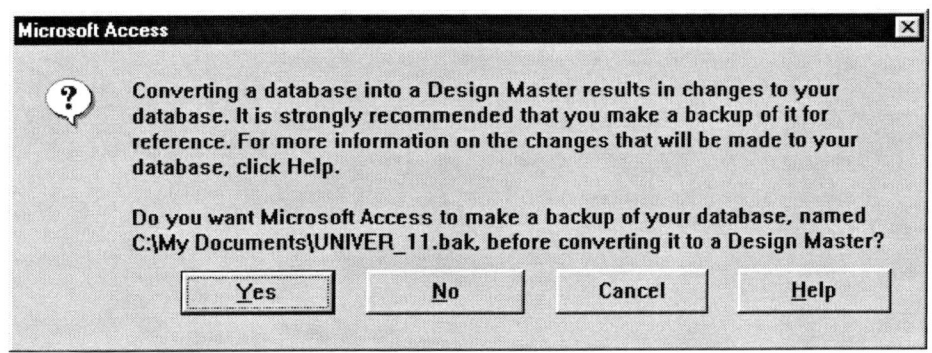

Replication warning message

• Click **Yes** to create a backup copy of the database	A backup copy is created.
• Enter the name and location of the first replica database (*example:* `c:\My Documents\Replica of Univer_11.mdb`)	
• Click **OK**	A copy of the design master is created as a replica and a message box is displayed.

LearnIT MS Access 2000 Expert — Page 315

Lesson 11

Replication confirmation message

- Click **OK**

    The **Database** window for the original database (now the Design Master) is re-displayed.

- Close the **Design Master**

Database Design Master

To create another replica, from the **Tools** menu, select **Replication** then select **Create Replica...**

Synchronising Replicas

Synchronisation takes place between two databases. You can synchronise a replica with the Design Master or with another replica in the set.

Synchronisation exchanges updated records and objects between two replicas. The exchange can be one-way or two-way, depending on whether amendments have been made in only one of the databases, or both.

To update a replica

Firstly, we will edit some records in the databases, in order to provoke a synchronisation conflict later on.

TryIT	Action	Result
	• In the design master (**UNIVER_11**), open the **Products** table • Change the name of **Chai** to `Breakfast Chai` • Close the database • Open the replica of **UNIVER_11** • Open the **Products** table • Change the name of **Chai** to `Afternoon Chai` • Delete the product **Chang** • Close the **Products** table	

Now we will synchronise the replica with the design master.

Lesson 11

TryIT	Action	Result
	• In the replica database, from the **Tools** menu, select **Replication** then select **Synchronize Now**	If any database objects are open, Access will prompt you to close them. The **Synchronize Database** dialogue box is displayed.

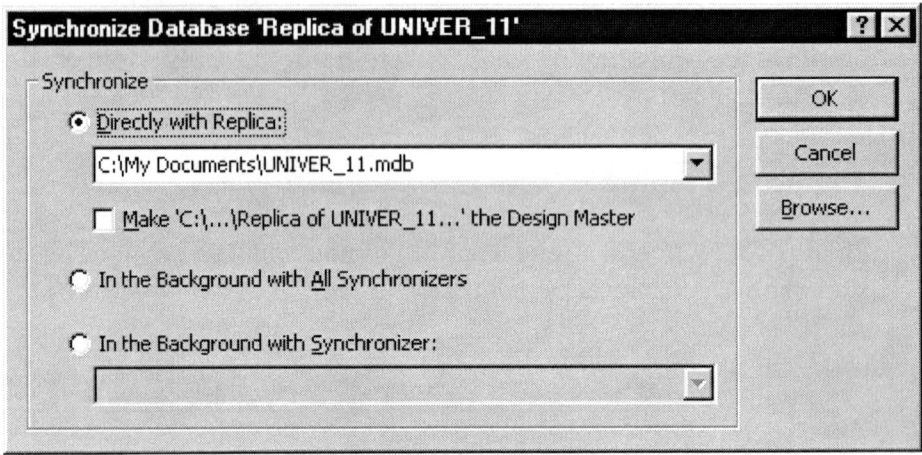

Synchronize Database dialogue box

The location of the design master is displayed automatically in this case, but at other times you may need to select **Browse** to locate the database with which to replicate.

	• Enter the name and location of the design master, if necessary	
	• Click **OK**	Access prompts you to close the database.
	• Click **Yes**	Access starts to synchronise the databases.

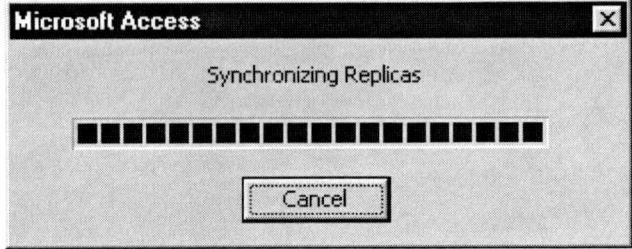

Synchronisation progress

When synchronisation is complete, a message box is displayed.

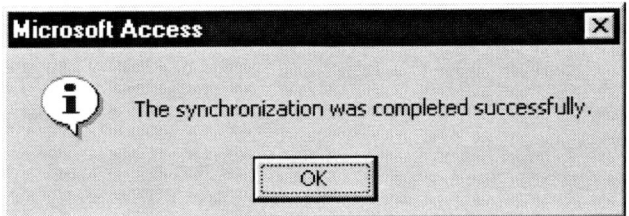

Synchronisation successful

- Click **OK**

The database is re-opened. If there have been any replication conflicts, Access displays a warning message.

To resolve replica conflicts

If Access has any problems synchronising the databases (for example, if it finds two different changes to the same record), it displays the message below.

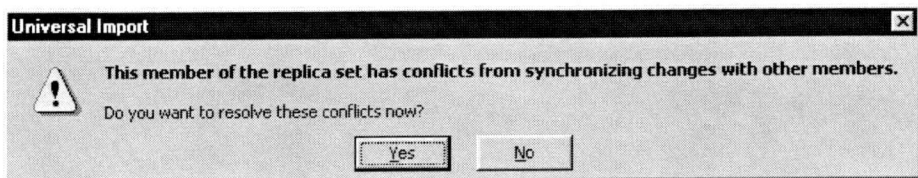

Replication conflicts warning message

■ If you click **Y**es, Access saves the conflicts in a special internal table

You can then review these conflicts.

Lesson 11

TryIT	Action	Result
	• Click **Yes** to the replication conflicts warning message	The **Replication Conflict Viewer** dialogue box is displayed.

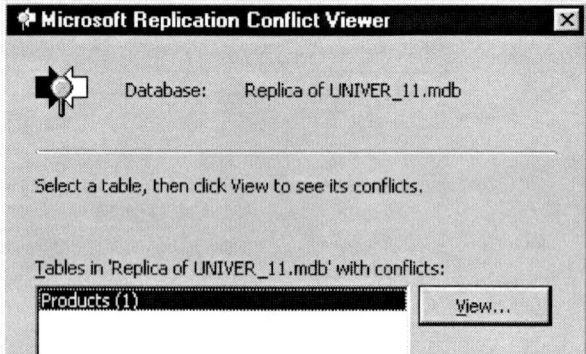

Replication Conflict Viewer dialogue box

	• Click **View...**	Access shows you the conflicting results.

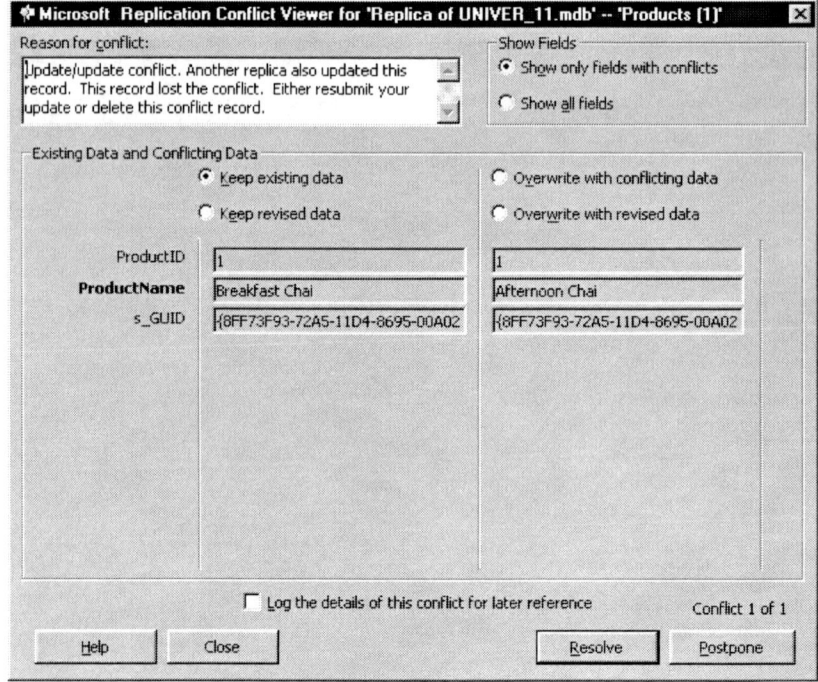

Replication Conflict Viewer

Existing and conflicting data

Access has automatically used the revision made in the Design Master as the winning change. The conflict viewer allows you to reject that change.

Note that the deleted record has not caused a conflict, but has been deleted from both databases.

The choices for resolving conflicts are:

Select	To
Keep existing data	Keep the revision from the other database
K**e**ep revised data	Modify the revision from the other database - enter the changes you want into the relevant fields
O**v**erwrite with conflicting data	Restore the original change made in this database
Over**w**rite with revised data	Modify the original change

You can log the details of the conflict for later reference, and you can decide to resolve or postpone resolving the problem until later.

- Select the **K**e**e**p revised data option button
- Click **R**esolve   The **Replication Conflict Viewer** dialogue box is displayed.
- Click **Close**   The **Database** window is re-displayed.

Converting Databases

In a multi-user environment, you may need to support users running different versions of Access, and frequently you may need to upgrade older databases to Access 2000.

Notably, an Access 97 database cannot be opened for editing in Access 2000, though it can be opened read-only.

When you open a database from a previous version of Access, Access 2000 prompts you either to upgrade the database file or open it without upgrading. You can also convert a database to the previous Access format.

To convert a database to Access 2000

TryIT 	Action	Result
	• On the **Standard** toolbar, click **Open**	The **Open** dialogue box is displayed.
	• Select the database **ACCESS97_DB**	
	• Click **Open**	The **Convert/Open Database** dialogue box is displayed.

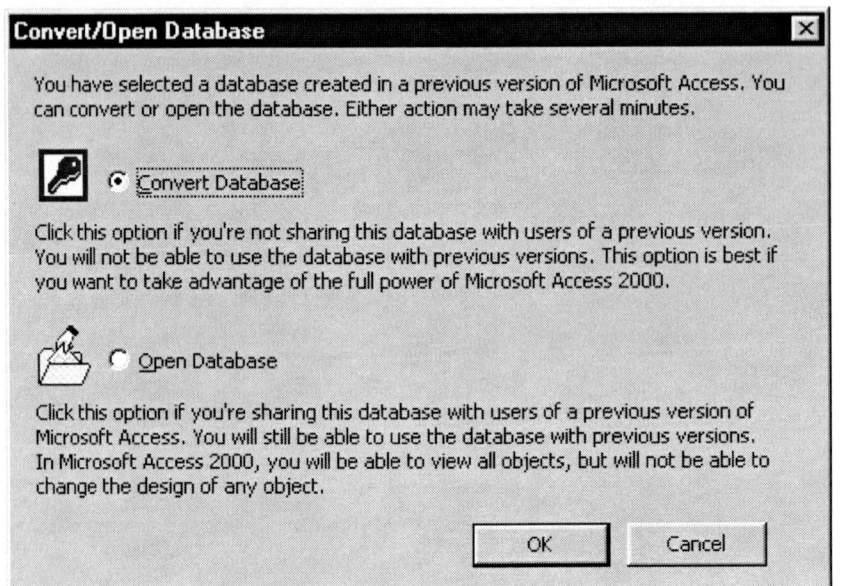

Convert/Open Database dialogue box

Database Utilities

- Click the option button **Convert Database**, to convert the database to Access 2000 format

- Enter a file name (CONVERTED_DB) then click **OK**

The database is converted to Access 2000 format.

If you open a database instead of converting it, you will be able to make alterations to the data but you will not be able to edit the design.

To convert an Access 2000 database to a previous version

You cannot open an Access 2000 database in Access 97, but you can convert an Access 2000 database to an Access 97 database (so long as it is not part of a replica set).

TryIT

Action	Result
• From the **Tools** menu, select **Database Utilities**	
• Select **Convert Database** then **To Prior Access Database Version...**	The **Convert Database Into** dialogue box is displayed.
• Enter the name (CONVERTED_BACK) for the converted database in the **File name:** box	
• Click **Save**	The Access 2000 database is converted to an Access 97 database.

When an Access 2000 database is converted down to Access 97, all specific Access 2000 functionality is lost.

Notes

Review Questions

(1) What is the Table Analyzer Wizard?

(2) What is replication?

(3) What happens when you try to open an Access 97 database in Access 2000?

Answers on the next page.

Lesson 11

Review Answers

(1) The Table Analyzer Wizard finds duplicate fields in one or more tables and splits the data into related tables

(2) Replicating a database creates a Design Master, where structural changes to the design of the database can be made, and one or more replicas where users can add or modify records, but cannot make any structural alterations

(3) Access checks whether you want to open the database or convert it. If you open the database, you cannot make any changes to the database or data

Skills Summary

Review

Congratulations on successfully completing LESSON 11. You have learned to use several database utilities.

Review objectives...

- ☐ Analyse a database with the **Table Analyzer**

- ☐ **Replicate** a database

- ☐ **Convert** a database

Lesson 11

Notes

Going Further

Documenting the Database Structure

In a large and complex database structure, it is important that you keep track of the various objects that make up the complete application. Access provides a method of doing this, called the **Documenter**.

The documenter allows you to select the objects that you wish to document, and produces a printable report.

To produce a documented report

- From the **Tools** menu, select **Analyse** then select **Documenter**

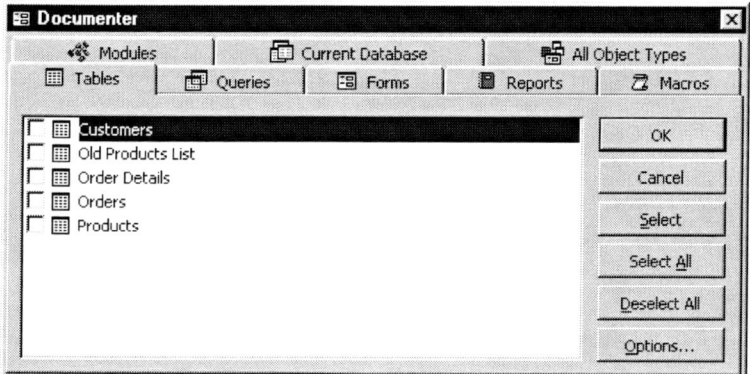

Documenter

The tabbed dialogue allows you to make selections from each of the six available object types. Global objects, such as table relationships and database properties are listed in the **Current Database** tab. In addition, the **All Object Types** tab allows you to view all database objects in a single list.

Each object can be selected and de-selected by clicking the checkbox against each object, or by using the **Select/Deselect** button. The **Select All** and **Deselect All** buttons work with all of the objects in the currently selected tab.

- Select the objects that you wish to document and click **OK**

After a while, the report is produced.

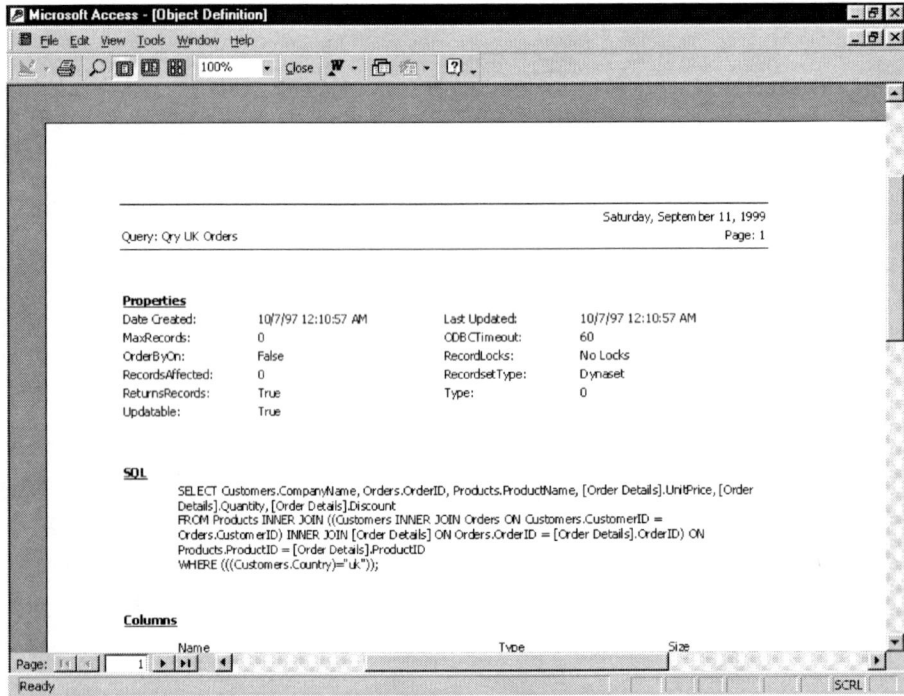

A sample documenter report

The report can be printed or exported (for example, to an RTF file for opening in a word processor) but not modified or saved in Access.

 To export the report for viewing and editing in a word processor, on the toolbar, click the drop-down arrow on the **Office Links** button and select **Publish it with MS Word**.

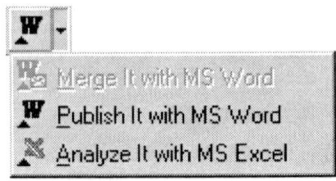

Office Links button

The report will be outputted to an RTF file and opened in MS Word, where you can edit and save it as normal.

The Performance Analyzer

The **Performance Analyzer** checks objects in your database to see if they can be made more efficient.

To analyse database objects

- From the **Tools** menu, select **Analyse** then select **Performance**

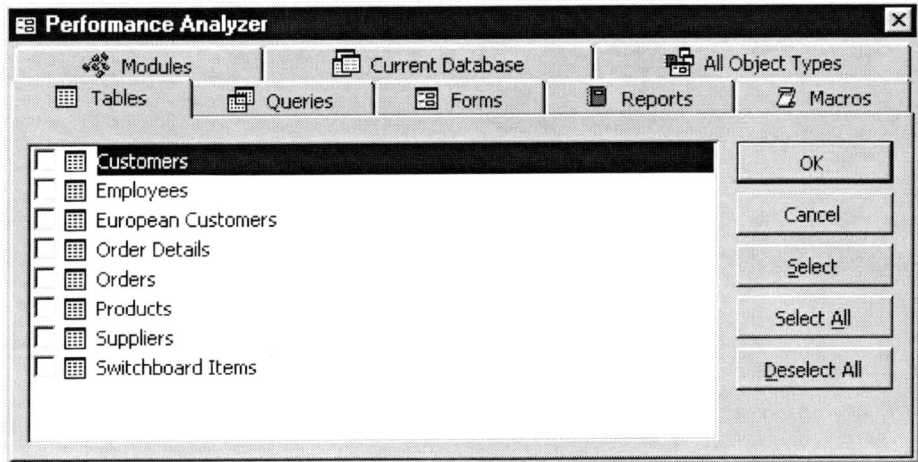

Performance Analyzer

This dialogue box works in the same way as the Documenter.

- Select the objects that you wish to analyse and click **OK**

After some processing, if the Performance Analyzer is able to make suggestions, a report dialogue box is displayed.

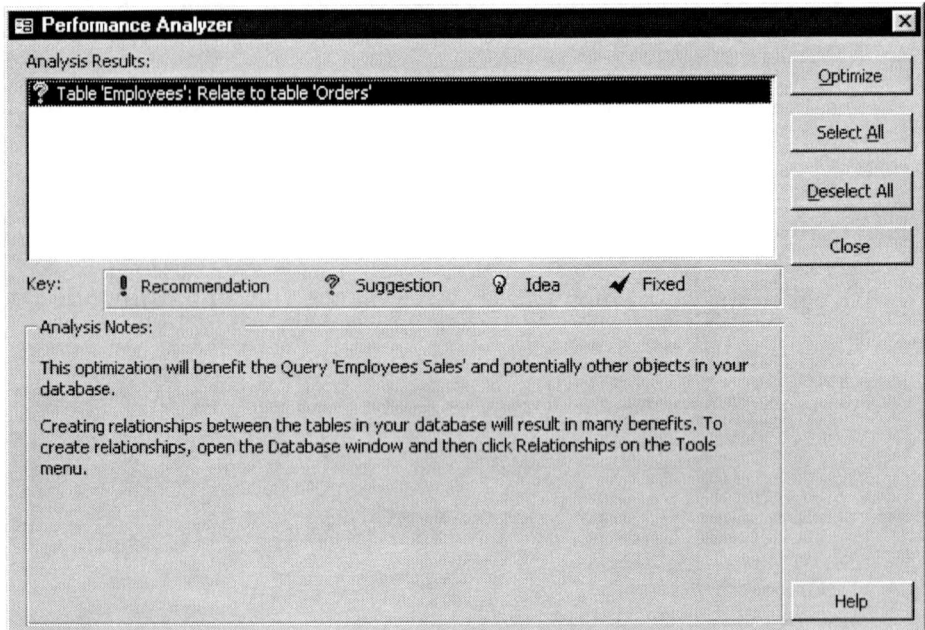

Performance Analyzer suggestions

The Performance Analyzer divides its help into three categories.

- **Recommendations** can be performed without taking other factors into consideration

- **Suggestions** may involve a trade-off in performance for other database features

- Both **Recommendations** and **Suggestions** can be implemented by selecting them from the list box and clicking **Optimize**

- **Ideas** are suggestions that you will need to implement yourself, by following the instructions in the **Analysis Notes:** panel

- Click **Close** when you have finished

Glossary

Term	Meaning
Action Query	A type of query that updates or alters records (for example, by appending them to a table or by deleting them).
Arguments	The parameters used to define macro actions.
AutoForm	A form automatically generated from a table or a query.
AutoReport	A report automatically generated from a table or a query.
Backup	It is important to make regular backup copies of the database to prevent loss of data.
Bound Control	Is tied to a field in an underlying table.
Calculated Field	A control that calculates expressions. They can appear on forms, and on reports that summarise data. A calculated control uses an expression as its source data.
Check Box	A box in a dialogue box that allows you to turn an option on or off.
Child Table	The table on the "many" side in a one-to-many relationship.
Combo Box	A control that allows you to type a value or select a value from a list.
Command Button	A command button is a button on a form or report that can automate your task. You can create a command button yourself or have the Command Button Wizard assist you
Compact and Repair	Tidies up, reclaims space and repairs errors in an Access database.
Control	An object on a form or report. Bound controls display data from the underlying table or query. Unbound controls can be used to add labels, lines, boxes and graphics to forms and reports, or to add a calculated control.

Appendices

Term	Meaning
Criteria	Conditions (or restrictions) that control which records to display from a query.
Crosstab	A type of query that displays summarised data grouped by two sets of headings (column and row headings).
Datasheet	The view of a table that allows you to enter or edit data.
Data Access Pages	Separate files stored outside Access in HTML format, but with a shortcut to the file in the database window, designed for the Internet or an intranet.
Data Type	Data types determine the type of data that is allowed in a field. There are ten data types.
Data Validation	The method of checking that data being keyed in meets the set criteria.
Date Format	The way a date is represented. D stands for days, M for months and Y for years. For example, d/mmm/yyyy would appear as 1/Jan/1999 and dd mmmm yyyy would appear as 01 January 1999.
Design View	The view used to make structural or formatting changes to database objects, including tables, queries, forms and reports. You cannot enter data in design view.
Encryption	Encryption uses built-in tools to ensure that the data is unrecognisable when viewed from text editors and word processors.
Export	Transferring data from the current database to another database or to a different file format, such as Excel.
Expression	An expression is a combination of symbols - identifiers or operators, and values - that produce a result.
Field	A category of information, such as invoice numbers or names.
Field Selector	The column heading at the top of a datasheet column that you click to select an entire column.
Filter by Form	Allows you to filter records by entering values in a blank view of your form or datasheet.

Glossary

Term	Meaning
Filter by Selection	Allows you to filter records by selecting values in a form or datasheet.
Foreign Key	One or more fields in a related table that refer to the primary key field(s) in the primary table
Form	A more user-friendly method of displaying data than a datasheet.
Format	The appearance of objects, such as fields or controls
HTML	The language used to create world wide web pages.
Hyperlink	A shortcut that jumps to tables or forms in the current database, another database, or to documents created in other applications and documents on the Internet or intranet.
Import	The means of converting into Access information created in other applications.
Join	A line joining a field in one table or query to a field of the same data type in another table or query. A join tells Access how the data is related.
Link	When you link to an object, you can make changes to it from Access, but the changes are stored in the original file.
List Box	A control with a list from which you can select an item.
Lookup Field	Provides a list of entries from which you can select.
Macros	A macro is a series of actions that run in sequence to perform a specific task on a regular basis.
Mathematical Operator	The part of a formula that determines how the formula is carried out, such as adding, subtracting or multiplying.
Navigation Buttons	Buttons at the bottom of a window that help you find your way around the window.
Object	An element in a database such as a table, form or report.
Option Button	A control that allows you to select one option from a group of option buttons.
Parent Table	The table on the "one" side in a one-to-many relationship.

Term	Meaning
Password	When a database has a password attached, it is not possible to open the database without typing the password.
Primary Key	A field that uniquely identifies a record in a database.
Properties	A set of instructions that determine how Access handles and stores data in a field.
Query	Extracts specific information from a table or another query.
Record	A collection of fields comprising one entry in a database.
Relationship	Matching values in equivalent fields in two tables.
Replication	Creating managed copies of a database for mobile users.
Report	A method of displaying data for printing.
Report Wizard	A series of dialogue boxes that guide you through the creation of a report.
Required Field	Determines whether an entry in the field must be made. If set to Yes, the field must be filled in.
Subform	A form within a form
Summary	A type of query or report that performs a summary calculation (such as summing or averaging) on values in one or more fields.
Table	An object in a data that allows you to display information in a database in a grid format. Tables are divided into rows and columns; rows representing records and columns representing fields.
Text Box	A bound text box displays data from a record source. An unbound text box contains a label for a field or an instruction message.
Unbound Control	Objects such as text boxes, lines and graphics or calculated controls added to a form or report.
Validation Rule	Sets limits or conditions on a field or control.
Web Page	A file that can be opened in a web browser. Web pages can be published on the internet for world-wide access or on a company intranet.

Appendices

Index

A

Action Queries, 101

Actions/Arguments, 238, 240, 241, 246

Active Server Pages, 214

Administration, 276

Analyzer, 310, 329, 331

AND Criteria, 121

Append Queries, 105

B

Backup, 281

BETWEEN Criteria, 137

Button Image Editor, 270

C

Calculations, 113, 157, 189

Cascade Update/Delete, 38, 39

Charts, 192, 198
 Modifying, 197

Child Table, 26, 32

Command Buttons, 238, 252

Compact Database, 284

Controls, 140, 145, 146
 Adding to forms, 146
 Aligning, 148
 Assigning menus, 266
 Calculated, 157, 189
 Chart, 197
 Command button, 238, 252
 Data access pages, 227, 230
 Deleting, 154
 Formatting, 152
 Graphics, 155
 Naming, 17
 Resizing, 148
 Selecting, 147
 Spacing evenly, 149
 Subform, 165
 Subreport, 202
 Validation, 54

Crosstab Queries, 126

D

Data
 Export, 92, 94, 214
 Importing, 84
 Linking, 84, 89
 Validation, 54

Data Access Pages, 20, 210, 219, 225, 227

Data Disk, 4

Data Types, 53

Database, 19

Database Administration, 276

Database Backup, 281

Database Conversion, 322

Database Design, 12, 17, 26, 32, 38, 40, 52, 264, 273, 310, 329

Database Security, 224, 276, 277, 281, 286, 295, 299, 306, 307

Appendices

Database Sharing, 276, 295, 299, 306, 307

Database Splitter, 288

Decryption, 286

Delete Queries, 106

De-normalisation, 16

Drag-and-Drop, 93

E

Encryption, 286

Events, 238, 260

Export, 92, 94, 214

Expression Builder, 57, 254

Expressions, 54, 109, 110, 113, 114, 115, 157, 189
  Examples, 113

F

Field Properties, 16, 52
  Modifying, 78

Field Size, 53

Filters, 119

Find Unmatched Query Wizard, 34

Foreign Key, 12, 30, 32

Format Property, 60

Forms, 16, 19, 140
  Controls, 145
  Data access pages, 219
  Design, 141
  Events, 238, 260
  Fonts, 153
  Graphics, 155
  Hyperlinks, 211
  Macros, 239, 243, 254, 260
  Multi-table, 160, 163, 165
  Properties, 151
  Record locks, 295
  Sections, 142, 144
  Splitting, 288
  Switchboard, 173
  Toolbars, 264

G

Graphics, 146, 155, 156, 189

Graphs, 192, 198

Grouping, 111, 179, 225

Groups, 276, 299, 306, 307

H

HTML, 214

HTML Templates, 216

Hyperlinks, 210, 211, 230
  Creating, 211

I

Import, 13, 33, 84, 85

Inner Join, 41

Input Masks, 58, 59, 60, 75
  Codes, 58

J

Join Types, 40

Joins, 43, 118

K

Keyboard Conventions, 9

L

Linked Table Manager, 91

Lookup Fields, 52, 61
  Fixed list, 76
  Properties, 66, 77

Lookup Wizard, 62

M

Macros, 20, 238, 241
    Command buttons, 252
    Conditions, 246
    Creating, 239, 249
    Examples, 243
    Expression Builder, 254
    Message box, 248
    Running, 238, 242, 252, 260

Make-Table Queries, 102

Many-to-Many, 27

Menu Bars, 264, 267, 273

Modules, 20

Mouse Conventions, 8

MS Excel, 85

Multi-Table Forms, 160, 163, 165

N

Naming Conventions, 17

Normal Forms, 14, 15, 16

Normalisation, 12, 13, 16, 26, 40, 310
    De-normalisation, 16

O

Object, 19

Office Links, 94

One-to-Many, 26

One-to-One, 27

OR Criteria, 122

Outer Join, 41

P

Parameter Queries, 122, 138

Parent Table, 26, 32

Passwords, 276, 277, 278, 280, 299, 304, 305

Performance Analyzer, 331

Permissions, 276, 299, 306

Primary Key, 12, 15, 16, 27, 30, 32, 38, 65, 66, 68, 69, 70, 312

Q

Queries, 16, 20, 100
    Action, 101
    Append, 105
    Calculated fields, 113
    Combining, 116
    Crosstab, 126
    Delete, 106
    Filtering, 119
    Find Unmatched, 34
    Indexes, 68
    Joins, 40, 43
    Make-table, 102
    Parameter, 122
    Summary, 110
    Update, 108

R

Record Locks, 295, 298

Referential Integrity, 32, 38

Relationships, 12, 26, 40, 44, 310, 329
    Cascade options, 38
    Creating, 27, 28, 30
    Many-to-many, 27
    One-to-many, 26
    One-to-one, 27
    Referential Integrity, 32

Repair Database, 284

Replication, 314, 317
    Conflicts, 321

Reports, 16, 20
    Calculated fields, 189
    Charts, 192, 197
    Data access pages, 219
    Design, 178, 180
    Documenter, 329
    Exporting, 94
    Grouping, 179, 180
    Multi-column, 186
    Pagination, 181, 185
    Relationships, 39
    Sections, 178, 180, 185
    Sorting, 182
    Subreports, 202
    Summary, 189, 191

Restore, 283

S

Security, 224, 276, 277, 281, 286, 295, 299, 306, 307

Splitter, 288

Startup, 175, 273

Subdatasheets, 44

Subforms, 160, 163, 165

Subreports, 202

Summary Queries, 110, 138

Switchboard, 173

Synchronising Replicas, 317

T

Table Analyzer, 310

Tables, 19, 329
    Child, 12, 26, 32
    Data validation, 57
    Exporting, 92, 94
    Exporting to HTML, 214
    Field Properties, 52
    Importing, 84
    Indexing, 68, 69
    Joins, 40, 118
    Linked Table Manager, 91
    Lookups, 61
    Make-table query, 102
    Modifying, 78
    Parent, 12, 26, 32
    Record locks, 295
    Relationships, 12, 26, 32, 38, 44, 310, 329
    Splitting, 288

Toolbars, 264, 267, 273

Toolbox, 146, 189, 230

Top Values, 138

Totals Query. See Summary Query

U

Undo, 154

Update Queries, 108

Users, 276, 295, 299, 306, 307

V

Validation Rules, 54, 55

W

Web Pages, 214, 219

Wildcards, 138

Windows, 3

Going Further

Appendices

Opportunities for Further Study

If you are working towards MOUS certification in other applications, or simply want to learn about other MS Office software, the LearnIT series includes manuals for Word, Excel, PowerPoint, Access, Outlook, and Windows.

Visit www.learnitbooks.com for further details.

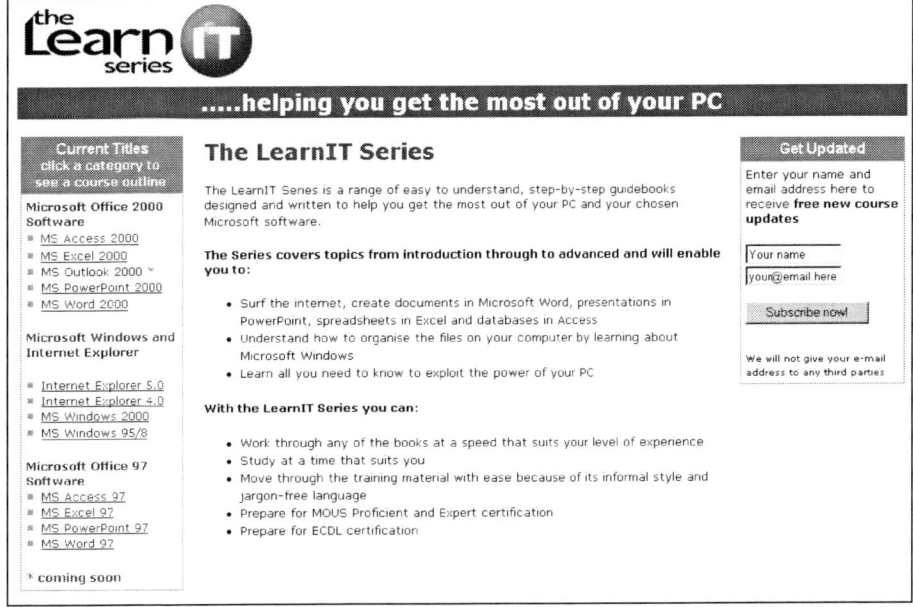

www.learnitbooks.com

Further Titles in the LearnIT Series

the Learn IT series consists of the following courses:

COURSE CODE	COURSE TITLE	MOUS	ECDL
L100eng	ECDL with Office 97		✓
L101eng	ECDL with Office 2000		✓
L103eng	MS Access 97 Expert User Part 1	✓	✓
L104eng	MS Access 97 Expert User Part 2	✓	
L105eng	MS Access 2000	✓	✓
L106eng	MS Access 2000 Expert User	✓	
L112eng	MS PowerPoint 97 Expert User	✓	✓
L113eng	MS PowerPoint 2000	✓	✓
L114eng	MS PowerPoint 2000 Expert User	✓	
L115eng	MS Word 97 Proficient User	✓	✓
L116eng	MS Word 97 Expert User	✓	
L117eng	MS Word 2000	✓	✓
L118eng	MS Word 2000 Expert User	✓	
L107eng	MS Excel 97 Proficient User	✓	✓
L108eng	MS Excel 97 Expert User	✓	
L109eng	MS Excel 2000	✓	✓
L110eng	MS Excel 2000 Expert User	✓	
L111eng	MS Outlook 2000	✓	
L121eng	MS Internet Explorer 5.0 User Introduction		✓
L102eng	Basic Concepts of IT		✓
L119eng	MS Windows 95/98 User Introduction		✓
L120eng	MS Windows 2000 User Introduction		✓

To order further titles, please visit our website for the LearnIT series courses www.learnitbooks.com